VALUE JUDGMENTS

ELLEN GOODMAN

VALUE

JUDGMENTS

FARRAR STRAUS GIROUX

NEW YORK

LIBRARY OF CONGRESS CATALOGING-IN-PUBLICATION DATA
Goodman, Ellen.
Value judgments / Ellen Goodman. — 1st ed.
p.   cm.
1. United States—Politics and government—1989–1993. 2. United
States—Politics and government—1993–   3. United States—Social
conditions—1980–   4. United States—Moral conditions.   I. Title.
E881.G65   1993   306'0973—dc20   93-1241 CIP

Acknowledgments

||||||||||||||||||||||||||||||||||||||||||||||||||||||||||||||||||||||||||||||||||||||||||||||||||||||||||||||

A few years ago, I bought an old advertisement for a comic book to hang on my office door. It's a cardboard drawing of Wonder Woman holding sway at a political convention with a headline that reads: "Wonder Woman for President—1000 Years in the Future!"

The poster was printed in 1943, exactly fifty years ago. In the 1940s, the idea of a woman running for President seemed like Buck Rogers futurism—a millennium away.

I bought this as a marker and a reminder. It's behind this doorway in a corner of the *Boston Globe* city room, and from this vantage point as well, that I write as a chronicler of social change.

Writing itself is a solitary profession. But these pages are the product of many lives. They wouldn't exist without the people who have shared their stories and ideas with me in conversations, in letters, or in their more formal counterpart, interviews. I want to thank them.

I also want to thank the people who share this life with me. My husband, Bob Levey, fellow-traveler and best friend. My daughter, Katie Goodman, whose adulthood delights and often surprises me. My sister, Jane Holtz Kay, and my friends Otile McManus and Pat O'Brien, who can read the running dialogues of our lives together in these columns.

There are other fingerprints on this book. My colleague Celia Lees-Low shares my daily work life more than anyone else. She is there through all the anxious moments of a breaking story, an errant fact, an irate caller, a canceled airplane. She makes it look easy.

The Washington Post Writers Group—more of a collective than a syndicate—operates with grace, efficiency, and great humor through all the lo-tech trials of editing columns and the hi-tech trials of computer transmissions. To Suzanne Whelton, Heather Green, and Christine Swiac, I wish a glitch-free future.

I was lucky for many years in working with Bill Dickinson, the head of the Writers Group, who—sensible man—has returned to Kansas and a mostly civilian life. He has been replaced by a new professional "stepfather," Alan Shearer, and we have "blended" with an ease that families would envy.

What every writer needs in an editor is not just a spell-check or grammar-check, it's a sanity-check. They don't build that into a software program, but it is built into both Alan and Anna Karavangelos, who have shepherded these columns into print.

I also want to thank Esther Newberg, a cant-free, straight-ahead agent and loyalist, for her advice and friendship. Finally, one of the pleasures of this book has been working with Jonathan Galassi. He remains proof that at least one book editor is what book editors used to be.

Contents

||||||||||||||||||||||||||||||||||||||||||||||||||||||||||||||||||||||||||||||||||||||||||||||||||||||||||||||||||||

VALUE JUDGMENTS

Introduction

||||||||||||||||||||||||||||||||||||||||||||||||||||||||||||||||||||||||||||||||||||||||||||||||||||||||||||||||||||||||||

Like many people who string words together for a living I am sometimes asked to explain what I write about. It's a simple, direct question. But I always find it hard to answer.

My columns vary as much as the news. They range as far as the chapter headings in this book: from people to politics, from family to ethics.

But what do you write (itals) about (end itals), they ask? What is the subject? the field? the specialty?

I never wanted to fit into one carefully marked cubbyhole. I didn't want to divide the world into Foreign Affairs or National Affairs, public life or private, Washington or home. I didn't want to become a subspecialist.

From the beginning, I deliberately set out to write about the world as we experience it, a place where life spills over the retaining walls, the way the smell of flowers and the fume of smoke drift over neighborhood fences.

On any given day, we may be at the office but thinking about our children at home. On any night, we may be surrounded by our own family, when the faces of strangers from the Persian Gulf or from Eastern Europe drop in for a disturbing television visit. I wanted to write about it all.

But over time, it occurred to me that if I absolutely had to choose one word to describe my subject, that word would be: values. I write, often, in search of, or in explanation of, values. It's the connecting thread through many of these pages.

I am not talking about bargains or values at the discount store, but, rather, ethics and standards, the qualities in life that mean the most to us. The things that matter.

The word itself, values, has become loaded down with heavy political and moral implications. It was usurped by the right wing, by the same people who took possession of another word: family. Stitched together, "family values" have often and ironically become fighting words. They divide the very people they should unite.

But to give up the language of values is to leave a powerful vocabulary to others, whether we agree with their definitions and their views or not. It's also to abandon the argument, and the struggle to mark out common ground in a country that often seems splintered.

I have called this book *Value Judgments*, in part, to take back the terms of the argument. Value judgments are too often associated with commandments, ten or more. The phrase implies a clear-cut, prepackaged set of one-size-fits-all moral strictures. When we think of value judgments, we think of knee jerks rather than struggles.

My own dictionary defines value judgments this way: "an estimate made of the worth, goodness, of a person, action, event or the like, especially when making such a judgment is improper or undesirable." The dictionary makes a value judgment against value judgments.

So did many of us who broke or drifted away from traditional values. Indeed, people who see the world in complex or personal terms often shy away from the words altogether. When you ask their opinion about another's behavior, many demur, "Oh, I don't want to make a value judgment."

But judgment needn't be the opposite of understanding or even compassion. To be valueless is not a compliment. The truth is that we all make decisions and choices. We use our own judgment, and base that judgment on our own values.

That is surely true in my life. Arguing with both hands, often wrestling with ambivalence and ambiguity, I spend my workdays writing what I think. About all the centrifugal forces of our society. About the pulls of individualism and community. About the appeals of tradition and change.

I write about designer genes and euthanasia. About gender gaps between what he says and she says. About the year of the woman that was not the year of the wife. About life in the fast-forward lane and on an island in Maine.

The pages in this book argue and wonder and often laugh their way through these times. During the past four years, the baby-boom generation came into its own, and into the White House. Parents began to see themselves as members of a counter-culture, forced to counter the impact of the culture on their own children. Character became the political buzzword covering a range of human imperfections, from infidelity to the hiring of illegal nannies.

In the long, slow process of change that we call the women's movement, these were the years when we met Anita Hill and Hillary Clinton. We debated the mommy wars and mommies at war. Some women hit the glass ceiling and others felt the backlash and still others were left without enough time even to attend a stress workshop.

At searing moments in these years, American men and women stood across a great dividing line yelling at each other, "You just don't understand." Sexual harassment and date rape were the topics of the office, the dinner party, and these columns. In some of these places, men and women began to understand.

Four years ago, I could not have predicted that the Vice President of the United States would mount a campaign against a fictional single mom, Murphy Brown. I would have been surprised to see a sign, "Better Dead Than Coed," on a (itals) women's (end itals) campus. More surprised to find someone marketing condoms for women.

I would not have been surprised—just saddened—to find the abortion wars escalating. To find that the women of my generation who struggled to gain access to institutions are still struggling to change those institutions. To find our daughters' freedom—these daughters of liberation—is limited now by a fear of violence.

In my own life, mid-life, as writer, wife, mother, daughter, I find myself still pursuing that elusive sense of balance. Like children who ask "Are we there yet?" my husband and I often ask each other, "Are we on an even keel yet?" We search for a balance between the internal rhythms of life and the external pressures of deadlines and airplanes. Between the supports and obligations of family life. Between service and pleasure.

Mid-life is, I think, a time for sorting out, for deciding what is important. In short, it's a time for thinking about our values.

This book is in that sense also a diary. It's about values. And it's about judgments.

AMERICAN
SCENES

||||||||||||||||||||||||||||||||||||||||||||||||||||||||||||||||||||||||||||||||||||||||||||||||||||

|||||| *This ideal of simultaneous
accomplishments fuels the favorite
fantasy of the decade: that if we were
only more organized, and blessed with
all the proper electronic helpers, we
would be able to squeeze at least two
lives into the time for one. Instead of
making choices, we think we can
make time.*

Eating Our Medicine

||||||||||||||||||||||||||||||||||||||||||||||||||||||||||||||||||||||||||||||||||||||||||||||||||||||||||

A friend and I go through the lunch line together. We pause at the salad bar while she carefully picks up six green florets. "Calcium," she explains. I thought it was broccoli.

I sit down at a table with a colleague who is deliberately spearing beige flakes of food with his fork. "Protein," he says. I could have sworn it was tuna.

I am on the subway when a student next to me reaches into a bag, grabs something yellow, and peels it. As if to explain her intense, even desperate chewing, she utters one word: "Potassium." It looked like a banana to me.

Forget about Paul Prudhomme and Julia Child. Never mind the sauces of France and the spices of Mexico. This is what eating is like in America today. Like taking medicine.

The haute cuisine of the body-conscious culture has become Nouvelle Nutrition. We don't exchange recipes so much as we exchange information. Pleasing our palates has become a secret vice, while fiber-fueling our colons has become a most public virtue.

If we had a menu for the way we now think about food, it would look like a prescription pad. Any day now, I expect even the supermarkets to arrange their aisles: complex carbohydrates to the right, simple to the left.

I cannot date the precise moment when we began to think of food as medicine. I know for sure that the nutrition I learned in school was as circumscribed as the four basic food groups. I got the general idea that as long as there were different-colored foods on our plates, we were okay. The only certified culinary cure of my childhood was chicken soup for the common cold.

For the most part, good nutrition was a synonym for bad taste. Cod-liver oil and cooked spinach carried the evil tracers of wellness. Things that were healthy came with a maternal stamp of approval. An occasional piece of liver. Endless glasses of milk. Please.

But somewhere along the way, we became a far more sophisticated, far more suspicious, food-fixated culture. The oldest anxiety about food—is there enough?—was translated into this new anxiety. The body is now regarded as a complicated, even fragile item—a human Jaguar—that won't operate right unless it is cared for with utmost precision by its owner.

The more we learn, the more we fine-tune our diet. Going to run tomorrow? Load up on some carbohydrates tonight. Got a test at two? Proteins at noon. Feel the 4 p.m. blues? Have a nice big piece of fructose. Trouble sleeping? You never should have had that amino acid.

Nouvelle Nutrition is more complex than a bowl of beans and rice. Even the television ads today read like entries in a medical journal. The caring American family is shown as they begin the day with a bowlful of antidotes for rectal cancer. That is followed almost immediately by a potion to prevent osteoporosis. We have legumes for lunch and balance our electrolytes with dinner. And we haven't even gotten to vitamins.

The epitome, or pièce de résistance, of food as medicine is, of course, oat bran. This is the good grain you should ingest to counter the bad cholesterol you ingest. Oat bran is the current four-star item on the Nouvelle Menu, having barely and recently edged out calcium among the most culinary cautious.

Admittedly, there are some advantages to the food-is-medicine school, although the taste of oat bran isn't one of them. It offers a balanced diet of worries. We don't just concentrate on the bad things in our food—from fat to Alar; we get obsessed with the good. It also, as a comedian noted the other night, offers a new set of excuses when you get caught with the munchies: I couldn't help it. I needed the zinc.

But there is something missing in any cuisine that asks us to think of a banana as a portion of potassium. There is something skewed about an eating regimen designed to do the most for every part of your body except the tip of your tongue.

What I need, creature of comfort that I am, is a regular dose of chocolate truffles. It has all the necessary ingredients for my health. My mental health. Put it before me and I promise to take my medicine.

MAY 19, 1989

Sex, No Sex

||||||||||||||||||||||||||||||||||||||||||||||||||||||||||||||||||||||||||||||||||||||||||||||||||||||||||

When Magic Johnson first started talking about AIDS, condoms, and abstinence, he got his words a bit muddled. "The best sex," he said at one point, "is no sex."

That wasn't exactly what he meant. Somebody out there may be getting ready to publish *The Joy of No Sex*. But Johnson was talking about the risks of sexually transmitted diseases and the one sure way to avoid them.

Still, in the months that have followed, months full of a sober and necessary discussion about sexual risks and sexual values, his original bungled phrase has stayed in my mind. There is something missing from the public discussion about sex. The current no-no, the one forbidden word, is not the anatomically correct name of a body part: it is the word "pleasure."

The debate among those who teach the young and single is deeply divided between two camps. Those who want to teach "safe sex" and those who teach "saved sex." The community is replete with intense arguments over what to say to young people.

On any given morning, one school in the country may be giving away condoms and describing birth control, while another school may be leading their students in a chastity pledge: "Do the Right Thing, Wait for the Ring." Religious leaders on one front may be preaching abstinence at Sunday-morning services, while on the other front the Harvard Divinity School celebrates AIDS Awareness Week with an art exhibit entitled "Sacred Condoms."

These arguments rage in communities from Shreveport, Louisiana, to Greenwich, Connecticut. The consensus that we have to give our young some sex education splits right down the middle. Should the education be from the chastity curriculum like Sex-Respect, or the caution and condom curriculum. Which break more easily: condoms or vows of celibacy?

But, for all the furor, both sides share the same subtext: danger. And only occasionally do we notice a problem with this shared anxiety. Perhaps, for example, when a nine-year-old boy tells a reporter here: "When I grow up, I'm not going to have sex because I don't want to die."

Sex—that word that we too often limit to mean intercourse—has both dangers and pleasures. In the sixties and seventies, we talked about pleasures and forgot about dangers. Many of our children, our daughters in particular, were not liberated by the sexual revolution but made more vulnerable—to pregnancy, to disease, to exploitation. But in the 1990s, we talk about danger and forget about pleasure.

"We use AIDS to clobber our young people," says Debra Haffner of the SIECUS, the Sex Information and Education Council of the United States. "We are trying to say to them you will die, therefore don't do it, rather than to talk about values, relationships, decision making. Pleasure? We don't talk about it at all."

None of this is surprising. When AIDS-infected "Uncle Eddie" makes front-page news for sexually exploiting young men in Philadelphia, pleasure is not the first thought on a parent's mind. When thirteen-year-olds are having sex and fifteen-year-olds are having babies, the most popular P-word is "protection."

And when the sexual messages of movies and TV and MTV are locked in a media time warp where sex is rarely safe and never saved, we see our own role as one of rebuttal. They talk about sexual license; we talk about sexual danger.

Sol Gordon, one sex educator who speaks the language of young people, even says, "I'm at a stage where I can't even talk about pleasure as a sex educator. I have to talk about health issues, life and death issues."

But to talk only of danger is to limit all of human sexuality to the sex act. To remain silent about sexual pleasure leaves the field to the exploitive distortions of the mass culture.

This may be a hard time for any sexual ethic more complicated than a bumper sticker. That may be especially true for those of us who believe in both postponement and protection *and* pleasure, each according to its time and place and person. Those who believe in caring and carefulness.

Yet there is nothing contradictory in teaching children about both the risks and the delights of sex. If we don't, we may leave them safe but crippled. Along with all the other anxieties of the age, add this to the list: We need to also fear the fear of sex.

APRIL 3, 1992

Wanting Out

||||||||||||||||||||||||||||||||||||||||||||||||||||||||||||||||||||||||||||||||||||||||||||||||||||||||||||||||||||||||

Somewhere on the evening news, in between stories of various disasters and ads for various bodily dysfunctions, there appears the airline pilot.

Well paid but discontented. Handsome as the anchor man himself, but weary with his working man's lot.

The pilot in this commercial vignette has come to his stockbroker to plan for the future before his horizons are reduced to Polident and Serenity.

He is in a rut—if there are ruts in the sky—going back and forth between Detroit and Minneapolis. Together he and his attractive financial planner chart a new route for his life: an escape route.

The ad has intrigued me, and not only as a break from the bran flakes. It comes on the heels of an ad last year by a brokerage house that featured a *cinéma-vérité* chat between well-heeled and burned-out executives. Only one had planned for what they all wished to buy: freedom.

I assume that businesses which deal with money for a living know what customers want to do with their greenbacks. In this case, the financial planners are not promoting Mercedes and mountaintop retreats. Their message about what many prosperous people in America want is simple. They want out.

Admittedly, this is hardly a sentiment limited to the working well-off. Nor is it entirely new. It's in the heart of many a lottery-ticket buyer. But when the American success story is an exit line, something is going on.

A few years ago, when broadcaster Susan Stamberg was asked what she wanted to do next, she answered in one word: "less." At the time I thought it was a wonderfully eccentric response. Now it is becoming the norm.

Blame it on the declining American work ethic if you like, a creeping laziness in the culture. That seems to be the favorite tack of the Japanese. Most of them, we are repeatedly told, work six days a week. Half of them don't take their allotted vacation. Thousands also drop dead at their desks, victims of *karoshi*, death from overwork.

But I attribute this longing for the door to an enervating combination of burnout and alienation, of overwork and underappreciation, a paralyzed economy and a gridlocked generation.

The case for exhaustion is made most persuasively in *The Overworked American*, where Juliet Schor chronicles the rise of work hours in the past twenty years. The average employed person is now on the job an additional 163 hours, or a full month. Indeed, our friendly pilot is an exception; his hours are regulated by law.

Overwork is due in large part to the economics of the workplace. Costs—pensions and health insurance—have made it cheaper to pay fewer workers overtime than to hire more workers. The growing gap between the poor and the rich is also a gap between those who are out of work and those who are overworked. Choose one of the above.

In part, overwork is due to the economy of the eighties. The long slide left Americans working more hours for the same lifestyle.

The sense of getting somewhere was replaced by the sense of the treadmill.

But alienation is not just a matter of hours. In the last year, I have heard an extraordinary number of stories about the atmosphere and attitudes in the workplace. Stories about simple callous mistreatment.

A decade of takeovers, mergers, downsizings, and restructuring has had a very personal cost. It's turned legions of blue- and white-collar workers into dislocated refugees, the boat people of economic upheaval. Neither they nor the survivors and witnesses are likely to put their loyalty into a corporation that deals with people as interchangeable digits.

At the same time that the economy has gone down, the demography has grown up. The baby-boom generation has met the mid-life crisis. Some are frustrated trying to balance overwork and family. Others at forty see the slots at the top occupied by forty-five-year-olds. Where do you go when you can't go up? Out?

The pilot of our commercial plot line isn't yearning to lie on a beach. He wants to buy his own plane and fly people from one beach to another. In the fantasy department this is an aviator's equivalent to owning a country inn.

But the alienation of even those who are making it in America is quite real. It's not their work ethic that's gone awry. It's the work, the overwork, the lack of respect, and the deteriorating relationship between worker and workplace. Until we deal with the people problem, this languishing economy can't fly. It can't even get off the ground.

MARCH 6, 1992

Bye-bye to the Eighties

||||||||||||||||||||||||||||||||||||||||||||||||||||||||||||||||||||||||||||||||||||||||||||||||||||||||||||||||||||

This is the week when all good journalists can be found busily writing their farewells to the decade. The task is unusually difficult in 1989 because the eighties ran out on us before we ran out of them.

Like a dinner guest who left before dessert, the decade ended before it was over. It ended when Ronald Reagan went back West. It ended again when the Berlin Wall came down. It ended when people looked up from the bottom line and noticed the hole in the ozone. It ended when a number of Americans stopped asking: What about me? and started asking: What about us?

I personally regarded the early departure of the decade with pleasure, since the eighties had worn out their welcome at my table somewhere into the soup course. Now, with barely a palate-cleansing pause, we have plunged into the nineties, with good news and bad news from points as distant as Berlin and Panama.

What were the eighties, anyway? For Americans, the decade past was a time of personal isolationism. The oldest tension in American society between the values of independence (self-made individualism) and the values of community (the desire for connection and caring) got way out of whack.

For much of this decade, we Americans were allowed, sometimes even encouraged, to landscape our lawns and ignore the environment. We were expected to pamper our children, to give them the perfect birth experience and flash cards for their cribs, while ignoring the schools and communities they would grow up in.

Our heroes were entrepreneurs, the Lone Rangers of business and politics and Hollywood. Our heroines were women who were praised for keeping the family economy sound, the children happy, and promotions rolling in, without leaning on or needing help.

Even our anxieties led us on a quest inward rather than out into the world. The staples of the televised talk shows of the era were about self-improvement and self-doubt. Many of the ethical debates were equally personal in their small scale—should we as individuals give alms to other individuals, the homeless street beggars?—because communities lost the will and the wallet to deal with these problems collectively.

I cannot date precisely when this long retreat to the single cell of self seemed to reach a turning point. But I suspect that it's been concerns about the future—from family at one end of the spectrum to the environment at the other end—that are making people think again about connections.

The dominant image switched at some point from the Iron Curtain to the greenhouse. The first had divided East and West into enemies; the second encompassed and endangered everyone equally. Public attention in turn is shifting from the Soviet threat to the environmental threat.

The Europeans these days may be more afraid of Chernobyl than of the Warsaw Pact. The Americans who thought they could buy the ultimate luxury item—insulation from problems—find it harder to feel secure in an air-conditioned car with pollution on the other side of the window. It has become more difficult to disconnect the fate of the American plains from the Brazilian rain forests.

In our domestic lives, all the attention paid to how American children are faring and failing has had its impact. For most of the decade, Americans expected every family to stand on its own, do for its own. But too many children were missing time and nurturing. They were like head shots on a million milk cartons. Gradually we may be returning to the belief that a family also thrives or shrivels in the larger human environment.

If Americans are becoming less self-centered, it may be because America is no longer the center. The economy has gone global; the superpower has become a player. It may also be because the vast baby-boom generation has come of middle age. They are no longer as concerned with the issues of youth, breaking away, independence.

They are becoming more involved with building, with family, with community, with caretaking.

Or it may be that independence in its purest form—isolation —can seem lonely and ultimately meaningless.

I don't want to be unduly, uncharacteristically optimistic. The news from Central America suggests a very different and unhappy sort of adventure abroad. The domestic, personal turnaround won't be easily accomplished. People don't change on cue the way we turn a page on a calendar.

But with energy and luck we may begin to right the vast imbalance of the 1980s, to see the connections between individual behavior and survival. In that case, we may even get a genuinely new New Year.

DECEMBER 26, 1989

Hello, Bill

||||||||||||||||||||||||||||||||||||||||||||||||||||||||||||||||||||||||||||||||||||||||||||||||||||||||||||||||||||||||

Washington — By mid-afternoon and mid-parade, hordes of people sweeping past the back of the White House had stopped for a moment to gawk at the moving van parked in the driveway. They peered through the wrought-iron fence and snapped pictures of this celebrity vehicle. They would bring these images home as mementos, proof that they were here the day Bill and Hillary Clinton took over the nation's most elegant piece of public housing.

The van somehow made this moment seem ordinary, down-home, a matter of boxes and "Honey, who packed the toothpaste?" It made change seem as routine as emptying out boxes and filling a new set of drawers. It made it look easy.

But it didn't and doesn't feel that way. If anything, this inaugural week was a mix of emotions about the possibilities of change, that word that President Clinton has worn like a talisman. It was a week of high hopes and tempered expectations. Optimism, but cautious optimism.

There was a desire to believe that things could change with the guard. Yet there was also an undercurrent—what John Irving might call an "undertoad"—of doubt.

I can't remember an inauguration quite like this. A week imbued with such earnest, anxious hope for what the brand-new President called "renewal"—and such sober accounting of the burdens that shackle the new to the old. With every endless chorus of "Don't Stop Thinking about Tomorrow," there seemed to be a reminder of yesterday. Yesterday's bills, yesterday's wars, yesterday's problems.

On opening night, as the fireworks sent up the word HOPE in a grand finale, even the children in the crowds lining Georgetown were reminded nervously of the "fireworks" over Baghdad. As black-tie revelers walked to parties in this gridlocked city they passed by street people who were at their usual posts, asking for their usual handouts.

As the new President told the nation, "There is nothing wrong with America that cannot be cured by what is right with America," someone in the crowd, which was as thick as in a rush-hour subway, thought of the deficit. And as the first baby-boom President talked about posterity—"the world for whom we hold our ideals, from whom we have borrowed our planet and to whom we bear sacred responsibility"—a certified Friend of Bill sighed, "I wish him well."

These nagging reservations were to be found not only among the Washington media, though many here seem unwilling to give the man a wedding night, let alone a honeymoon. They were also found in the fine print of the polls, which showed, as one pollster put it, that "Americans don't expect miracles." They were there, as well, in the subtext of conversations.

The same, belated, understanding of the seriousness of our country's problems that brought this new man to office now tamps down any unbridled belief in success. The country is faced with a question that often comes at mid-life: How do you make a fresh start in the middle?

Maybe such questions are always asked at a moment when a new generation comes into its own—its own responsibility, its own inheritance, its own time, its own place in the middle. Maybe it's the obvious question of personal middle age, when so much of our life is already formed and yet there is much we want to do.

In his speech, the forty-six-year-old President tipped his hat at the generation "whose steadfastness and sacrifice triumphed over Depression, Fascism, and Communism." But this is a middle-aged country now, with waste sites that are more visible than new frontiers. The legacy comes with debts, and much of the "new" work to be done is old. It's cleanup work: cleanup of the environment, cleanup of the deficit, mending and repairing the human seams. In a world that won't stand still.

At mid-life we don't get a clean slate. As a mid-life country we begin where we find ourselves, with obligations from the past and to the future. With an understanding of how tough the tasks are.

As the new people in the White House unpack their belongings, the trumpets of renewal, the clarion calls to heroic beginnings are grander than our feelings. The words that I have heard the most are more measured, more furrowed, and more middle-aged:

"I just hope he gets a chance."

JANUARY 26, 1993

Bean Counters

||||||||||||||||||||||||||||||||||||||||||||||||||||||||||||||||||||||||||||||||||||||||||||||||||||

After all was said and done, after all was added and subtracted and shuffled around a bit, Bill Clinton did what he promised. The class photo of his cabinet presented a more diverse portrait of Americans than had ever been assembled around a Presidential table.

This was the official breakdown: six white men, three black men, three white women, two Hispanic men, and one black woman. That's fifteen secretaries, and a whole lot of counting going on.

But before we put aside the numbers and get on with the policies, one last observation about the way we divvy up Americans these days.

With all due respect to the President-elect, who let off steam at the "bean counters," the people "playing quota games and math games," bean counting is not a new political pastime. The demands for diversity, for a cabinet and government that "looks like America," go back over our history.

What is different is our image of what America looks like. What has changed are the beans.

Without much notice or fanfare, the concept of diversity in America gradually and then fundamentally shifted. It is no longer a matter of geography, religion, nationality, or even class. When we talk about diversity now, we are talking about race and gender and, in the case of Hispanics, ethnicity.

There was a time when geography was so important that the Constitution wouldn't allow a President and a Vice President from the same state. More than one chief executive tried to please the north and the south, the east and the west points on his constituency compass. Diversity was a collection of white males from different places on the map.

As for religion, our grandparents were conscious and self-conscious. The first Catholic made it to the White House in 1961. That same year, Senator Abe Ribicoff turned down the Attorney General's job because, he told Jack Kennedy, it would not help the cause to have a Jewish Attorney General putting Negro kids in schools in the South.

Now, quick, tell me the religious background of three or more Clinton cabinet members? Our grandparents would have known, would have instantly counted any beans of their own religious persuasion, especially if that religion was a minority. Religion is not a moot issue in this country, but in political terms it's muted.

As for nationality, the old urban ticket of political patronage —Italian, Irish, Polish—was no easy balancing act. But as they were admitted, assimilated, Americanized, many European Americans stopped counting. At least out loud.

Today, in the new diversity game, an Italian Catholic male is another white bean. Donna Shalala's roots in a Lebanese-American family are no more politically salient than her birth as a twin. The newly designated Secretary of Health and Human Services is a woman bean.

It is the job and the curse of outsiders to be bean counters— to feel their exclusion acutely and to plead their grievance. The people who have felt locked out most want someone "of their own" at the table. As a symbol and a representative.

This new math can admittedly lead to some odd calculations. We count Robert Reich, the designated Secretary of Labor, as another white male insider. Yet, at four feet ten inches tall, he had his own struggles to win.

We list Warren Christopher, the designated Secretary of State, as an Establishment male, though he was raised one of five children by a widowed salesclerk. We list Mike Espy, Secretary of Agriculture, as an outsider, though his family owned twenty-eight funeral parlors. There's more than white and black in our backgrounds. We are individuals as well as beans.

But there is still something in the historic record that is reassuring about the future. Critics say that the claims of diversity are splintering America, dividing and subdividing us into our warring parts. Yet Americans have become less—not more—conscious of region, religion, nationality. It can happen with race and gender as well. As we are included, we stop counting.

For now, though, the Clinton cabinet does look a lot like America. It's not exactly a melting pot. But it's a pretty interesting bean pot.

JANUARY I, 1993

Fault Lines

||||||||||||||||||||||||||||||||||||||||||||||||||||||||||||||||||||||||||||||||||||||||||||||||||||||||||

The man was talking about what he calls the "resegregation" of American life. He was a veteran of the civil rights movement, and went South as a student in the sixties when whites and blacks fought American apartheid together.

The man went on to make his life in a Midwestern university, where he was my guide one spring day. Indeed, he taught about race in America until he felt discredited on account of his skin color—white—and went into administration.

Walking me into the student union, he said, "Look." The tables in front of me were nearly as segregated as a lunch counter in the Alabama of the 1960s. There was just one table where black and white undergraduates ate in noisy camaraderie. They, my guide explained, were members of the varsity team.

Pausing, he counted on one hand the number of places where blacks and whites interact on his campus these days: in sports, in the arts, or, he added ironically, in race relations class. A few years back, there was a shantytown on campus, a makeshift protest against investing in South Africa. Now he was almost sorry the university divested, because it had been one of the few actions that brought students together.

I brought this story home to a woman who disputed only one phrase: resegregation. We never desegregated, she says. An academic and black, she knows very few people who ever had social lives that easily traversed the color lines.

As a mother, she sees her grade school kids with friends of all hues but her college students subdivided by skin color. So she also wonders when it happens and why. Many of her black students believe they can integrate only on white terms and turf. Many of her white students feel unwelcome by blacks. Many feel unwelcoming.

Who was defensive and who was racist and who was just uncomfortable? And why this great silence today between blacks and whites about race relations in America?

Both these academics, now enjoying the summer that is their chief professional perk, can cite incidents over the past year. Graffiti, hostility, tension. Yet they would agree that these are by no means the worst days on campus or the worst years. They remember the KKK, Mississippi, legal segregation.

But they also know that nearly every campus holds a volatile mix of attitudes that in no way resembles a melting pot. In some places, whites believe that their black classmates were admitted because of their race. In others, blacks believe that whites believe that.

On many universities, the black search for identity—their own place on a white campus—can end up fusing blackness with victimization. In many universities, white classmates resent the racist label brushing them indiscriminately.

There is today a high degree of racial consciousness and a sorry lack of a language, of a forum, of a common ground where people can talk honestly about race. These two facts have given many campuses the look and sound of two cultures. And in these segregated places there may not even be faith anymore in the value of integration.

Neither of my guides believes that campuses are unique in their sharp segregations. Quite the opposite is true, they say. Look around the office. Look around town.

In Washington, it is still almost impossible for blacks and whites to talk about the trial of Mayor Barry. To most whites in the nation's capital, the case was *about* the mayor and his alleged use of drugs. To most blacks, the case was *about* the entrapment of a black leader. Across the great divide of the race, the words defied interpreters.

Even in journalism, bylines often come color-coded. White journalists are awkward writing about blacks, as if race were a qualification. Black journalists are often both required to write and discredited for writing about "their own."

And in our cities there are neighborhoods as separated by race as ever in our history. There are people who speak for the "black community" and for the "white community" as if their apartness was an accepted and permanent reality.

But universities have often thought of themselves as models, communities of scholars. At best, they are expected to uphold their own values. At a minimum, they are places where we are to think and talk deeply about what troubles the "real world."

The universities are reopening. They start each new year with a fresh curriculum. But what troubles the real world as much as anything these days is race relations. It's a problem that exists on a scale as large as a city. But it can also be seen—and changed— on a scale as small as a dining-room table.

SEPTEMBER 4, 1990

A Tower of Psychobabble
||||||||||||||||||||||||||||||||||||||||||||||||||||||||||||||||||||||||||||||||||||||||||||||||||||||||||||||||||||||||||

It is notable that the clearest, maybe even the sanest words heard at the Woody and Mia custody trial so far were offered up by Moses: "Everyone knows not to have an affair with your son's sister."

This searing, flat-out judgment did not come from *the* Moses. It came from fourteen-year-old Moses Farrow Allen. This phrase was not inscribed on a stone tablet. It was written in a letter to somebody he once called Dad.

Nevertheless, the boy's vision was as unclouded as his pain when he wrote, "You have done a horrible, unforgivable, needy, ugly, stupid thing." It stands in stark contrast to the rest of this bizarre trial being conducted in a dreary New York courtroom under the strictures of the law and in the language of Shrinkese.

Indeed, in that courtroom it's possible to hear the way that once-arcane vocabulary has infiltrated our everyday conversation just as English has infiltrated French. Under the linguistic rules of Shrinkese, good and evil are now translated into "appropriate" and "inappropriate." Right and wrong have become "good and bad judgment."

The use of Shrinkese in this "head case" is predictable. It may be the native tongue of the entire extended and distorted Allen–Farrow clan—a tribe that comes with a battery of psychologists, psychiatrists, and therapists in tow. These children seem to have been assigned a shrink at birth or adoption, the way other children are assigned a patron saint.

But this week in the wrangling over custody the court was further treated to the testimony of son Satchel's therapist speaking in this tongue. By the time it was over, Dr. Susan Coates had offered a national lesson from the Tower of Psychobabble.

Was Woody evil, a lawyer asked. "I would say this was someone whose judgment is very impaired," she demurred.

Was he bad? One "could not generalize about a person without multiple, multiple bad acts."

Was Mia wrong in her rage? "I felt that for her to see Mr. Allen as an all-bad person was an overreaction."

Was there a solution? "What is critical for the children is they find a way to have a mother and father and that each parent find a way to emotionally empower that tie."

Every time the psychologist was asked a question about the ethics of right and wrong, she seemed to, uh, shrink the moral dimensions down to their clinical dimensions. She dropped any accent of criticism. Indeed, the closest she got to expressing an opinion about a man who slept with the daughter of his longtime mate and the sister of his children was to say, "I couldn't understand why he couldn't understand" what the impact would be.

Well, I hear you, Dr. Coates, as they say in Shrinkese. I know where you are coming from. Though maybe Woody couldn't understand because he spent so many years in therapy being understood.

I rarely side with people who want to put good and evil stickers on every piece of human behavior. There are enough zealots in the world searching for biblical proof that Spandex is a creation of the devil. It's important to understand a criminal as well as punish a crime. It is wise to distinguish between a bad act and a bad child. The word evil doesn't roll off my tongue either.

But there are times, and this is one of them, when I wonder whether our adoption of Shrinkese as a second language, the move from religious phrases of judgment to secular words of acceptance, hasn't also produced a moral lobotomy. In the reluctance, the aversion—dare I say the phobia—to being judgmental, are we disabled from making any judgments at all?

In Woody Allen's lifetime and often with his running commentary, we have made an extraordinary transition. From moral absolutes to moral relativism. From exorcists to therapists. When in trouble—marital misery, infidelity, abuse—we are often sent or even sentenced to a shrink. Moral problems become medical ones, and yesterday's sinners become today's patients.

And sometimes, just sometimes, people like Woody Allen, a fallen-away Jew, and Mia Farrow, a fallen-away Catholic, fall into something else. A therapeutic mode that erodes one set of moral bearings without replacing it. A world that emphasizes the need to understand each other but not necessarily to understand right and wrong.

Woody Allen slept with a mother and a daughter, threw a grenade into the family vortex, and now says that he should have custody of three children, bring them home to an apartment where their sister would be stepmother. And this is what passes for a confession of guilt about starting his relationship: "I think I did make a mistake. An error of judgment."

I'd rather give the last word to Moses.

APRIL 4, 1993

R e d e f i n i n g   S i n
||||||||||||||||||||||||||||||||||||||||||||||||||||||||||||||||||||||||||||||||||||||||||||||||||||||||||

I don't know who first put together those little words "sin" and "taxes," but it was an inspired moment in public relations. With one stroke, the tax collector was set squarely in the camp of the righteous, and the tax protesters were allied with the devil.

Of course, sin taxes always conveyed a slightly mixed ethical message. With one hand, the government wagged its public finger of disapproval and promised to price people onto the straight and narrow. With the other hand, it scooped up a piece of the action.

But those were the days when drinking and smoking were considered evil. When a sin was something that put your soul in jeopardy. When we all expected to pay big-time for any offenses —after death.

Now, of course, we pay the most devout attention to our medical behavior. Our chief vices are the ones that put our bodies in jeopardy. We may still expect to pay big-time for our offenses—but it's with a premature death.

So there is something symbolic in the current proposals to help pay for health-care reform by taxing the habits of the unreformed. We are being offered a new generation of sin taxes for a new definition of sin.

I have no problem with this as a revenue plan. The dollar-a-pack tax on tobacco suggested in the Senate would raise $10 billion a year. Adding a little something to the bar bill might help us get in the black. But I am queasy about the ties that bind evil and illness, virtue and health.

Sometimes it seems that the harshest moral judgments of our era are reserved for medical misdemeanors. People who wouldn't dream of judging others by their sexual preference or bank balance casually calculate personal worth according to the health commandments. But when you consider the average American medical balance sheet, there's a lot of good with the bad in any profile.

It's not just a matter of bald spots, which, as a friend gasps, have just become the medical mark of Cain. Nor is it a question of apple-shaped bodies that may or may not be a sign of impending breast cancer in women and an omen of heart disease in men. These are in our genes; they are not our choices.

But what of Americans who eat off the high end of the food chain and the fast end of the restaurant chain more often than they should. We may be risking trouble, but are we sinners? An act may be foolish or dangerous, but is it evil?

One misbegotten study after another suggests that the worst thing we can do to ourselves, aside from lighting up another cigarette, is to swallow another glob of fat.

We now have a bible of fat grams with a permanent place on the best-seller list. The tabernacles inside tell us a tablespoon of butter has 11.5 grams of fat and a Big Mac has 35. If we are going to reward and punish people for breaking medical taboos, then surely we should charge a penny a gram for Brie.

On the other hand, if it is true that moderate portions of red wine can reduce the odds of a heart attack, then should we declare it a virtue? Perhaps we should offer a tax break for two glasses a day. Under the medical deduction, of course.

The odd thing is that Americans remain selective in medical morality tales. All sorts of risky behaviors escape the mantle of right and wrong.

Our health-care dollars go without comment to mend the broken bones of the horseback rider, even the bungee jumper. We don't regard the skier as a sinner. Indeed, we may perversely regard his indolent brother as the greater danger.

But the notion that we should justify taxes as a fine on people who mistreat their bodies is enough to make an IRS man start counting his blessings. And our character flaws.

I am happy to tax cigarettes. I'm happy to tax the billboards and the ads. Happier to dump the subsidies for growing tobacco.

Call this tax a prepaid health plan for smokers—buy your Marlboros now, get your cancer treatment later. Call it preventive medicine—the higher the cost, the fewer kids who pick up the packs. Call it popular.

But don't call it a case of good versus evil. For heaven's sakes, don't call it a tax on sin.

MARCH 4, 1993

Split-Screen Lives

||||||||||||||||||||||||||||||||||||||||||||||||||||||||||||||||||||||||||||||||||||||||||||||||||||

I am watching an ad for a new television set that offers a screen within its screen. The beauty of this technology, I am told, is that it lets the viewer watch one channel while scanning the others.

But this particular electronic creature gives you more than a window of opportunity into the wide world of network and cable television. If you are into double vision, it actually lets you watch two channels at the same time.

I confess that I have trouble finding one program I want to watch, let alone two. But I am convinced that this is a product of superb marketing strategy. It is attuned to the updated and speeded-up notions of efficiency and time management which now rule our lives.

Remember the quaint needlepointed idea taught by childhood teachers? The idea was that we should do "One Thing at a Time." To this day, many of us fight losing battles with our children in a vain attempt to convince them that they cannot learn multiplication tables while listening to New Kids on the Block and watching MTV.

It is time to admit that most adults are leading split-screen lives. Nobody who is anybody just does one thing anymore. Our burgeoning breed of one-minute managers, inputters, and maxi-mizers of potential have come to believe that those who do two things at once get twice as much accomplished.

Busyness itself is no longer a symptom of workaholism but a badge of efficiency. Such twofers as dialing and driving have become status symbols for executives. It isn't considered ditzy anymore to drink coffee, apply makeup, and insert contact lenses while com-muting to work. It's seen, perversely, as being well organized.

Time is now regarded as a precious and rare resource, so wasting it is the modern sin of human ecology. We are expected to conserve, even recycle, every minute, and to use several of our five senses at a time. So it is that we have come to breakfast with the newspaper and our kids, lunch with business associates and printouts, and shower with a waterproof radio.

This double and triple shifting comes with its own technology. We are able to watch one television program while taping a second, vacuum while talking on a portable phone, bike twenty miles on an Exercycle while studying Swahili from a tape, and log on to our portable computer in an airport waiting room. And so we do.

What's behind all this is the true passion of the times: a lust for productivity. Remember the pursuit of the elusive simultaneous orgasm? We now pursue the illusion of simultaneous accomplish-ments.

There is a course offered in Cambridge, Massachusetts, that teaches students several languages at the same time. That is nothing compared to the curriculum we set up for ourselves. Those who pass today's finals must be able to spend time with their kids while losing weight and making three new business contacts during one intensive hour at the gym. Is it any wonder we are suffering from performance anxiety?

A recent *Psychology Today* article suggested that there was a damaging link between the pace of walking, talking, and working in various cities and the rate of coronary heart disease. My own sense is that well-being isn't a matter of how much time it takes to do one thing; it's a measure of how many things you are trying to do at the same time.

I try to imagine sometimes what an updated version of Charlie

Chaplin's *Modern Times* would look like. These thoroughly modern times place a wider range of demands on every individual. We are supposed to be responsible for work, family, lowering our cholesterol, raising our computer literacy, actualizing our lives, and becoming ecologically sensitive—all at the same time.

This ideal of simultaneous accomplishments fuels the favorite fantasy of the decade: that if we were only more organized, and blessed with all the proper electronic helpers, we would be able to squeeze at least two lives into the time for one. Instead of making choices, we think we can make time.

When life is as split as the new television set, the second screen does show you a whole lot of options. But when it's on, funny how much harder it seems to focus on the big picture.

NOVEMBER 28, 1989

A S i m p l e r L i f e

||||||||||||||||||||||||||||||||||||||||||||||||||||||||||||||||||||||||||||||||||||||||||||||||||||||||||||||||

Casco Bay, Maine — Visitors have flown in this morning. We are awakened by the noises of two of these transients, sea gulls tap-dancing on the roof of the cottage. When their dance is over, they scream their self-satisfaction and leave to cruise the rest of the cove.

I get up slowly, crawl down the length of the bed alcove, and reach for the shorts and T-shirt that hang on the wall pegs. I fall into them like an old familiar chair. They have been waiting for me since last summer and the summer before.

There is one style up here: Maine. It only changes with the weather. There is nothing to mix or match. The shoes are relics of earlier musseling ventures on the rocks. The one appropriate accessory is an old baseball cap that is unquestionably a fashion don't.

We come here to slow up and pare down. There are no travel

guides and Triptiks and express checks in our summer plans. We choose to rid ourselves of clutter for a while, to slough off the chores and obligations, the people and things that must be dealt with, the choices and decisions that confront us with their urgency. We want to get life down to a four-room cottage on an island. To simplify.

Wasn't that what Thoreau wrote when he built his home at Walden Pond? I look up his words in the tattered book on the shelf. "Our life is frittered away by detail. . . . Simplify, simplify." His retreat from "details" opened the spaces of his life. And so does ours.

Our vacation is defined in part by what we do not have. These are things that the island does not have: a traffic light, a movie theater, a burglar alarm, a bank machine, a Benetton. These are the things that the cottage does not have: bedroom doors, pantyhose, cloth napkins, neckties, videotapes.

We are not roughing it by Walden standards. There is electricity and running water in the cottage; a shower of sorts is rigged up to the tub. One of the "staples" of our diet is lobster, the luxurious shedders and hard-shells from our neighbor's traps. And this year we improved the kitchen with a newfangled addition: a plastic trash can.

But here we have happily limited our options the way we limit the items on our dinner menu. We cannot dash out for tacos or frozen yogurt. We can't debate the allure of sushi or pesto sauce. Indeed, we chuckle over the *Gourmet* magazine recipes that call for arugula.

We are just a boat ride away from the mall culture of mainland America. But the waters form a protective barrier against consuming. The loss of access, the downsizing of our home, our community, our lives, defines this time out. Simplify. Simplify.

A few weeks ago, a friend who has been a Moscow correspondent told me what she will miss about her family's time in that capital: the absence of choices. After all her letters describing the shortages and hassles, I laughed. But I also understood.

In her world, there is no consuming to be done, no lawn to be mowed, no extra rooms to be cared for, no lessons to be chauffeured.

For a Western family, this temporary less can feel like more. More time. More togetherness.

Up here, I wonder how many American lives, freer and richer, are frittered away by detail. The extra rooms that demand cleaning, the lawns that demand attention. How many family lives are scattered over aisles and miles of choices that become demanding necessities. Places to get to, prices to pay, things to want. How much easier it seems in our four-room cottage to live smaller.

Is this summer talk? Island life is not easier for the teenagers who take a boat to school or for those who get sick on a winter's night. The pace of our life here has as much to do with leaving work as with leaving the malls and the makeup.

But these are the days we store up. Days when there are mackerel in the cove and raspberries on the bushes and hours in the hammock. They will stay there all winter, permanently hanging in our minds like old clothes on the wooden pegs, carrying another image of life, another message. Simplify. Simplify.

AUGUST 8, 1989

PEOPLE
WATCHING

||||||||||||||||||||||||||||||||||||||||||||||||||||||||||||||||||||||||||||||||||||||||||||||||

|||||| *Gossip was once about people we had actually met. Now it has gone upscale and national. Celebrities are the people we have in common. Talking about their behavior is a way of talking about ourselves, or at least our values.*

The Hillary Watch

||||||||||||||||||||||||||||||||||||||||||||||||||||||||||||||||||||||||||||||||||||||||||||||||||||||||||||||||

It was a miserable, gray, icy winter morning in a city suffering from three major epidemics: the February blahs, the flu, and another rash of no-school days. Indeed, the Boston that greeted the head of the Task Force on Health Care Reform was a coldbed of Seasonal Affect Disorder.

But Hillary Rodham Clinton came here on her appointed rounds for one of a series of trips billed as "pulse-taking" sessions. She is out taking the pulse of the public, and clearly, the public is taking the pulse of this new sort of First Lady.

Here and everywhere that she travels, there seems to be a mutual checkup, and an ongoing public discussion about what makes her tick. Hillary-analyzing threatens to become a chronic condition.

It's over a month since the Little Rock lawyer moved to the White House. Seven months since the candidate's partner was locked in a chocolate-chip cookie bake-off with Barbara Bush. A year since Bill Clinton's wife was introduced to the American public as a woman who was "not Tammy Wynette."

But the dissection of Hillary's character and motives remains something of a full-time specialty, particularly among those who write character prescriptions for a living. Even in the medical mecca of Massachusetts, Hillary Clinton—her name, her job, her hair—can produce more free association than a Rorschach blot.

I am not surprised by the intensity of the interest in the First Lady who has now been on more magazine covers than Cheryl Tiegs in a good year. Hillary belongs to a generation of women whose changing lives have been under constant examination and self-examination for over twenty years.

The roles that most women her age are struggling to bridge in their everyday lives—balancing work and home, juggling children and jobs, success and acceptance—are now being played out against the most rarefied and public backdrop of the White House. We are witnessing the high profile of the first full-fledged professional woman to serve as First Lady and the first First Lady to take such an open part in public policy making.

The newspapers and television bring us daily portraits of Hillary the hostess, Hillary the mother, Hillary the health honcho. We see Hillary setting a table, and Hillary setting an agenda. It's as if the long-dormant and much-debated superwoman had finally broken through the glass ceiling.

But what bothers me is the way the talk about this woman so often seems to turn into a hunt for the seven early-warning signs of power grabbing.

Remember when she became head of the health-care panel? One magazine warned: "She risks being accused of using her marriage as a route to advancement." Another woman sleeping her way to the top.

Remember when she set up shop in the West Wing of the White House? Her move was universally described as a power trip. Remember when she took her briefcase to Congress? The newspaper headlines hung on one word: clout.

After her very first "pulse-taking" trip, the Sunday-morning pundits hinted darkly about a Hillary run amok because she has no "accountability." And even now those who administer weekly political potency tests assert that as the First Lady gets more power, the Vice President has less.

The fixation on female uppityness is common enough to rank as a cultural disease. Women who struggle long hours at low wages may be praised as virtuous or self-sacrificing. Somewhere on the way to the top they are often mysteriously rediagnosed as power-hungry and self-aggrandizing.

But this case deserves a second opinion. Hillary Rodham Clinton moved from primary family wage earner to full-time—truly full-time—volunteer. The task she has taken on is not some beautification program sure to yield praise and popular support for her effort.

Indeed, at the end of a grueling day in Boston, after listening to hours of health-care horror stories, the clearly weary head of the task force said, "We are not going to be able to propose to you . . . a system that has everything in it you want."

The woman has volunteered to walk into the propeller of health-care reform. Does that sound like a savvy career move? Or does it sound, possibly, remotely, like a public service?

Yes, I know. Diagnosticians, even amateurs, are always searching for what's wrong. But when the First Lady takes on a task that may be, literally, thankless, it's pretty strange to scrutinize her continually for symptoms of power hunger. This habit might even be called unhealthy.

FEBRUARY 25, 1993

Dr. Seuss: A Legacy of Imagining

He was a subversive, of course. Not a doctor, unless you count an honorary degree. Most certainly not a "Modern Mother Goose," the unhappy rubric pasted on one obituary. Only the most literal and dullest of booksmiths would dare confine Dr. Seuss's appeal by calling him a "children's writer."

The Theodor Seuss Geisel who died at eighty-seven in bed in his mountaintop home—a rambling Seuss house if there ever was one—was subversive in the way that people who really speak to children often are. They cut through the treacle, the mush, and the fear. They side with the young and dismiss the rest of us for what we are: "obsolete children, and the hell with them."

This is the beauty, after all, of the writers who built Oz and Wonderland as well as Whoville. They re-created what Seuss called the "logical insanity" of a child's world out of their memory and imagination.

What is it like for the people who inhabit a world full of chairs that are too big for them and rules they don't understand? What does it feel like to be as small and complicated as a speck of dust in Horton's hand? "A person's a person no matter how small."

Dr. Seuss, the creation and creator, was unlike most adults. He remembered. He retained a sense of the absurd, including the absurdity of the idea that growing up means losing your humor. So, while too many adults spend their time teaching children the seriousness of the situation, he managed to sneak under the heavy door of learning, asking, "Do you like green eggs and ham?"

The Loraxes and Grinches, the Cats in Hats and elephants on nests, began life not so far from Mulberry Street in Springfield, Massachusetts. The boy's sense of the absurdity of the adult rules came from his father, slated to be named president of a brewery on the very day Prohibition began. The fantastic menagerie grew out of Geisel's visits to the zoo when his father became, instead, Superintendent of Parks.

Geisel spent the Depression drawing an endless series of cartoon ads for insect killer—all bearing a single cutline: "Quick, Henry, the Flit." But in 1936 he sat on the deck of a cross-Atlantic ship and turned the mind-numbing rhythm of the engine into the beat behind "And to Think That I Saw It on Mulberry Street." That began his running, giggling, and sometimes warning commentary on the world.

If governments ignored the little folk, Horton heard a Who. If there were Hitlers in the world, well, Yertle the Turtle was brought down by a single burp from his lowliest subject. If the environment was in danger, one child listened to the Lorax. And if the adult world worked one way, children worked another.

He drew inhabitants for these places that resemble a collection of runaways from some mad genetics institute. He even gave them their own language, so they snuffled and snarggled, cried with cruffulous croaks and made smogulous smokes.

But the subversion that pleased him the most was when he replaced Dick and Jane and their dreary little reader world with the rambunctious, irrepressible Sam-I-am. He excised Spot for a Fox in Socks.

Dr. Seuss was not universally loved. There were educators who thought that making up words was improper. There were loggers who thought the Lorax was dangerous. To which I say: Quick, Henry! The Flit!

The world tells children to act their age all too often. School is Serious and Reading is Important. Today the Books are Relevant, the Subjects are Real Life. It's rare that an adult escapes all this, rarer still that someone comes along piping a message that says: Imagine This. Thing One and Thing Two.

Ted Geisel has died. But in Dr. Seuss's reading room it is still possible to laugh and think at the same time. In his pages, even parents still get permission to delight in the sounds of silliness. He has left a legacy of Truffula trees, ziffs, nerkles, Grinches, and stolen pleasure. "I think I have helped kids laugh in school and at home," he said. "That's enough, isn't it?"

OCTOBER 1, 1991

Jean Harris: Clemency for Prisoner 81-G-0098

To give you an idea of how long ago Jean Harris became Prisoner 81-G-0098, try a few cultural markers. It was before Charles married Di, and before Thelma met Louise. It was before *Smart Women, Foolish Choices*.

It was before *Fatal Attraction* played in the movie theater and sexual harassment played in the Senate hearing room. Before co-dependency became a twelve-step program and, of course, before the battered woman's defense was admissible in court.

When Jean Harris was convicted of killing "Diet Doc" Herman Tarnower in the winter of 1981, we hadn't even figured out that crash diets were crashing failures. Tens of thousands of

Americans—even Julia Child—were following the dictates of the Scarsdale Diet book which Tarnower had dedicated to Jean. And also to "Suzanne, Phyllis, Terry, Elizabeth, Janet, Barbara, Elaine, Frances, June, Sharon, Ruth . . ." Just some of the other women in his life.

For long months, Jean Harris, the headmistress of Madeira and scorned mistress of Scarsdale, was the star of the tabloid firmament. She was a fifty-seven-year-old upper-crust blues heroine whose man done her wrong. She was every woman who was ever dumped for another, younger woman after fourteen years.

There were otherwise reasonable women who didn't care whether Harris dunnit or not: she was the victim and they wanted her acquitted. There were others who saw Harris as nothing more than another jealous, murdering woman: they wanted her convicted.

In court, Harris testified that she was trying to kill herself, not her scornful lover. Later, her advocates claimed that she was not herself that day but an addict in withdrawal from the amphetamines Tarnower had prescribed.

But in the end the only opinion that mattered was the jury's. They found her guilty of second-degree murder. Fifteen years to life.

I thought then and think now that Jean Harris was a woman who had learned too well how to swallow mouthfuls of humiliation in return for tidbits of attention. She was every woman who hung on to a relationship by her fingernails while her self-esteem eroded like a crumbling windowsill on the eighteenth floor. She fell into the abyss.

Now, after nearly twelve years in prison, 81-G-0098 has been granted clemency by the governor who had refused it three times before. As she was heading into coronary-bypass surgery, Mario Cuomo set the sixty-nine-year-old woman on the path to freedom. He attributed his act to her health and to something else: her "above-average behavioral record during her incarceration."

The irony is that Jean Harris became a model prisoner by fighting the prison model. The irony is that she was "rehabilitated." Not by the system, but in opposition to it.

"One fights to stay whole in prison," she wrote from her cell.

Indeed, the self-esteem that eroded in long years of her destructive relationship with Tarnower was, remarkably, rebuilt in resistance to prison's attempt to destroy her.

In one of three books she wrote, Prisoner 81-G-0098 described, in unsparing, unself-pitying detail, the petty tyrannies of "correction officers." She described the constant humiliations of strip searches, the deadening routines of waiting before as many as eighteen locked doors on each walk to and from meals.

With black humor and compassion, she saw life around her in society's warehouse for the criminal, the insane, the abused and abusive who were allowed one bizarre courtesy—to be called "ladies." "How do you teach anything to a human being stripped of all personal dignity?" she asked.

Yet she found an answer. In prison she also became an advocate for reform, organized programs as if it were her school, taught classes for pregnant mothers, worked at the prison children's center. The old headmistress ran up good marks even in the hostile "learning environment." She earned that "above-average behavioral record."

In the years that Harris spent behind bars, we have become more sensitive to emotional abuse. We label people as "victims" with both more sympathy and more abandon.

In some ways Jean Harris's strength is a rebuttal to those advocates who chose to see her as "a victim." In other ways, it's proof that even a seed of self-esteem can grow again.

But, either way, this woman has done her hard time. "Remorse has become an appendage to me," she said once. "It's like another skin, and I live in it and I always will."

It's 1993 and time to free Prisoner 81-G-0098.

JANUARY 3, 1993

Blondie Gets a Job

||||||||||||||||||||||||||||||||||||||||||||||||||||||||||||||||||||||||||||||||||||||||||||||||||||||||||||||||||||

On Labor Day morning 1991, Blondie Boopadoop Bumstead, thirty-five years old and holding, had an epiphany over her coffee cup. Worn out from cooking and cleaning lo these many decades, the suburban housewife of comic-strip fame suddenly figured a way out of her domesticity. "I could go out and get a job."

Bing! Light bulbs flash! Cameras roll! Sweetheart, get me the *Today* show!

Not since Nora left the Doll's House has one wife's change garnered quite this much attention. But Nora was ahead of her time. Blondie isn't exactly a trendsetter among her peers. More than three-quarters of the women in her age group (where she has lingered longer than Jack Benny) are already in the work force.

Nevertheless, this is something of a landmark. Blondie began comic-strip life over sixty years ago as a gold-digging flapper. Back then, Dagwood Bumstead was the daffy heir to a railroad family that owned, as it was said, the right side of the tracks, the wrong side, and the tracks themselves.

When the Depression deepened, these true lovers got married despite Poppa Bumstead's disapproval. Disinherited, Dagwood got a job. They moved to the suburbs, had two kids, a dog, and remained in their thirties ever after.

In some ways the Bumsteads have been emblems of the American family and the American economy. Dagwood, for all his ditziness, has had one job his entire work life. Even in the eighties, as other American companies downsized and streamlined, this long-abused white-collar worker kept his job. While other companies were being taken over, Dithers and Co. dithered along. Even Dagwood's metabolism and eating habits managed to stay the same.

As for Blondie, over the years this white-collar wife also kept her supportive role. She never did get proper credit for her invention of the Dagwood sandwich. She never got any kudos for getting her husband out of the house every morning and into the car pool.

But now that she's decided to get a job, she's doing the "nets," making all the talk shows. Even the Secretary of Labor is interested in how this newest entry will fare in the workplace: "Some of the skills Blondie had will have to be rehoned." Indeed.

Once again, Dagwood and Blondie are getting back in touch with what's happening to the American family that lives paycheck to paycheck: two paychecks.

How, then, can we help Blondie to mark her momentous entry into the working-woman world after all these years? A few tips and tidbits are in order.

The good news is that things are better for working women. The gap between male and female wages has narrowed. The bad news is that it's narrowed mostly because men's wages are falling.

Despite all those years when she was at home with Dagwood and the kids, Blondie's earning capacity won't be much worse than that of other women. If she is typical, her earnings will peak at about age forty to forty-five at $22,000. This is, however, just about what the average man earns between twenty-five and twenty-nine.

On September 9, this longtime kitchen worker decided—at least for the moment—to become a caterer. She will be joining the fastest-growing part of the American economy, women-owned small businesses.

This will supply her with a lot of flexibility. She can be there when Alexander and Cookie get home from school or from the mall. But she'll get none of the perks: vacations, pensions, health insurance. If Dagwood can hold on at Dithers, if Dithers doesn't wither, they will discover the basic economic fact of life in the nineties: two workers equal one good job.

About the household drudgery she's trying to avoid? Well, if she follows the pattern, Blondie will do less housework than before.

But she'll still do most of the work that gets done. Home will become her second shift.

In any case, with luck, this was the last week Blondie will ever have to ask Dagwood for pocket money. If the studies are right, as an employed spouse, she'll start sharing financial decisions. Her job will give them an extra ounce of two-job security, keep the refrigerator stocked with sandwich stuffing, and if Blondie makes it in business, they may even be able to afford to get the kids out of the strip and off to college.

Oh yes, one final piece of advice to this wife: Ms. Bumstead, when you get out there in the work world, for gawdsakes, don't let the guys still call you Blondie.

SEPTEMBER 10, 1991

A Glorious Voice for Change

||||||||||||||||||||||||||||||||||||||||||||||||||||||||||||||||||||||||||||||||||||||||||||||||||||||||||||

In the end she will be remembered less for her sound than for her symbolism, and I suppose there is some sadness in that. Every obituary of the great contralto Marian Anderson, who died Thursday at ninety-six, will focus on the special moment when her artistry interacted with our history.

On a cold Easter Sunday afternoon in 1939, this Negro—not black, not African-American, not yet—stood before a crowd of 75,000 people in front of the Lincoln Memorial. She would write later that "there seemed to be people as far as the eye could see."

When the racially mixed crowd in the racially segregated capital of America grew still, she felt as if she was choking.

By that day Marian Anderson was already in her forties. She had been born in Philadelphia before the turn of the century. Her father, a coal and ice dealer, had died when she was ten, and her mother, who had lost her teaching certificate in a fire, had worked scrubbing floors.

By then Anderson had already been refused admittance to a Philadelphia school of music. No Negroes need apply. She had already been forced to take the voice that stretched over two octaves of depth, power, and gentleness, to Europe just to find an audience.

She had already been told by the conductor Arturo Toscanini, "Yours is a voice such as one hears once in a hundred years." And—perhaps this mattered more—she had already earned enough money to call Wanamaker's and announce that her mother would not be scrubbing floors anymore.

But in the winter of 1939, the Daughters of the American Revolution, the very people who proudly traced their ancestry to breakaway Republicans, barred Anderson from singing in their auditorium, Constitution Hall.

Nearby, an appalled Eleanor Roosevelt, a certified D.A.R. herself, heard the news and quit in a very public protest.

E.R. was then a First Lady embroiled in enough controversy to dwarf those of Hillary Clinton. The year before, at a segregated Southern conference, she had moved her chair into the aisle between the black and white sections. Now she and Harold Ickes, the Secretary of the Interior, decided to find a place for the concert, although the First Lady herself wouldn't attend.

So it came to be that late that Easter afternoon a wary Anderson, a woman who "didn't like a lot of show" and was uncertain about safety, came to stand behind six microphones and eight electric heaters at the Lincoln Memorial, feeling as if she might choke.

But soon she felt "a great wave of good will pour from these people, almost engulfing me," and then did all she had ever really wanted to do in her whole life: she sang.

First she sang "My country 'tis of thee, sweet land of liberty." Then she sang Schubert and then spirituals.

It would be four more years before Marian Anderson got her concert in Constitution Hall. It would be another fifteen years before segregation cracked. She wouldn't become the first black to sing with the Metropolitan Opera until 1955, when her voice was past its peak.

Later she would say, "Other Negroes will have the career I dreamed of." But they would have it, in part, because of her dreams.

"There is a quality in the women of her generation," a cousin once said. "A stoic quality. You rise above whatever indignity is present." She did that. Indeed, Marian Anderson's lifetime spanned an era from stoicism to activism, from ragtime to rap, from segregation and lynchings to civil rights and gang wars.

She wanted to sing, just that, the way Jackie Robinson wanted to play ball, just that. The way Rosa Parks wanted to sit down. Just that.

"Music to me means so much, such beautiful things," she said. "It seemed impossible that you could find people who would curb you, stop you from doing a thing which is beautiful."

But there are times when it requires bravery just to hit a ball. There are also times when you cannot sing or be heard without changing the world first. She lived through those times.

Marian Anderson didn't want to make political history. She wanted to make music. The woman who should have been known simply as the singer of the century will be better known as a sound of historic change.

But in the end she was a daughter or perhaps a mother of another American revolution. In more than one way, for ninety-six years, this glorious voice was heard.

APRIL 11, 1993

Madonna: Siren or CEO

|||||||||||||||||||||||||||||||||||||||||||||||||||||||||||||||||||||||||||||||||||||||||||||||||||

It's past midnight. The football game is over. The local news is over. Forrest Sawyer is asking the news junkies who are still awake to watch *Nightline*: "Has Madonna finally gone too far?"

On the big screen, the same screen where Secretaries of State and terrorists get to say whether they have gone too far, comes a Madonna I've never seen. Conservative black jacket with a collar up to her chin. Power shoulder pads. Gold buttons. Proper little gold earrings. Sleek hair pulled back. Right hand grasping the appropriately serious prop: a pen.

Except for the slim band of dark roots beneath the platinum, except for the voice—early *Working Girl*—she might pass for the CEO of some Wall Street firm. Or she might pass for someone trying to pass for the CEO. That is the thing about Madonna. Look for her identity and you find another image to add to the Rolodex of Madonnas.

Nightline was doing what MTV had refused to do, showing her video "Justify My Love." And Madonna had come dressed to justify her video by saying: It was (1) artistic and (2) better than the other horrors that grace MTV without such fuss. "Why is it okay," she said, "for ten-year-olds to see someone's body being ripped to shreds?"

To this viewer, who refuses to get into the debate about which is worse, sex or violence on TV—lousy choices—the Madonna video was definitely an R but not quite an X. It was clearly fantasy and clearly not the sort of thing you want the kids to find when they're channel-surfing after the Peter Pan tape.

But tonight it's not the black-and-white video Madonna fantasies that fascinate me. It's the contrast with the black-dressed and blond-coiffed Madonna.

Madonna the executive is speaking about Madonna the artist, Madonna of the satellite feed is talking about Madonna of the hotel bed. There are other variations on the theme of Madonna, more incarnations in the life of Madonna, more colors to the chameleon.

The woman before me has earned $90 million in four years from the subsidiaries of her own talent: Boy Toy, Siren, and Slutco. The woman has revamped her image every two years like an engine: Material Girl to Blond Ambition. And still she has icon status among those who see her as the bad girl, the sexually assertive woman, the powerful play mogul. Ask for the real Madonna and she would stand up a pantheon of her selves.

Says Dr. Lynne Layton, who teaches popular culture at Harvard, "She speaks to many women who feel pushed into one aspect of their femininity—'Don't soil your dress, always be nice.' Madonna has many different versions of femininity and seems comfortable with all of them."

When Madonna first brought her underwear and ambition to the stage, it was said that the multiple Madonna appealed to adolescent girls because they try on identities like lipstick. Years later, she still appeals to young women feeling the stress of expectations. Women who try to be all things to all people: sexy but dressed for success, maternal but independent.

But what bothers me in all this is a belief that she offers the wrong answers to the questions, or the crisis, of identity. Especially female identity.

If the work of growing up is finding a center, integrating the parts, Madonna spotlights the fragments and calls them a whole. If the business of adulthood is finding yourself, she creates as many selves as there are rooms in her video hotel. If we must evolve as grown-ups, she switches instead, like a quick-change artist between acts. And if there is a search among Americans for authenticity, Madonna offers costumes and calls them the real thing.

Multi-Madonna is the survivor of a rough childhood, of religious guilt and a bad marriage. She has purposely become a female with the nerve to be "bad" and the will to be powerful. She is, in short, sexy and hard-nosed, brassy and vulnerable, S and M, victor and victim, dressed in bra and black dress.

But the fight against being "pigeonholed" can also be an excuse for confusion. The star of this show after all makes little attempt to reconcile the contradictions of her life and psyche. She insists instead that all the fragments of a self be accepted.

In the end, watching the Madonnas pass before us over the years is a bit like watching the three faces of Eve . . . as a role model. That's not an answer for women trying to integrate their lives.

Has Madonna gone too far? Not in a video for adults. But in real life, she has a way to go.

DECEMBER 7, 1990

Einstein's Wife

||||||||||||||||||||||||||||||||||||||||||||||||||||||||||||||||||||||||||||||||||||||||||||||||||||||||||||||

When I first heard about Einstein's wife, the story sounded like a parody of feminist studies. A coven of historians searching through the archives come to a dark conclusion. It wasn't Einstein who discovered relativity. IT WAS HIS WIFE!

Mileva Maric, fellow student and first wife of the famed Albert, is starring in one of the hottest controversies to hit the dry, footnoted world of historians and scientists. Ever since the American Association for the Advancement of Science held a panel on the subject last month there have been letters, counter-letters, and counter-counter-letters. People have taken sides as if the Einsteins were Donald and Ivana.

Speaking for Mileva are Evan Harris Walker and Senta Troemel-Ploetz. Walker, a physicist, contends that the basic ideas for relativity came from Mileva. Troemel-Ploetz, a German linguist, says that the ideas may have been Albert's, but Mileva did the math.

Speaking for Albert are some irate Einstein scholars. John Stachel, keeper of Albert's letters, says that Mileva was little more than a sounding board.

Of course, the Albert and Mileva Affair has its own place in history. In 1929, Virginia Woolf began the famed *A Room of One's Own* by asking what chance a sister of Shakespeare would have had to become a great playwright. Over the past decade, scholars have studied the lives of great men's wives.

Women from A to Z—or from Anonymous to Zelda (Fitzgerald)—have been reclaimed. Some of Zelda's best writing was found between Scott's pages. Clara was discovered to be a Schumann in her own right, not just Robert's. Camille Claudel emerged as more than a marble block in Rodin's way.

Mileva Maric Einstein, described in a popular biography as the "gloomy, laconic, and distrustful" Serbian peasant, was due for a comeback. It turns out she was one of the rare women admitted to the Polytechnical Institute in Zurich in 1896.

But the case for her as co-genius is shaky. It depends on letters in which Albert referred to "our" theory and "our" work. It hinges on reports of his mathematical weakness and her strength. And rests on a divorce agreement in which Albert promised her his Nobel Prize money. That's not enough to change the credit line on the theory of relativity.

The tragedy of Mileva's life is real enough. But it's of a more personal and a common dimension. It's a parable of two young people who begin life as intellectual soul mates. "How happy I am to have found in you an equal creature who is equally strong and independent as I am," wrote Albert. But somewhere along the way, life and love had an unequal effect in their lives as man and woman, and as scientists.

It's possible to read between the outlines. Pregnant and un-married, Mileva flunked her final exam. Their first child was born out of wedlock and presumably was adopted. By the time their second and third were born, Mileva had become wife, caretaker, and often supporter of the family. Her scientific work stopped, his soared. Finally, the famous Albert left her for another woman and Mileva spent the rest of her life struggling to support herself and her children, including a psychotic son.

There is something familiar about this tale of the two Einsteins. It's aroused such passion it also strikes a very current chord. The scientist, pacifist, humanist was also the product of a time when women's lives and talents were submerged as routinely as their last names in marriage.

We can round up generations of wives before and after Mileva whose star faded or was eclipsed, who went from scholar and co-author to typist to a name on her husband's dedication page or his obit or nothing. Few women marry geniuses, but many have spent their lives in the shadow of "great" men.

Today when couples are struggling to be equals not just at the beginning of their marriage but for life, the young Einsteins raise questions for more than the history buffs. Their story touches those who want marriages of mutual caretaking and individual achievement and wonder if it's possible.

What happens, furthermore, in our own world to those who become caretakers? There is more than a little fear that they'll be left behind . . . or left. And what do we think of the well-cared-for achievers. Are they "greats" or tainted exploiters?

We judge our own lives by these standards and often rejudge the lives of others. "We've had the myth of Einstein as a saintly figure," says Dr. Stachel. "Now we're getting Einstein as the demonic figure." We had the myth of the wife as a nobody. Now we are offered the "myth" of the wife as martyr.

When Einstein died, his brain inspired such awe that it was removed for study. But modern standards add another dimension to his biography. In his personal life, Albert was no Einstein.

MARCH 16, 1990

Donald and Ivana:
Trump This
||||||||||||||||||||||||||||||||||||||||||||||||||||||||||||||||||||||||||||||||||||||||||||||||||||||||||

Until now I had repressed any bad feelings for Donald and Ivana Trump on the theory that their marriage had one major redeeming social virtue: by choosing each other, they had saved two other people.

But my excuse, like their marriage, is now history. In the past week, their Trump-eted separation blasted everything else—the uprising of Eastern Europe, the fall of Mike Tyson, and the resurrection of Nelson Mandela—off the top of the tabloids.

All this comes not a minute too soon for the lifestyle sections of the rich and famous. They don't have Leona to kick around anymore. Zsa Zsa has paid her dues to society. Hollywood is into babies and twelve-step rehab programs. And the Washington scandals of the day are less about sex than S&Ls.

So it is that Americans who have never flown Trump, read Trump, or played Trump are talking and reading about Donald and Ivana as if they lived next door. Was she indeed becoming, gasp, another Leona? Was he unfaithful? Would the prenuptial agreement hold? Who would get custody of the Plaza?

Once again, in the global village, it is clear that celebrities— a category that now lumps Dan Rather, Sting, and the Mayflower Madam together—have become our neighbors. Americans may know more about them than they do about the folks on the next block. (Quick, name all the neighbors, their occupations, lipstick color, and infidelities. Time's up!)

Gossip was once about people we had actually met. Now it has gone upscale and national. Celebrities are the people we have in common. Talking about their behavior is a way of talking about ourselves, or at least our values.

Take the Trumps. (Okay, I'll say it . . . Please.) In the eighties, Donald Trump represented a boyish, open-faced, unabashed, go-for-it love of the Great More, the Eternal Bigger. As a celebrity, he was living proof to Americans that an unexamined life was probably a prerequisite for making money.

To say that the Trumps had it all was something of an understatement, and understatement was not the Trump style. He was the one who renumbered the floors on his Tower to make it ten stories higher. Don and Ivana had over $1.7 billion, three children, 345 rooms in all their houses to call their own, and our attention. They weren't shy about it.

To some extent, Americans used the Trumps to air their ambivalence about wealth in a country in which everybody calls himself or herself middle-class. To some, Donald was, as Ivana said before the split, "the people's billionaire." To others, he was, as *Spy* magazine wrote, "the short-fingered vulgarian."

As for the missus, some saw Ivana as a poor girl from Czechoslovakia who found love, marriage, and money in America. Others saw her as the rich lady who considered herself thrifty because she bought $3,000 designer dresses wholesale.

Either way, in a fifty-room apartment high above Fifth Avenue, the Trumps seemed wholly removed from the more pedestrian problems of life. As celebrities, they got to glitter and the rest of us got to debate the cost and value of the glitter.

Now they get to suffer, thereby fulfilling the great American hope that money can't buy happiness. Under the guise of gossip, we can watch the celebrated split the way we watched their celebrated lives—at a safe distance. The Trumps now become a glitzy text for daily commentary on the way less pricey partnerships unravel.

There are already some classic divorce scenarios. Ivana, the self-described "European wife," once happily accepted "a salary of $1 a year and all the dresses she could buy" from Donald. Now she says that a $20 million agreement isn't enough.

Donald, a proud husband once, put Ivana in charge of the Plaza because she was "rock-strong and solid." Now he lets friends suggest that she did little but pick out wallpaper.

Add a lot of zeros to the checkbook and this sounds like any marital partnership unraveling, any couple you know revising the story of their marriage with hourly bulletins. Take away the public relations men and the lawyers and it sounds like our friends pushing us to choose between the Bride's Side and the Groom's Side.

Of course, the question this time is whether it's more dreadful to be married to a woman who has her carpet vacuumed before she steps into the room. Or worse to be hooked up to a man whose social outlook is: "Even if the world goes to hell in a handbasket, I won't lose a penny." Donald Trump once described his work style this way: "Boom—like a cobra." In this celeb match, we are asked to choose between the mongoose and the cobra.

Nevertheless, in some way, the media care and maintenance of the Supercelebs, the fascination with their Triumphs and Trials, is the way Americans talk out the mores and morals of society. If future historians want to know what we were like, they'll go to the *People* magazine files, not to *Foreign Policy*. Leave them a note to look under "Trump, Donald and Ivana."

FEBRUARY 20, 1990

Jackie: Oh!

||||||||||||||||||||||||||||||||||||||||||||||||||||||||||||||||||||||||||||||||||||||||||||||||||||||||||

The woman is in a state of high gush. Never mind that she has interviewed Prime Ministers and grilled Presidential candidates, that she eats her subjects with a side dish of cynicism. This is the ultimate news bulletin:

"I just saw Jackie," she breathes into my phone. "She looks fabulous!"

I do not ask: Jackie Who? I know. Everybody knows. Everybody has seen her, if not in person, close up enough. She's on the cover of *Life* and *Vanity Fair*. She's on both covers of *A Woman Named Jackie*, the best-seller that everybody loves to hate and refuses to admit they have read. Every gossipy, intrusive, unreliable word.

Jackie is turning sixty on July 28. Sixty. This is not the sort of event that colleges hold symposia about. There is nothing of national meaning or international significance for this life marker.

But for at least one month, Americans will gape at her photo the way they gape at the person who comes back to their college reunion looking, dammit, exactly the same. Fabulous.

Jackie, sixty and skinny, celebrating her fifteenth birthday as a forty-five-year-old, looks like the young girlfriend on the arm of her fifty-nine-year-old companion. Jackie, sixty and surviving, her fifteen minutes of fame have extended to thirty years of speculative, bitchy biography.

She has gone from being Jacqueline Bouvier to Jackie Kennedy to Jackie Onassis to Jackie O. The last name of the most famous woman in America sounds like a simple exclamation of admiration, a vowel of awe. Jackie: Oh.

Jackie came into the public eye in a pillbox hat and never left. She became famous as a wife and widow. She became infamous as a wife and widow. She became famous again and permanently for being famous. By now her life is more familiar than many members of our family. How many of us know about our father's infidelity? How many know our own sister's shoe size? We know Jackie's size: 10.

Jackie O has rarely made a move in public that wasn't photographed, rarely had an employee who couldn't be paid for her private memoirs or had a friend who could talk about her without feeling like she was name dropping. She has led the most private of public lives, the most public of private lives.

So what do we say about this sixty-year-old survivor? One brief admiring word about her success at mothering. A pro forma acknowledgment of her success as a working grandmother and a dutiful daughter. And then to the big stuff: Gawd, she looks fabulous!

The photos in *Life* are f-stops along every year from 1929 to 1989. The last twenty of them look the same. The only things that have changed are the hemlines and the language. At forty she was glamorous, at sixty she is "still" glamorous.

This is what sixty looks like?

How many women search these pictures for clues of the cost of maintenance, the way they search along her hairline for evidence of a scalpel. How many single-potato-and-caviar dinners account for the dress size? How many lunches passed up, how many yoga sessions have replaced desserts? How much time spent jogging and how much at the hairdresser?

The most energy-, money-, and time-consuming activity is the struggle against aging. There isn't a woman in the world who doesn't know that. Vanity is an expensive vice and beauty an expensive virtue. There is hardly a woman of any age who hasn't wrestled with that cost accounting. Ours and hers.

How many million women wake up saying this is the first day of the rest of their diet? How many resent the glorification of youth and yet blame themselves for aging as if it were a personal lack of willpower? How many have felt the ambivalence? Faulting ourselves for caring about looks. And for not caring enough. Wondering when we get permission to stop caring, stop fighting.

When the new First Lady came into view this January, there

was much ado about her gray hair, her laugh lines, her dress size and lifestyle. At sixty-four, she looks her age. We want her to wear it comfortably. When the old First Lady comes into view, just four years younger, there is much ado about her skin, dress size, glamour. We want to know how she does it.

The truth is that most women want to want to look like Barbara Bush. But they truly want to look like Jackie. We want to stop fighting against age—pass the chocolates and the footrest—and we want to still look young. We want to be admired for our character, lines and all, and thought of as glamorous. We want to let go and stay the same.

Now Jackie has another birthday carrying another sort of message across the cover stories. This is what sixty can look like. This is what we're supposed to look like at sixty? Oh, Jackie, oh. She looks, dammit, fabulous.

JULY 28, 1989

ABOUT
WOMEN

||||||||||||||||||||||||||||||||||||||||||||||||||||||||||||||||||||||||||||||||||||||||||||||||||

|||||| *The much-heralded new choices
for women—circa 1972—now seem
like hard decisions circa 1992. Full
time, part time, mommy track, child
care, one paycheck or two—each
option comes with an elaborate and
unsettling cost accounting that goes to
the psyche as well as the pocketbook.*

The Theory of the White Male Rat

||||||||||||||||||||||||||||||||||||||||||||||||||||||||||||||||||||||||||||||||||||||||||||||||||||||||||||

This is a story that begins with white male rats. No, it is not a political fantasy created by those who regard "white male rats" as redundant. The subject here is science and sex.

It turns out that most of the basic research that teaches us what is good and bad for human beings begins with rodents of the male persuasion. Their female counterparts are usually excluded because of what might be called "raging hormonal imbalance." Their female physiology is more complex.

I didn't come across this information through personal experience. I have never seen a female rodent with PMS, let alone hot flashes. Nor have I ever before worried that they were denied equal employment opportunities as research subjects.

Rather, the tale of the white male rat was reiterated at the congressional hearings of the House Subcommittee on Health and the Environment this week. These creatures were a small if furry part of the larger saga. In research, female humans are also excluded from most studies done on "people."

The pills women swallow, the diets that we follow, the exercises we adhere to—the health plan that is prescribed for us—are for the most part based on research done on a thoroughly male model. Remember the cholesterol study? Its 4,000 subjects were men. Remember the smoking study? The 15,000 subjects were men. How about the aspirin study? Its 22,000 doctors were all male.

The end result is that women with heart disease—the number-one killer of women—and all sorts of ills are by and large treated as if they were men. And while this experience might be refreshing in a paycheck, it could be dangerous in a checkup.

The hearings that brought the tale of the neglected females of two species to the public consciousness were called because of a government study pushed by the congressional women's caucus. The study showed that the National Institutes of Health had failed to fulfill its own four-year-old policy to include women in clinical trials. The scientists who planned, proposed, and funded research had paid little more attention to it than a smoker pays to a warning on a cigarette pack.

But it turns out that the exclusion of women as subjects for research is only one piece of a profoundly skewed research program. Not only are men studied more, so are their health problems. Diseases like ovarian cancer and osteoporosis remain second-class subjects. Even breast cancer, which kills 40,000 women a year, gets only $17 million for basic research.

All in all, about 13 percent of NIH's $5.7 billion budget goes to study the health risks of the half of the population that is female. While every woman in America will go through menopause, hormone treatment has little priority in terms of federal dollars. While every woman ages, the latest study—entitled "Normal Human Aging"—has no data about women at all.

"I've had a theory that you fund what you fear," says Representative Patricia Schroeder, who along with Representatives Olympia Snowe of Maine and Henry Waxman of California has kept a spotlight on this issue. "When you have a male-dominated group of researchers they are more worried about prostate cancer than breast cancer."

The fund-what-you-fear bias in health research goes straight through the medical system. After all, who decides what we should study, what is important and who is important? The dearth of female researchers, female reviewers, female doctors and administrators at NIH has directly resulted in a dearth of research on women's health issues.

But conversely, the rise of women in medical and policy-making positions in the rest of the world has put these issues in the public eye. This summer, the congressional women's caucus will be presenting a health package that calls for more research.

In fairness, medical science is not all that different from any other business in America that is just beginning to adjust to women. There is the dual notion that you can either treat women just like men or exclude them altogether.

According to the rat theory, many researchers lament that including women with all their peculiar plumbing is too complicated, and too expensive. But in the long run, research that is valid for only half the human species is no bargain. So the next time you pop a pill, or follow the doctor's orders, check carefully for the telltale paw prints of the white male rats.

JUNE 22, 1990

Condoms   for   Her
||||||||||||||||||||||||||||||||||||||||||||||||||||||||||||||||||||||||||||||||||||||||||||||||||||||||||||||||||||||

From all reports this is a medical breakthrough, although breakthrough is probably a bad word to use when you're talking about condoms.

In any case, somebody called it "a great day for women." The buzzword of the week was "empowerment." All eleven members on the FDA panel recommended the tentative approval of the first condom for women.

Well, forgive me if I don't get my "Sisterhood Is Powerful" T-shirts out of storage to celebrate the invention of this vaginal pouch. I share the more subdued attitude embodied in the name of the device. It's called "Reality." Maybe it should be called "Bleak Reality."

About five years ago when alarm about the heterosexual transmission of AIDS first broke through the walls of denial, sexual entrepreneurs began marketing male condoms to women. The most straightforward of the ads featured a woman saying, "I'll do a lot for love, but I'm not ready to die for it."

The message in the marketing was pretty clear. Women who had taken on the full responsibility for birth control were urged to take on more responsibility for disease control. The condom which once made an impression in teenage male wallets was repackaged for female purses.

Now it's 1992. Almost two-thirds of the AIDS cases worldwide have been transmitted heterosexually. Magic Johnson is infected with the HIV virus. And the new, improved line of defense we are offered is a device that eliminates any male responsibility at all.

This is the much-touted advantage of the female version of the condom. It may be expensive. It may be awkward to use. But it circumvents the need to even "negotiate" with a man.

Dr. Mary Guinan, who works in AIDS and other sexually transmitted diseases at the Centers for Disease Control, is quite open about the female advantage. "We need protective devices for women," she says. "Then they don't have to negotiate something with a man. They can do it themselves."

This is the new Reality. The success of the female condom is predicated on the failure of male-female negotiations. The "empowerment" that comes with a vaginal pouch is proof, if we needed it, of women's lack of power in relationships.

Dr. Guinan wearily admits to the power gap she has seen in many forms and many populations. Not long ago she asked a roomful of peers—all women doctors—how many thought they had equality in sexual decision making. Only 20 percent raised their hands.

Today one of her patients is a thirty-year-old woman married to a hemophiliac with AIDS. He refuses to use condoms and she continues to have sex with him. She is more reluctant to hurt his feelings than he is to endanger her life.

Drawing such parameters, Dr. Guinan asks, "Do you think a woman can negotiate condom use with a crack user? They have to have something of their own so that the guy won't beat them up." Indeed her chief reservation about the female condoms is that they can be seen or felt by male partners. "The next step is a condom that a man can't detect."

The medical facts show that women are more vulnerable to

sexually transmitted diseases than men. Even AIDS is not an equal opportunity virus. It is easier for a man to infect a woman than the other way around.

But a decent product can still be a lousy sign of the times. This one points to the stark unevenness of social change. The most current sexual armament coexists with the most ancient sexual passivity.

After all this time, it is still simpler for many women to insert a condom than to assert themselves. It's simpler for women to take care of themselves than to say "no" or "not now" or "not without protection" to men who aren't caring or careful.

How many women in the past two decades have found it easier to change their own behavior than to change the men in their lives? How many have found it easier to alter the way they behave independently than to alter the way they behave in a relationship?

This time it's condoms for women. "We can't afford to wait until society becomes enlightened," Dr. Mervyn Silverman of the American Foundation for AIDS Research says quite properly. "I'd hate to see a lot of women die because we were waiting for nirvana."

So, this is Reality. One step forward in female protection. One step backward in male responsibility. Something new and something very, very old.

FEBRUARY 7, 1992

A Woman in the House

||||||||||||||||||||||||||||||||||||||||||||||||||||||||||||||||||||||||||||||||||||||||||||||||||

Maybe this is the best way to think about it: When two adults move in together in mid-life, the common wisdom says that it's best not to move into his place or her place but to find theirs. In politics, however, said Ruth Mandel, the head of the Eagleton

Institute, "women are moving into his place, uninvited and unwooed."

Those who nodded with familiar amusement at this analogy were seasoned women politicians from across the country gathered last week at Harvard's Kennedy School for a conference on leadership. All of these women know what it feels like to move into his place—the city hall, the state legislature, the Congress. All of them have struggled to feel comfortable there, to fit into one room, to redecorate another more to their taste.

So, as is often the case when women get together, the talk was not just of strategies for success but of values, not just "how to" move up but "why to" and "whether to" and "is it worth it to?" There were echoes of conversations heard all the time now among business women and professional women, those who are struggling to get into the system while questioning it, those who want to be accepted as one of the boys and want to change the way the boys operate. Those who don't know if they can do all of this at the same time.

The women at the conference included, still, a large number of "firsts" and "onlies," women at the cutting edge of change. They held high the recent evidence of how elected women can make a difference: It was the women in Congress who had stood up days before, one after another, pressing their colleagues to restore Medicaid funding of abortions for victims of rape and incest. It was women legislators in Florida who had led the fight to defeat their governor's attempt to limit abortions.

But there was also the palpable sense that women are not moving ahead as fast in politics as in other professions. There was the deep concern that it is harder for political women to "make it" and "change it."

The most moving description of the dialogue carried on inside the heads of women who live in the institutions built for and by men came from the highest-ranking woman at the conference. In a speech rich in depth and emotional honesty, Governor Madeleine Kunin of Vermont, who has been successful by every common measure, talked as a woman and governor, a woman governor, about inner skirmishes in a dual-value system. She spoke to the conflicts

she fears may inhibit women from moving into and up in politics.
"We would like to change the rules of the game," Kunin said,
"and sometimes hold ourselves back because we don't approve of
the way it is played. But then we find if we don't play by their
rules, we don't play at all.

"We would like to be the advocates of political *perestroika*—a
less adversarial and more consensus-built system—that is what we
are more comfortable with. But the bottom line in politics is crude
and demanding. It's win or lose. Nothing in between.

"We can't expect the few women in political life to change the
values and the rules of the game alone, although that is sometimes
precisely the expectation. If you haven't changed the world, what's
the point of your being there?"

Living with these contradictions is uncomfortable for any woman
in a "man's place." "That is what is hard," she told her colleagues.
"Reconciling one's internal self with the demands of the political
system, which is based on male traditions and is still largely male-
defined."

Kunin fears that these contradictions may be the largest hurdle
for women advancing in political life. "It is not lack of polling data
or campaign contributions which keeps many women from ascend-
ing higher on the political ladder. It is fear and loathing for the
political system itself."

Perhaps this same "fear and loathing" holds women back at the
edge of real breakthrough success in other institutions. "Fear and
loathing" of the "system" that leads to the corner office of the CEO.

The governor countered her melancholy and honest assessment
of women's place with a description of what women can accomplish
in political life and how much they are needed: "Women's voices
must be heard as we debate, plan, and decide the future of our
states, nation, and world." But her eloquence about the inner conflicts resonates at this moment in social change.

This is what women are learning. After the first flush of excitement, after they've made the commitment and moved in, it
takes a long time for a house, or a House, or even a governor's
mansion to become a home.

O C T O B E R   2 0 ,   1 9 8 9

Barbara Bush Comes to Wellesley

|||||||||||||||||||||||||||||||||||||||||||||||||||||||||||||||||||||||||||||||||||||||||||||||||||||||||||||||

There won't be a boycott this commencement day. There won't be boos or banners strung across the Wellesley campus. It isn't that sort of a place or that sort of a protest.

But when it was announced that Barbara Bush would talk at commencement, it turned out that the First Lady was not every senior's dream speaker. A petition circulated around the 120-year-old women's college, and 150 members of the class of 1990 said they were "outraged by this choice."

"Wellesley teaches that we will be rewarded on the basis of our own merit, not that of a spouse," read the petition signed by this dissident quarter of the class. "To honor Barbara Bush as a commencement speaker is to honor a woman who has gained recognition through the achievements of her husband, which contradicts what we have been taught over the last four years at Wellesley."

With those words, the speaker became the subject of a college debate about women's roles and role models: Barbara Bush or Mrs. George Bush. Woman of Achievement or Wife of Achiever. The wife beside the husband or the woman behind the man. Can anyone check all of the above?

Whatever this says about college etiquette and "outrage," I don't think it's bad to end an academic life on a women's campus with such a final exam. The women are leaving this environment debating whom they admire, what they respect and why. The last multiple-choice question of their college career is also the first in the rest of their lives. As the college president, Nannerl Keohane, put it, "It's at the fulcrum of the kinds of issues we've all been wrestling with."

The petitions were right in one respect. The best and the brightest of our young women, like their male counterparts, have indeed been rewarded on the basis of their own "merit." At the core of academic life is the notion of individual achievement. Students rise and fail on their own. They have been encouraged to know and speak their own minds, plot their own lives.

But in their peripheral vision, young women see ahead a year or ten, to the time when their lives won't be exclusively their own. They will be made in concert with others, especially husbands and children. It's still not clear whether you can own a life and share it, whether the compromises sure to come will include ambition.

So there may be more anxiety than disrespect in the protests. On the way to becoming a first woman, could they be diverted to becoming someone's first lady?

Barbara Bush, of course, grew up in another era. She left Smith with an MRS., not a B.A. She made a life as wife, mother, volunteer. She moved with her husband from Maine to Texas to China, from the loser's circle to the White House. Her mother had taught her that you have two choices in life: "You can like what you do, or you can dislike it. And all my life, I have chosen to like it."

Times have changed since then. Our daughters are handed a much longer list of choices and a much harder list of decisions. We tell them to like what they do or change it. We value acceptance less and change more.

But Mrs. Bush has lived within certain constraints and also stretched them. As First Lady there are limits to what one can say and she has stayed within them. There are also depths to what she can do and she has plumbed them. If Barbara Bush has "gained recognition through the achievements of her husband," no one can say that she has rested on his laurels.

This may be something to share with a generation that hasn't yet assumed any title more circumscribed than that of student. Eventually they too will make choices and feel constraints. How will they take a role and make it larger?

"Every role comes with certain circumscribed notions of what it means," says President Keohane of First Ladydom. "We take them and pummel them into our own." This is equally true for the young Wellesley graduate when she becomes a doctor and when she becomes a wife. In our era of change, none of the titles quite fit; the definitions of mother and CEO, volunteer and lawyer all need a bit of pummeling to fit our lives.

So in many ways this may be a proper match for a commencement day. In the audience, a class of women with diplomas as fresh as a new deck of cards. Each holding fifty-two options, wondering which ones to play, how many at once, and whether it's easiest at solitaire. On the podium, a woman who took some of the cards that were dealt her and rearranged them into the best order. A woman who has played her hand with grace and character.

APRIL 24, 1990

The Cost of Fear

"This is what I am getting my daughter for Christmas," says my friend, placing a newspaper ad on the table that we share for our annual holiday lunch.

The ad contains no teddy bears or Santas. Her daughter, like mine, is grown. Rather it shows a young woman next to a broken car in an isolated area. The model, with an anxious look on her face, is urgently saying into a car phone, "Please hurry, it's getting dark!"

My friend's gift idea is, of course, the phone. She wants to give her twentysomething daughter—the same child who once longed for a Cabbage Patch doll and then yearned for a pair of silver earrings—a bauble of added security.

I understand this choice, although my friend's taste usually runs more to funky hats than to hardware. Car phones themselves, once sold as a basic for work, are now featured as a dress-for-security accessory. They are sold for protection.

But this afternoon, as I pass the ad back, it occurs to me that her worries about safety are not seasonal. Nor are they restricted to the car and its occupants. Indeed I share them.

I tell my friend about a conversation I had with my own daughter. She, the wanderer, had just called to describe in detail her new apartment. I, the worrier, had asked for the most important detail: "Is it safe?"

She had talked about cabinets in the kitchen and curtains on the windows. I had asked about alarms on the door and grates on the windows.

The two of us, mother and daughter, stopped and calculated the hidden "safety tax" on her last two apartments. Hadn't the difference between pretty safe and not so safe places been about $100 a month? Wasn't this a sort of gender tax?

Now my friend and I go on. We tabulate the everyday costs of being female and sometimes afraid. Do we count the extra lock on one friend's door? Self-defense lessons for another? Cajun pepper Mace for a third? Do we include the times we took taxis instead of streetcars?

What is the price list for other women? How many jobs are passed up because they are in places or at hours considered unsafe? How many places do women *not* go to—movies, dinners, friends —on how many nights, out of how much anxiety? And how do we calculate this cost of safety?

The world is not always safe for men either. We know that males who are young and black are at the greatest risk of criminal harm. But we also know that feeling unsafe—at home, at work, on the streets—pervades women's lives more completely.

Last fall, when two groups—the Ms. Foundation and the Center for Policy Alternatives—surveyed women across race and class and age, they found that worries about personal security were second only to worries about economic security. Indeed the two worries were often connected.

In public, activists and policy makers still tend to divide such concerns into their parts. Rape, sexual harassment, battering, crime.

But add them together and give them one proper name—personal safety—and a quarter of all women will admit that this is their top concern. Some, poor Latina women in particular, worry more about safety than even about paying their rent.

This is one women's issue that can cut across all lines because it cuts across all lives. It can link together a woman with the cellular phone on her Christmas list and the woman who cannot leave her housing project apartment after dusk. They share the gender tax and, often, the fear.

My friend and I finish our pre-Christmas lunch in a not so festive mood. We are women who feel confident at work but tense in an empty city parking lot. We know others who have broken the glass ceiling, but feel afraid—and sometimes ashamed of feeling afraid—of footsteps in the dark. We have raised daughters to be strong and yet daughters who must beware.

Now we are learning that women cannot feel free unless they feel safe. Trying to communicate that message will take much more power than a cellular phone.

DECEMBER 15, 1992

Beauty   and   the   Breast
||||||||||||||||||||||||||||||||||||||||||||||||||||||||||||||||||||||||||||||||||||||||||||||||||||||||||||||||||||||||||

I arrived at adolescence in the era of training bras and angora sweaters. I never did figure out what these bras were training us for—Womanhood? the Great American Breast Fetish?—but now I look back to that era, reluctantly, as the good old days.

Thirty years ago we gossiped about which of the girls in our class and our *Seventeen* magazines were wearing falsies under their blouses. Now we gossip about which of the Miss America contestants and *People* magazine subjects are wearing falsies under their skin.

The hourglass figure, that fantasy of the 1950s femininity, has been transformed into a muscular anorexic with a C cup in the 1990s. And since this is a model that rarely comes off of nature's shelf, it is being manufactured.

Some two million American women—one in every sixty—have had their bodies cut open and implants put into their chests. Last year alone, 150,000 paid their surgeons between $3,000 and $5,000 for this piecework. Less than a third of the women were cancer patients undergoing reconstructive surgery. The overwhelming majority were trying to "enhance" their self-image by enlarging their breasts the new-fashioned way.

Remember in *A Chorus Line* when a young dancer bragged that the operating room—"tits and ass"—not the casting couch, was the secret of her success. In real life, breast implants are now a success accessory that you can buy in your nearest surgical shop. They have become the most common cosmetic surgery on the market and silicone is the most popular product in the line.

Now the safety of silicone is going to be reviewed by an advisory panel in a three-day session. This week, the FDA is likely to air more about the risks of this procedure than many patients have ever heard.

The FDA will hear about implants that harden and implants that migrate, about infections and bleedings, ruptures and replacements, arthritis and scleroderma, numb nipples and hard-to-read mammograms. They'll hear reports that say the odds of serious trouble are very, very small and reports that say they're too large. And they're likely to hear that the research on silicone implants is still skimpy.

As for the benefits? Congress has already been inundated with women worried that their breasts might be banned. A campaign by the American Society of Plastic and Reconstructive Surgeons has mobilized support to "help all women retain the right to decide for themselves about breast implants."

Like many in the American public, I have two sets of feelings about breast implants: one about the choices confronting cancer patients and another about cosmetic patients. But I am of one mind about public policy. There should be a single standard of safety for silicone and a single standard of choice. If implants are safe, women should be able to choose them.

But what bothers me about the buyer's market in bigger breasts is not just the danger. It's that this boffo biz is based on insecurity. It's built on a diversifying data base of self-hates. Cosmetic surgery is the lucrative business of fixing an ever-expanding list of things that are "wrong" with women.

"What we have had in the past ten years," says Naomi Wolf, the author of *The Beauty Myth*, "is a determined drive by the cosmetic surgery industry to make women feel their breasts are inadequate."

The very same plastic surgeons now urging women to protect their right to prostheses began pushing them in the 1980s. Their association's press releases described small breasts as "deformities" that were "really a disease." The diagnosis was "a total lack of well-being" and the prescription was an implant. A surgical cure for a cultural disease.

Cosmetic surgeons for their part run ads that often make breast implants sound as simple as buying contact lenses. And for a time, the women's magazines joined in with feel-good-through-simple-surgery stories.

Some women do indeed feel better with implants. But there is a symbiotic relationship between a culture that makes women feel bad about their bodies and a business that makes them feel better. We know that every time we belly up to the blush-on counter. This time we are not talking about face powder.

The advisory panel may end this week without enough evidence for a ban or for a silicone seal of approval. But we'll all know more about the personal price of "beauty." And the more a woman is informed, the less she may give consent to this surgical fashioning of femininity. We're not in training any longer.

NOVEMBER 12, 1991

Tailhook: Running the Gantlet

||||||||||||||||||||||||||||||||||||||||||||||||||||||||||||||||||||||||||||||||||||||||||||||||||||||||||||||

Major Rhonda Cornum has a way to understand what happened to her. It was war, after all.

An enemy shot down her plane in the Persian Gulf War, breaking both her arms. An enemy bullet lodged in her right shoulder. And an enemy hand violated her body, vaginally and rectally.

When she talked about her ordeal as a prisoner of war last week, the strong-minded flight surgeon said that the indecent assault ranked as "unpleasant, that's all." Other POWs were beaten, shocked with cattle prods, starved. There is a word to describe her endurance: bravery.

But what of the military women who suffered from what can only be called the "friendly fire" of sexual assault? The women who were attacked by the men on their side, our side. The women brutalized by their officers, or their peers. What of the American men who treated American women as if they were the enemy.

One of them, Jacqueline Ortiz, a twenty-nine-year-old reservist, told a Senate panel last week that she was "forcibly sodomized" by her sergeant in broad daylight near the Iraq border. She said, "I would rather have been shot down and killed that way than have to deal with what I deal with daily."

Another, Paula Coughlin, a thirty-year-old Navy lieutenant, has told the country that she was passed down the now-infamous gantlet on the third floor of the Tailhook convention hotel as naval pilots grabbed her breasts, pulled at her pants, and chanted, "Admiral's aide, admiral's aide!" She said, "I thought, I have no control over these guys. I'm going to be gang-raped."

Should this behavior shock us? In the past few years, one study after another has shown that two-thirds to three-quarters of military women have been subjected to everything from sexual "joking" to physical assault.

But the war in the Gulf brought home images of military men and women performing their jobs in the rough and egalitarian camaraderie of wartime. In the wake of that war, Congress lifted the ban against women flying combat missions.

Now the dark underbelly of this story. Along with advancement, harassment. Along with the new Army, the last bastion. Call it backlash. Or just call it the gantlet.

The tale of the Tailhook has captured public attention because it was not the act of a single criminal, a military renegade. The men who ended up mauling some twenty-six women—half of them fellow officers—were our elite, the aircraft carrier pilots, the top guns, the present and former hotshots. So were the men who watched and did nothing.

Rosemary Mariner, the president of Women Military Aviators and a member of Tailhook herself, compares these assaults to what happened to blacks in the old South. She calls them a "tar and feathering."

She believes the atmosphere was poisoned not just by booze and strippers and porno flicks. Psychological permission for the disparagement of women was also granted at the Tailhook symposium, says Mariner, when a chant went up against women pilots on aircraft carriers—"No Women in TAC Air!" No senior aviator stopped it.

Such hostility was seen two years ago when a female Naval Academy student was chained to a urinal by male midshipmen. It was seen three weeks ago when an obscene banner directed at Representative Patricia Schroeder, a member of the Armed Services Committee, was unfurled at Miramar Naval Air Station in California. The backlash, the gantlet is not just on the third floor of the Hilton Hotel in Las Vegas.

But it finally came into focus there, among an elite. "Pilots are in a very dangerous job," says Judith Stiehm, who wrote *Arms and the Enlisted Woman.* "They develop strong special bonds and the military has used manliness as an essential part of bonding. But how do you prove you are a man if women also do it?" The men at Tailhook were, she says, engaged in the oldest and most widespread sort of harassment: "Peers making life so miserable they run the person out."

When Paula Coughlin saw the men in the hallway, it never occurred to her to be afraid. After all, she was one of them. A pilot, an officer. Now the woman who gave a name and a face to this crime won't let them run her out.

The Navy Secretary's head has rolled. Jobs have been cut and many promotions held up. But in the deeply scandalous investigation, 1,500 men of Tailhook have maintained an oath of silence more like the Mafia than the military. Only two men have been identified.

Many in the Navy have found it easier to close ranks against women than with them. That silence carries the message about the gantlet as backlash. That silence carries the message that women are the outsiders, indeed the enemy.

For the honor of Major Rhonda Cornum, and every woman who signed up to fight for the country, the Navy must know: This will not stand.

JULY 7, 1992

Better Dead Than Coed I

||||||||||||||||||||||||||||||||||||||||||||||||||||||||||||||||||||||||||||||||||||||||||||||||||||||||||

When the news came that Mills College would not be accepting men, there were cheers and champagne all across the Oakland campus. The young women in their counterrevolutionary T-shirts— "Better Dead Than Coed"—had won the day. They had been temporarily saved from that fate worse than death.

But on the other coast, this observer suffered from a case of déjà vu. Where had I seen those T-shirts before? Just last month, on the all-male campus of the Virginia Military Institute.

What would I say if the students of VMI were to pop champagne bottles and celebrate victory against the lawsuit to admit women onto that male bastion? I would call it a defeat.

So the Mills College case raises more than a few questions about the battle for equality. Is there a double standard being raised on the field? Are we to cheer the fall of the last male strongholds while defending the remaining female cloisters? Are male traditions bad and female traditions good? Is segregation bad for men and good for women?

I don't want to press the analogy between VMI and Mills College too far. VMI is a tax-supported institution and public money is being used by a school that excludes citizens on the basis of sex. Mills College is private, and private institutions have more legal leeway to structure themselves as they will.

But over the past decade, in the name of equality, some who favor admitting women into male colleges have also fervently argued against admitting men into female colleges. The defenders of women's institutions describe their campuses as oases in a sexist society. They say that the attention and encouragement women receive there make them better equipped to go into the world on an equal footing with men.

A good deal of research is mustered to support their belief that all-women's environments may produce more than their share of scientists, professionals, leaders. And if that is true, the double standard may actually be a double path to the same goal. Men's colleges may be bastions of male tradition, while women's colleges are on the front lines of feminist change.

I understand these arguments. In women's classes, women do ALL the talking. On women's campuses, they hold ALL the leadership positions. Indeed, when women's colleges go coed, they seem to lose that edge.

Nevertheless, it occurs to me these days that the ringing defense of women's colleges has a separatist clang to it. The argument carries the sounds of discouragement with the pace of change in coed institutions, perhaps even with the possibility of equality in the world. These days, do many prefer the cloister—some variation on the theme of the mommy track?

Susan Rieger, a legal studies professor who calls herself "the honorable opposition" at all-female Mount Holyoke College, says, "I think the ideology is mostly patronizing. It says, if we put you into a classroom with men you aren't going to do as well. You aren't going to edit the newspaper. You are going to be discouraged from science." Ironically, she says, that message grows stronger as the evidence may be growing weaker, as more women succeed in coed schools.

Women's colleges were founded because women were barred from most colleges. Today, only a handful of schools exist for men only. But the early and eager assumption that equal admissions would produce an instant equal environment has led to disappointment and impatience.

Indeed, the notion has emerged among some that if a woman goes to a coed school she will automatically—dare I say naturally?—remain a second-class citizen. There is a suggestion in the sales pitch that she is better off with her own kind.

"Separatism has become more attractive in the past few years," says Wendy Kaminer, who has written about this in A Fearful Freedom. "The notion that for whatever reasons we can't be equal in the same place at the same time reflects some resignation that I don't share."

Nor do I. The discouragement with change and the goal of equality is premature. And defeatist. There are, after all, only 125,000 women attending 94 women's colleges. These schools can remain a lively alternative. But the most important work is to change the learning environment on campuses where the vast majority of women go to school with men.

Mills College, neither dead nor coed, has raised some lively issues about equality even among its own defenders. Consider the role of Warren Hellman, the chairman of the board. In the past, Hellman quit two all-male clubs because they refused to admit women. Last week, he announced that Mills would remain male-free. Both times he was applauded by women.

MAY 25, 1990

Better Dead Than
Coed II

||||||||||||||||||||||||||||||||||||||||||||||||||||||||||||||||||||||||||||||||||||||||||||||||||||||||||||||||

The Virginia Military Institute is no Walden Pond. Trust me on this. I have been to the school and seen it in all of its spartan, neo-Gothic plainness.

Nevertheless, federal judge Jackson L. Kiser invoked the spirit of Henry David Thoreau when he upheld the right of this college to ban women. He said, "VMI truly marches to the beat of a different drummer and I will permit it to continue to do so."

A different drummer? Any drummer at VMI is probably playing John Philip Sousa. The row of cannons, the Stonewall Jackson statue, the parades, the institutionalized hazing, the rigid hierarchy are not what the Concord philosopher had in mind when he sang the praises of nonconformity.

But the misuse of Thoreau's words is just a part of the strange tale of the VMI case. Ever since a girl asked for admittance to the 152-year-old state military academy, an entire battalion of men have tried to protect their tradition. They've done it by speaking the language of those who pressed for change.

A year ago in a campus interview, the gentlemanly superintendent, General John Knapp, based his claim to remain all-male on the values of "diversity" and "equality." Diversity among institutions, that is, and equality among men.

In court this spring, the VMI lawyer—Robert Patterson, himself a graduate—argued that the school should be saved from the government's desire for "needless conformity." It should be given "the same protection as the spotted owl and six-legged salamander."

There was no attempt to deny sex discrimination, no attempt to prove that women can't perform in a military academy. Underlying the argument was the notion that we have come so far in changing society that places like VMI and The Citadel in South Carolina are an endangered species. Even VMI's famed "rat line" system—the ritual abuse of freshmen "rats"—was more to be saved than censored.

You don't have to read far to catch the subtext: Male bastions have been so successfully breached, their power so eroded, that what was once the establishment is now the last alternative. What was once the norm is now daringly different. A drumroll please.

The VMI which I visited did indeed seem much more of an anachronism than a threat. But the attempt to portray the institution as beleaguered, up against a feminist wall, may ring a bit hollow in a state where VMI grads form a powerful old-boy network.

What is going on is very much in keeping with the current passion to compete for the role of victim—especially the victim of reverse discrimination or political correctness. VMI hasn't taken quite so much pride in being an underdog since the Battle of New Market, when their Confederate schoolboys took on the Yankees.

The other argument co-opted is the one usually put forward by all-women's colleges. Judge Kiser sounded like a brochure from Smith when he concluded: "Providing a distinctive, single-sex educational opportunity is more important than providing an education equally available to all." Lawyer Patterson kept talking about Wellesley: "There's evidence that single sex schools are very beneficial."

But while all-male and all-female colleges do hang together on some of the same arguments—they both talk about the value of educational options—they make very strange bedfellows. Most women's colleges put themselves in the avant-garde of women's rights, while VMI and The Citadel defend what is most benignly called a traditional male environment.

Legally, the women's colleges are private, while VMI is publicly funded to the tune of $8 million a year. Virginia's taxpayers are forking over money to a school that bans their daughters. That's the very essence of illegal sex discrimination. It's likely that the district court decision will be overturned in a higher court. But it's not certain.

Meantime, Judge Kiser has decided that we all have something to lose if the last "rat" disappears from the educational environment. The interest in saving these rodents overrides the interest in equal opportunity.

Frankly, I doubt that the rat would be any more deeply mourned than that other extinct species, Jim Crow. Some traditions need honoring. Some need burying.

If VMI can't evolve, then perhaps it can be a museum, a Sturbridge Village of Ye Olde Male Ways of Doing Things. Look, kids, see the young men in uniforms shave each other's heads. See the older students heaping abuse upon the younger. Hey, Pops, where were all the women?

JUNE 21, 1991

The Might-Be Mommy Track

|||||||||||||||||||||||||||||||||||||||||||||||||||||||||||||||||||||||||||||||||||||||||||||||||||||||||||||||||

Johnson Controls didn't have a mommy track. What they had was something different. It was a Maybe, Could Be, Might Someday Be a Mommy track.

The company had a policy that assumed every fertile woman was a pregnancy waiting to happen. They banned these women from working in jobs with high exposure to lead on the grounds that some unborn—indeed unconceived—children might eventually suffer damage.

Johnson called this a "fetal-protection policy." So have many other companies. But it is not too cynical in these lawsuit-phobic days to call it a "company-protection policy."

In either case, the Supreme Court came up with another name for this policy. They called it sex discrimination and said it's illegal.

With rare unanimity, the court ruled (March 20) that Johnson can't ban every fertile woman—from menses to menopause—because of fear of health risks or lawsuits. They said that federal laws against sex discrimination clearly prohibit an employer from barring women from hazardous jobs.

To have lost this landmark case would have been disastrous for the millions of women who work in any remotely hazardous workplace, whether with lead or computer chips, in hospitals or even airplanes. As Justice Harry Blackmun wrote, "Concern for a woman's existing or potential offspring historically has been the excuse for denying women equal-employment opportunities."

But if the Johnson Controls case closes one chapter of history, it doesn't by any means close the book. In the wake of this decision, women have shored up their right to equal treatment in the workplace. We still haven't decided what that equal treatment should look like.

Remember when women set their eyes on the prize of equality? The target of the early laws against sex discrimination was the double standard. Many assumed that the single-standard-bearer was male. Equality would arrive in all its golden glory when women were treated exactly like men.

That never seemed like a wholly attractive option. Some women who saw how their male counterparts lived divided into two camps. One said, if that's equality, I'll pass. The other held on to the ideal of equality, but began to frame it as part of their vision of a different life for both men and women.

This has been at the crux of the argument between those who settle for mommy tracks and those who want parenting trails, between those who would opt for maternity leave and those who hold out for family leave.

The Johnson Controls story is part of this debate. Women who work with lead can indeed endanger a fetus. But so can men. Johnson tried to turn questions of the workplace into questions of gender. Their mommy-to-be track created sex discrimination without solving the problem of fetal damage.

The court in turn resolved the issue of inequality but not of safety. They ruled that women have the equal right to decide whether or not they want equal work at equally hazardous jobs and even whether some want to equally risk damaging their fetuses. Talk about your dubious rights.

Justice Blackmun wrote, "Decisions about the welfare of future children must be left to the parents who conceive, bear, support and raise them rather than to the employers who hire those parents." That's fine as far as it goes, but does it mean that bosses can be irresponsible as long as they are equally irresponsible to all workers and their offspring?

"This decision denies employers the right to make corrections that are at best half a loaf," says Phyllis Segal, president of the NOW Legal Defense and Education Fund. But, she adds, "if we are to value healthy offspring and deal with workplace safety, we need a whole loaf."

The Supreme Court wiped the ancient, stale crust of sex discrimination off the table. The case not only had threatened women's rights but, as often happens, had clouded the real issue of the dangerous workplace.

The question moves now from the courts to workers, employers, legislators and regulators. What will this equal workplace look like? Safe or hazardous? Men and women both share a stake in the outcome.

MARCH 26, 1991

The Women's Movement: Stuck . . .

||||||||||||||||||||||||||||||||||||||||||||||||||||||||||||||||||||||||||||||||||||||||||||||||||

A young television producer calls to ask about the state of the women's movement. She is working on an update on where women are now and how they feel. I feel this way: instantly wary.

In *The Washington Post*, Sally Quinn has declared feminism dead—again—this time murdered by its own leaders. In *The New*

York Times, Bill Safire had declared that a "new, natural womanism" has risen from its ashes. The role models are political wives who choose freely to stand behind their men.

On the best-seller lists are books women have bought to figure out whatever happened to the women's movement and what happens next. Number one on the list, by Gloria Steinem, is about the enemy within, low self-esteem. Number four, by Susan Faludi, is about the enemy without, backlash.

We are in for another wave of analysis, another chapter in the running commentary that follows women's lives like sociological ambulance chasing. We take the pulse of women regularly. The state of the women's movement—dead, dying, resurrected—has become a media staple like the monthly makeover feature in fashion magazines.

But the problem is not that American women are going backward or even off-track. What is missing in the women's movement is the movement. What feels strange, uncomfortable, wrong to those women whose lives personified change is the current lack of change.

It's 1992 and women feel simply stuck. Stuck juggling work and family. Stuck below the glass ceiling. Stuck in institutions they fought to enter but can't change. Stuck with rules they are allowed to follow or to break, but not to rewrite.

One generation ago, many middle-class women at home saw work as a ticket to independence. It was a way we moved, ahead of our mothers, out of the house. Now work is what we get up in the morning and perform.

That second income promised to lift families out of a hole, allow some breathing room for men, and offer balance in women's lives that had been devoted and limited to caretaking. Now that second income is a necessary part of a decent family wage.

The much-heralded new choices for women—circa 1972—now seem like hard decisions circa 1992. Full time, part time, mommy track, child care, one paycheck or two—each option comes with an elaborate and unsettling cost accounting that goes to the psyche as well as the pocketbook.

Feminism never promised us a rose garden. It offered a struggle against women's status as the second sex. To American women it held out the hope that we could, in the vernacular of the seventies, "have it all." Now women are often told we asked for too much. We are rarely told that we've accepted too little.

The reality is that the women's movement stood on two legs. With one, we kicked open the doors. With the other, we were to change the system. But the second is still dragging way behind the first. It is no wonder we are limping.

Women have gained access to the institutions, but not enough power to overhaul them. We got rights to make our way as individuals, but pitifully few supports to help care for our families.

We challenged the idea that women couldn't fit in as governor or mine worker or doctor. But we still haven't overcome the idea that we have to fit in . . . or get out.

Some of us got to breathe the rarefied air of a corporate office. But we didn't get to change the atmosphere. While many got husbands to help, few got husbands to share.

The fact that legal rights were easier—although hardly easy—to win than caretaking help has left a lot of women dangling. We are told that everything is possible—in theory—but find that it isn't in real life.

And for the past dozen years, instead of moving forward, the leaders of women's groups have had to use their energy to protect the gains made and the rights already won. It's a dozen years during which we've seen the feminization of poverty, the erosion of abortion rights, the stressing of family life.

So we come to this time feeling stuck. We are dragging that second leg behind us like a weight on social change.

There has been an inclination to blame the women's movement for women's discontent with the status quo. To criticize those who offered another vision instead of blaming those who thwarted it. Indeed feminism is often blamed for the success of its opponents. The stories about how it is ahead of, behind, outside of the mainstream are legion.

But what does happen next? Will women stay stuck for some time, juggling, balancing, trying to accommodate our lives into the existing structure the way we might adjust our bodies into "unisex" jeans? Will we continue separately, each trying to fit the pieces of her life into a fragile whole?

A full generation after the women's movement began, where do you look for the signs of change?

FEBRUARY 25, 1992

. . . And Moving

|||||||||||||||||||||||||||||||||||||||||||||||||||||||||||||||||||||||||||||||||||||||||||||||||||||||||||||||||||||||||||||||||||||

A friend says with a fine and frustrated humor that she has achieved exactly the right look for the nineties. Her consciousness is all raised up with no place to go.

From time to time, it will appear in a letter to the editor or to a senator. When Anita Hill is pilloried or the man at work says something outrageous or she reads about leaking breast implants, it will spontaneously combust over lunch or on the phone with friends. And then she will return to the everyday concerns of her desktop, her family, and her bills.

This friend is not unique. She describes the dress code for the moment of transition. Today the attention to the debate about every detail of a woman's life—whether she is a rape accuser or a candidate's wife—is higher than ever. But the concern is fragmented, haphazard, disconnected from programs or leaders.

Only at times do we wonder: What gets the momentum back into the women's movement.

Movements, they say, like revolutions, gain their energy from rising expectations, and that was true for the wave of feminism that began in the late sixties. Women who found each other and fueled change had been educated for one life and relegated to another. Betty Friedan's middle-class housewives and the "coeds" of the student revolution both chafed against second-sex status.

But when women shared the status of outsiders, it was easier to share the goal of getting inside. To keep their eyes on the prize.

Now women are both inside and outside. A movement that celebrated individuality suffers from its divisiveness. The prizes themselves are scattered, illusive, and often subject to second thoughts about men, women, values, and rights.

Nevertheless, what is growing under the cover of uncertainty, under all the restlessness about women's lives, is another set of raised expectations. Today's "problem that has no name" is the gap between the expectations built up in the last twenty-five years and a reality that has changed far more slowly.

It's a gap that has grown among both veterans of the women's movement and those who have been labeled "post-feminists." If this movement is to move again, the energy will come from all those people who live inside this gap, sharing more common ground and common frustrations than they may recognize.

They are young mothers, daughters of feminism, who expected to stay on the fast track and left it for motherhood because their firms and companies expect seventy-hour weeks. They are women in their twenties who grew up assuming independence and find their freedom limited by fear of male violence in the dorms and on the streets.

They are women who find it impossible to believe that "they" might take abortion rights away. Women who look in vain for a skirt among the suits at a Senate hearing or an international conference. Or sometimes find one.

They are women who have made it into the inner circle of men only to become conscious of how hard it is to make a difference. They are women who struggled with their own self-image only to watch their daughters immersed in a magazine of messages about female flaws and products for improvement.

They are women as well who are discouraged by the realization that "they don't get it," angered by an image on MTV, turned off by a blonde joke, and exhausted by the sheer tenacity of the way things are. And they are also the men who share the lives and perspectives of these women.

Margaret Mead once said that the only way to solve the disruption that comes from change is with more change. For the past ten years, we've attempted to salve the disruption by thwarting further change. And it doesn't work.

A constituency for a second generation of change exists now in the expectations gap. Those who populate this fertile territory are not monolithic. But there is broad agreement on the directions for change if not on the details.

What is needed is both leadership and the clear restatement of an agenda that puts the pieces of lives together. That agenda begins with the need to maintain rights—including abortion rights—won over the past twenty years, but it doesn't stop there.

It places a priority on family policy in both Washington and the workplace to help families catch up to the changes in society. It includes as part of this whole a strong and unified opposition to violence.

And underlying all of it is the insistence that women be heard. That our voices and our life experiences count at last in all the places where our future is decided.

FEBRUARY 28, 1992

The End of the Year of the Woman

||||||||||||||||||||||||||||||||||||||||||||||||||||||||||||||||||||||||||||||||||||||||||||||||||

All good things must come to an end. So we now bid a fond farewell to the much hyped, celebrated, and scrutinized Year of the Woman.

But before this historic year recedes into memory, allow me to offer a final word. At the risk of snatching a defeatist crumb from the jaws of victory, there was one thing about the past year that made me nervous about the future. It was the way women ran for office on a "different" platform.

Let me run the year-in-review tape.

The common wisdom of 1992 said that voters were looking for change. It said that women personified that change. They were change agents because of what they were not: one of the boys.

The claim that women were "different" also took on a moral meaning. Different meant better, which meant purer, more caring, more honest, more trustworthy. You get the idea.

In fairness, female politicians had long suffered from a double standard. They had to prove again and again that they were as smart and as tough as men. Remember 1984, when Geraldine Ferraro told the country in the Vice Presidential debate that she too could push the nuclear button? Women had to run like men.

By 1992, most women running for office were happy to finally find some profit in a double standard that favored their sex. One candidate for the Senate ran an ad with the tag line "You bet I'm different." Another used pink lettering in her television ad. A third ran as the "mom in tennis shoes."

Virtually every woman made note of her gender. Finally poor Rich Williamson, the man who ran against Carol Braun in Illinois, whined that sex "should not be an issue."

Political coverage too began to sound a bit like sociobiology. A commentator on the normally sober *MacNeil/Lehrer NewsHour* said that women were "*born* commanders." A political consultant said that "women are *by nature* less inclined to throw the first punch" in their ads.

It was as if estrogen had been prescribed as the perfect antidote for the country's testosterone poisoning. There was even a claim that biology was political destiny after menopause. An anthropologist wrote in *The New York Times*: "The biological changes wrought by menopause will bolster their [women's] interest in power and increase their ability to use it." Hold those hormones.

This different tack was pretty successful in 1992, but you don't have to be a worrywart to find troubling omens in the victory confetti. The new double standard has some dangers.

For one thing, women on this political pedestal seemed particularly vulnerable to the first charges of imperfection. In at least three major races women suffered a precipitous slide in support when they came up short of the high standards—whether they were tardy on taxes or too quick with negative ads.

Under the politics of difference, it seems, women candidates could be saints or sinners—a political variation on the theme of woman as either virgin or whore. The higher a woman rose on the helium of moral superiority, the faster she could fall.

Secondly, in the long run, it is hard to make the case for electing women on both the grounds of equality and those of superiority. Suffragists tried this at the beginning of the century. At first, some argued that women should get the vote as a matter of fairness. Later, others argued that women should vote because they were caring beings who would usher in a new moral order.

The moral claim to voting rights or to office has one advantage. It offers a strong and idealistic message. But it inevitably places a double burden for change on women. The high expectations can produce dismal disappointments. How long before we read the first story asking why six women in the Senate haven't yet changed the institution?

Finally, the language of difference also reeks of stereotypes, even if they are self-stereotypes. It speaks of differences between men and women but not among people. It places gender above individualism.

In general—and generalization—there are differences in the life experiences and perspectives of men and women. I have long argued that we should bring those experiences to the table. But we can't assume that those differences are rooted in our biological past or destined for our future.

Change is not just a matter of righting the raging hormonal imbalance in government. When all is said and done, change is an equal opportunity employer.

So as this year of the woman winds down, I take less pride in the notion that women and men remain different. I put a bit more hope in the idea that men will join women in making a difference.

DECEMBER 22, 1992

LIBERTIES AND CIVILITIES

||||||| *What is typical of our era is the cacophony of voices, once left out, now scrapping for a piece of the pie to call their own.*

When Names Hurt

||||||||||||||||||||||||||||||||||||||||||||||||||||||||||||||||||||||||||||||||||||||||||||||||||||||||||||||||||||||

Providence, R.I. — In the end, expelling Douglas Hann may have been the easy part. It's proving much harder to exorcise him. The ghost of this Big, Bad Man on Campus still casts a malevolent aura over the Ivy League quadrangles of Brown University.

On Wednesday, Hann was the context and subtext for a Public Affairs Conference here on what has come to be called "hate speech" on campus. Does a student have a right to cast a racial epithet or a sexual slur, to wave a Confederate flag or wear a swastika? Does a university have the right to enforce a code of community behavior?

All the questions were in the conference air. What happens when the right of one person to say whatever he wants conflicts with the right of another to be free from harassment? What happens when free speech comes up against community values?

These lofty matters were not at the front of Hann's besotted mind last fall when he celebrated his twenty-first birthday—the entry into mature manhood—by getting sloshed and yelling expletives and epithets in the quad. His equal opportunity tirade managed to encompass blacks, Jews, and homosexuals: or, rather, "niggers," ". . . Jews," and "faggots."

This was not Hann's first experience with boozy bigotry. A year earlier, his sentence for such misbehavior was to attend a race relations class and counseling for possible alcohol abuse. The lessons, need we note, didn't take.

A two-time loser, Hann was permanently expelled last month out of Brown and into the media spotlight. If Hann had been dismissed merely on the grounds of being a drunken and disorderly lout, few but his fraternity brothers would have missed him. But he was also cast asunder for breaking a code that prohibits "inappropriate, abusive, threatening or demeaning actions based on race, religion, gender, handicap, ethnicity, national origin or sexual orientation."

Vartan Gregorian, the elfin and engaging president of Brown University, emphasizes the word "actions." He protested many times during the evening conference that his school had punished the student's behavior, not his speech.

This is an interesting distinction for sophists. But our pal Doug's action was screaming in the courtyard. His outrageous behavior was accomplished with his mouth. So the question remains whether this university, or about a hundred others, should have codes that punish students for what they say.

Frankly, I didn't find this as easy a call as some of my other free-speech panelists. There is a time when one person's freedom to say anything he wishes can inhibit another's freedom to participate in the same class or community, or to say anything at all. Imagine sharing a class with someone calling you "faggot." The First Amendment can collide with the Fourteenth. Free speech can inhibit equality.

There are times when speech is as damaging as a punch in the nose. The notion that sticks and stones are more lethal than names doesn't sit well with what we know of psychology. The mind takes blows as painful as the body. "Nigger" hurts.

The cure isn't to decide which is more important, free speech or equality, but to find some balance. And balance depends on weighing the amount of harm done in each incident. The harm done by gagging the free exchange. The harm done by the specific insult, threat, abuse.

Because of the need for a case-by-case balancing act, codes don't work. They are either unnecessary, as in the case of Doug the Drunken Lout. Or they are too uniform. They are either intimidating. Or useless. Indeed Mary Rouse, who administers such a code at the University of Wisconsin, went to great lengths to tell the Brown gathering how rarely it's implemented.

When thinking about codes, it's important to consider the campus as well as the Constitution. What I have witnessed is not so much contentiousness as an uneasy peace—and quiet.

Blame it on politically correct repression—the whipping dog of the moment—but there is little real conversation around issues of race and gender. There is mostly silence, occasionally broken by epithets hurled across the emptiness.

Confederate flags are hung at Harvard and T-shirts are printed with women's butts at Emory. Students who are unable to deal personally with their own classmates ask the university to write codes to fight their battles and make the campus Utopia.

Not even Utopia bars conflict. What is needed on campus is more speech, not less. At Brown these days they are at least talking about talking. It's the legacy of a most unlikely and uncivil donor: Douglas Hann.

Doug, old man, don't drink to that.

MARCH 19, 1991

The Case of the Pink Daiquiri

||||||||||||||||||||||||||||||||||||||||||||||||||||||||||||||||||||||||||||||||||||||||||||||||

If we ever adopt a national motto, it will probably read like this: "Mind Your Own Business." Not a very poetic sentiment, nor very patriotic. But it's succinct, and to the point.

Americans value the right to be left alone, certainly by their government and often by each other. We are easily outraged by intrusion into our lives, invasion of our privacy. The word "busybody" is not a compliment within our borders.

This is what two young servers in Seattle learned when an extremely pregnant customer ordered a drink in their restaurant. In the now-famous Case of the Pink Daiquiri, the servers asked her twice if she was "sure" she wanted a drink. One ripped the label off a bottle of beer that warned about the dangers of alcohol to a fetus, placed it on the table, and said, "This is just in case you didn't know."

The outraged customer complained about being treated "like a child abuser" and the servers were fired. Instead of serving a pink daiquiri, they got a pink slip. Mind your own business.

Case closed? Well, not exactly. There is another American value that hasn't quite achieved the status of a motto but is every bit as widely shared. That's the notion that somehow we're connected. As a community we have some concern for each other's well-being.

This is why the state of Washington required the sign that hung in the same restaurant lobby warning about the effects of alcohol on a fetus. This is why in forty-one states bar owners can be held responsible for the accident of a driver who tanks up at their stop. This is why in twenty-three states party givers can even be responsible for partygoers.

And this may be partly why the two young servers interfered in the life of the would-be daiquiri drinker. One person's busybody is another's caring soul.

There is no clear line that says when private behavior is a fair matter of public concern and when public interest in private life becomes intrusion. In this country, we try to respect freedom but avoid the charge of neglect. We dislike coercion but feel some responsibility for each other.

The compromise we have settled on is the catchall phrase called "education." Society, we say, is supposed to give each citizen the tools to understand what's best for him. Citizens in turn are supposed to use them.

The most popular educational tool these days is the ubiquitous "warning." Americans are inundated by hundreds of little signs to let the consumer beware. Warnings on movies and medicine, on beer bottles and cigarette packs, and even on jobs.

That compromise too can be shaky. In the past month, the Supreme Court ruled in the Johnson Controls case that as long as women workers were warned about the dangers of lead to the fetus, they had the same rights as men to risky jobs. Does this mean that a warning is enough? Is it all an employer has to do?

The same Supreme Court said it will decide if the warning on the cigarette pack protects manufacturers from lawsuits by sick smokers or their families. Can you sell anything, even something lethal, as long as you warn the consumer? Can consumers blame the manufacturer for their own decisions?

The Case of the Pink Daiquiri is even trickier. Teetotalers notwithstanding, there is such a thing as moderate drinking. There is also such a thing as Fetal Alcohol Syndrome.

At least one mother has already sued (unsuccessfully) a distillery claiming that she was hooked on Jim Beam. It's possible that one could sue a bar owner or even a server, claiming they are as guilty for a genetic disaster as for a traffic accident. The same duo who were fired for putting a warning on the table could be sued for not warning a woman.

From what I have read, the Seattle servers were intoxicated with self-righteousness. The almost-mother was sipping guilt. They were obnoxious; she was defensive.

The woman, who gave birth to a healthy son the next week, had reportedly been careful in her pregnancy. The worst fetal damage is done early. Any woman banned at a bar can drink at home. They shouldn't have hassled her so nastily. She shouldn't have gotten them fired. It was probably a case for Miss Manners.

These are delicate negotiations that go on as part of a bigger negotiation. We want to be treated as independent adults *and* be protected from danger. We are expected to care for each other *and* to respect each other's privacy.

"Education" is still the best compromise we've got in this conflict. So the next time a server tries to impress a customer with the wisdom on the beer label, offer some careful words in return. Caution: Even warnings can be dangerous.

APRIL 5, 1991

Free Speech;
Private Speech

|||||||||||||||||||||||||||||||||||||||||||||||||||||||||||||||||||||||||||||||||||||||||||||||||||||||||||||

It's been a long time since I believed that "names can never hurt me." By kindergarten we all learn that words can be as damaging as sticks and stones.

The vocabulary of prejudice in particular can be as destructive as a physical weapon. Words like "wop," "kike," "nigger," "bitch," "fag" are thrust deliberately to wound another.

But so are the other words with which we tongue-lash each other these days. "Racist," "bigot," "anti-Semite," "homophobe," "sexist." In theory, these words were created and stockpiled as an arsenal of self-defense. Yet we use them as aggressive implements all their own. They have become a public and preemptive strike. A deadly silencer.

In the past few weeks, Andy Rooney was struck by one of those accusing words. He was cast, and cast out from CBS, as a racist for allegedly telling a magazine that "blacks have watered down their genes."

Next, Ann Richards, candidate for governor of Texas, was colored in racist hues when some heard through her Texas twang the remark that "no judge and no bureaucrat has any business in determining whether a white woman has an abortion." Political linguists pored over the tapes to decipher if she said "whether a white woman" or, as Richards claims, "whether or why a woman."

Then, in Massachusetts, Boston University president John Silber, running for governor, was attacked by a rainbow coalition. Once, for calling the city of Lowell the Cambodian capital of America. Twice, for comparing Jesse Jackson's oratory to Hitler's. Thrice (perversely), for alluding to racism among Jews. And finally, for sexism in using the phrase "sons of bitches."

These were just the most public cases of the past month. Charges of "anti" or "ism"—the big verbal guns to be drawn out against serious attacks—now seem to be the Saturday-night specials of discourse. They are part of a random civic violence.

Who was caught in the verbal nets this time? Rooney, who was arrested in 1942 for integrating the back of a bus. Richards, whose autobiography is a civil rights story. And Silber, who is, to all appearances, an equal opportunity misanthrope.

For the most part, those who speak up for these and others accused of some bigoted remark have hinged their defense on the First Amendment. Freedom includes the rights of Americans to say things that are cruel or stupid, outrageous as well as inspired. In Eastern Europe, after all, neo-Nazi skinheads now roam uttering anti-Semitic remarks. People there are discovering the hateful side of free speech.

But what I am struck by is something else: the disparity, the gap between our current hypersensitivity to public speech and our relative and lingering insensitivity to private speech.

This year a slew of truly racist, sexist, anti-gay, anti-Semitic acts took place on campuses across the country. They were followed by protests and then by administration speech bans and then by debates on the First Amendment versus Harmful Speech. The pattern became familiar.

I wondered, then and now, how many of the students had ever personally confronted someone else's stupidity and bigotry eye to eye. Had the undergraduate spoken up when her friend was called a Jewish-American Princess? Had the young man ever challenged his buddy on a casual slur about their black teammate? Had a female student who'd been harassed at a fraternity party ever phoned the president of that house with a personal complaint? Had the black who'd been hassled in a campus bookstore called the manager before calling the protest meeting?

In our work lives, in our social lives, it happens time and again. Something is said. Not knowing how to reply, whether to reply, we say nothing. We may avoid the people, avoid the situation, but they go on, not knowing their offense.

The right to free speech was never meant to silence opposition. I can defend your right to say what you think and fight to change what you think. If over the years, Americans have learned to hold their tongues and change their minds, it is partly because of the personal reactions to bigotry. On the other hand, those who truly ply hate in public have often tried it out first in private.

Names can hurt. To hurl them indiscriminately in the name of self-defense is dangerous. It seems that we have become trigger-happy in public. What we need is more courage against prejudice in private.

FEBRUARY 27, 1990

To Be or Not to Be PC

||||||||||||||||||||||||||||||||||||||||||||||||||||||||||||||||||||||||||||||||||||||||||||||||||||||||

She was accused the other day of being politically correct. Maybe it was the string bag in her hand. Maybe her use of the word "person." Or her ticket stubs to *Dances with Wolves*. Maybe it was because she was known to favor such things as multiculturalism or diversity.

She says that she was "accused" because this was not a friendly exchange. The label was delivered with a sneer and carried the aura of an epithet. Once attacked, she was expected to cringe with denial.

This brief encounter confirmed what she had suspected for some time. It wasn't even trendy anymore to be politically correct. Indeed, it had become wrong to be right. Or wrong to be too right, which is to say too left.

Once the term PC had described an idealism that was at worst excessive, occasionally even silly. But at best, an ongoing impetus for change.

But that was before the rash of articles declaring the New McCarthyism, the New Stalinism, the New Hegemony (wonderful word that), and the Fascism of the Left on American campuses. She had counted now some half a dozen cover stories and several dozen major articles about these repressive progressives.

According to the current theory, a faculty raised on sixties dissent was spending the nineties rooting out the very last vestiges of racism, sexism, heterosexism, Eurocentrism, even looks-ism and species-ism. In the process, no dissent from their dissent was allowed.

Undergraduates in their care were similarly said to be in hot pursuit of the very last racial slur, sexual leer, or environmentally unsound T-shirt. They had become conformists in their belief in diversity, narrow-minded in pursuit of multiculturalism, and utterly vicious in the fight against cultural insensitivity.

All this was dire proof that liberal commandants were suppressing free thought and intellectual debate. Proof that their establishment had produced a corps of storm troopers intent on, gasp, bashing intolerance.

Who would have dreamed that being politically correct would become such a character flaw? Who would have thought that we would come full circle at such a dizzying speed? That it would become trendy to be anti-PC, or APC if you prefer.

Frankly the woman was always surprised at the power struggles that emanated out of academia. There are reasons why the colleges refer to the rest of the country as "the real world." Nowhere else in America do people believe so passionately in the power of ideas.

Universities are not only idea factories, they are also communities. Most take seriously the commitment to shape an ideal small society.

In the past decade the gap between these ivory-tower societies and the increasingly conservative real world has widened enormously. Their relatively progressive aura has made some colleges seem a touch more unreal. They have become both the last liberal bastion and the last juicy target for conservatives.

Now comes the movement against the evils of too-goodness, the terrors of political correctness. Just in the nick of time.

Conservatives had nearly run out of liberals to attack. Now they can experience the pleasure of bashing bigot-bashing.

Undergraduates had nearly run out of ways to rebel. Now they can show they are free thinkers by writing diatribes against minorities, hanging Confederate flags, and yelling epithets against homosexuals in the dorms. They can stand up against the pressure to accept sexual equality and ethnic diversity.

Indeed, upon graduation the anti-PC students will be able to go instantly from being rebels on campus to being full-fledged members of the Establishment—without having to change ideology.

Frankly, this woman had never worried too much about the excesses of progressive campus virtue. After all, it's already politically correct to hold campus conferences questioning political correctness.

But she does worry that PC is the L-word of the nineties. The movement against it is another way of trashing idealism, putting a lid on change, pushing back what in a less heated phrase might be called humanistic values. Even progress.

So, pin this one on her unrepentant string bag: PC Pride.

APRIL 2, 1991

A   Cultural   Clash

||||||||||||||||||||||||||||||||||||||||||||||||||||||||||||||||||||||||||||||||||||||||||||||

There were times when the Mapplethorpe trial in Cincinnati produced testimony worthy of the title attached to the museum exhibit: "The Perfect Moment."

Perfect Moment Number One: Prosecutor Frank Prouty holds up two photographs, one of a man with a bullwhip in his rectum. He asks the art director who chose these images for the show: "Would you call these sexual acts?"

She answers: "I would call them figure studies."

Perfect Moment Number Two: Prouty questions museum director Dennis

Barrie: "This photograph of a man with his finger inserted in his penis, what is the artistic content of that?"

He responds: "It's a striking photograph in terms of light and composition."

Perfect Moment Number Three? This one occurs when even the most devoted defender of free expression lifts her eyes from the page to offer her own art criticism to the great curator in the sky: "AAAARGGH!"

There was never any doubt in my mind that the trial over Robert Mapplethorpe's photographs would bring "a cultural clash" into the courtroom. SoHo meets Cincinnati.

But at the trial, the testimony often sounded like a linguistic battle, a tale of two tongues: one side speaking art; one side speaking English. It sounded less like a case about obscenity than about class, elitism, artistic sensibilities, and common sense.

Americans often divide like this when dealing with art. One group thinks that Andy Warhol's Brillo box is brilliant and the other thinks it's a scam. Each believes the other a pack of fools, though one may be called snobs and the other rubes. Guess which one is larger?

The divide is bad enough when the argument is about Brillo. But when it's about bodies, watch out.

The seven photographs at issue in this trial contain some grotesque subjects. In one of them a man urinates into another man's mouth. Show me somebody who can look at that photograph and think about the composition, the symmetry, the classical arc of the liquid and I'll show you someone with an advanced degree in fine arts. This was the sort of thing said in Cincinnati.

In the wake of this, it is remarkable that the verdict was not guilty. A jury without a single museumgoer, artist, or student of "What Is Art?" decided that the museum was protected turf in the legal quarrel over obscenity.

But the trial in Cincinnati and the troubles at the National Endowment for the Arts are partly the result of the art world's own chic insularity. They come because the art community speaks its private language to a circle so small, so cozy, and so closed as to be dangerously isolated.

Perfect Moment Number Four: The prosecution asked how art was determined—was it merely the whim of the museum?

The witness, a museum director, said no, it was the culture at large. And this is how he defined the culture at large: "museums, critics, curators, historians, galleries."

I agree with the decision and with those who defended the museum's right to show these photographs. To leave the dark side out of a Mapplethorpe show would be like leaving the tortured black paintings out of a retrospective of Goya's work. It wouldn't be legitimate to pick and choose the sunny side of the work—the calla lilies and celebrities—and show it as the whole.

Indeed, as the director also said, Mapplethorpe set out to capture the line between the disgusting and the beautiful. There is room in life for the deliberately disturbing. The museum's room—a glass case in a separate gallery—was tame enough.

But even in the moment of victory, there is still a warning here. This trial and the funding woes of the NEA are not just the fault of Jesse Helms on the rampage. They are the fault as well of an art community that prefers to live in a rarefied climate, talking to each other, subject only to "peer review" and scornful of those who translate the word "art" into "smut."

In many cities, there is still the knock of the policeman at the door. Having failed to make its case in public, the art community ends up making it in court. In the history of art, this is not a perfect moment.

OCTOBER 9, 1990

Free the Sperm 14

||||||||||||||||||||||||||||||||||||||||||||||||||||||||||||||||||||||||||||||||||||||||||||||||||||

No matter what people say, all trends are not born on the West Coast. Nor does the prevailing wind of change spread each of California's ideas across the country. At least, let us hope not.

This is the latest bulletin just in from the Pacific. A brand-new movement has been born, or should I say conceived. It is the movement to "Save the Sperm." Not the sperm whale, you understand, the sperm male.

This week, fourteen prisoners on death row in San Quentin officially filed a suit against the state of California, claiming the right to procreate by artificial insemination. These convicted and condemned killers want to have their sperm preserved for insemination with a willing woman.

Moreover, they insist that the denial of their "right to reproduce" amounts to "cruel and unusual"—and therefore unconstitutional—punishment. Under the shadow of the death penalty, they are demanding the right to create life.

This is a case so stunning in its sheer chutzpah that it left two ACLU lawyers I called—one on each coast—utterly and unusually speechless. Only twice before, in Virginia and in Nevada, had anything similar even been tried.

Yet in some ways, it was inevitable. We have, right there on the cutting edge of the country, a synthesis of assorted and dearly beloved trends in modern American life. Another entry into the ever-expanding list of individual "rights." Another tale of our national obsession with genes, sperm, ovum, and the technology of reproduction. And another example of the exploding number of bizarre lawsuits.

Just listen to Carter King, the intrepid lawyer who has taken on the cause of the condemned sperm. "Procreation is a basic right," he says from his office in Reno, Nevada. "We let everyone procreate, even lawyers, even politicians."

But seriously, folks, he adds, "While the law demands an eye for an eye, executing all future generations is extreme."

King states his moral claim on behalf of spouses, would-be mothers, and even would-be grandparents of the death row inmates. "I'm suing for the women," King says. "They have the right to procreate with anyone they want to. I'm suing for the grandparents who will be deprived of the right to be grandparents. This family shouldn't be wiped out because their son committed a terrible crime."

Admittedly, there are any number of men on the outside for whom fatherhood is just a sperm donation. There are many women who expect nothing more from men than their genes. The jails are full of such casually fathered children.

But until now, there has been no unlimited right to procreation. Women cannot join their egg to any sperm they choose. Warren Beatty, for example, is currently taken.

As for the plaintiffs, several of them did their best to forcibly "donate" their sperm in civilian life. They were rapists as well as murderers.

Carter King may believe that his murderers have been born again in favor of life. But the notion that their "family shouldn't be wiped out"? That rings a bit hollow in the case of plaintiff Darren C. Williams, who shot and killed an entire family—a woman, her daughter, and two grandsons—in a murder for hire. (By the way, it turned out to be the wrong family.)

The idea that these men have a right to be fathers also pales in the case of plaintiff Randy Haskett, who wasn't a terrific uncle. He killed his ten- and four-year-old nephews, after they saw him rape and try to kill their mother—Haskett's stepsister.

As for the right to be a grandparent? Well, that is probably moot in the case of plaintiff Richard Stewart. He murdered his mother, thus reducing her chance to be a co-plaintiff.

Of course, the suit doesn't say how many children these men are entitled to have with how many women. There are three hundred men on death row in California alone.

Nor does it say anything about women prisoners. In the name of equality, women on death row would have the same right to reproduce. Presumably they could stay pregnant, thus postponing the date of execution until menopause.

But this rhetoric of rights and reproduction implies that the same state that can kill these men must save their sperm for immortality. It's a theory of valuing life from the moment of ejaculation to the moment of execution.

Did you ever wonder exactly how far things could go in the American legal system? Now you have an answer straight out of San Quentin. Westward Ho!

JANUARY 10, 1992

Say You're Sorry
||||||||||||||||||||||||||||||||||||||||||||||||||||||||||||||||||||||||||||||||||||||||||||||||||||||||||||||||

When I see yet another account of oil-slicked seabirds washed up on slippery beach rocks in Alaska, I wonder about L. G. Rawls. The chairman of Exxon must see these photos too. When he looks up from the bottom line, out from the circle of lawyers who have surrounded him, what does he think?

I am not the only one who has wondered about him and his inner circle of executives. More than one economist or ecologist, making a cross-cultural note, has said that in Japan the CEO of such a disaster would have resigned in shame and sorrow. Japan is no paragon of virtue—recent government scandals have proved that—but the country is ruled by moral consensus. Ours seems to be ruled by the ethic of lawsuits.

In litigious America, guilt is no longer defined as something you feel but, rather, something that must be proved. We rarely hear a high corporate executive admit moral blame. Here, having a lawyer means never really saying you're sorry.

Chairman Rawls did apologize. Sort of. More than a week after the disaster, he published the most impersonal of personal apologies. I can imagine the wrangling between the public relations and legal staffs behind the words of that hollow statement: ". . . I want to tell you how sorry I am that this accident took place."

"This accident" that "took place" sounded as distant from his moral domain as his desk was from Prince William Sound. But it's more than Captain Hazelwood of the *Exxon Valdez* said, lawyered into silence. To apologize might be to incriminate.

I am not demanding the resignation of Rawls and his inner circle. But it does seem to me that when a disaster occurs, the people in charge have some duty to do more than call their lawyers.

They have a duty to pay their respects with time and energy, to spend weeks, months, scrubbing the rocks and sea life with their own hands, and paying last respects to the lost life.

I think this is true for Chairman Rawls as well as for the crew of the *Exxon Valdez*. I thought it was also true for the Union Carbide people who devastated Bhopal and never laid a personal compassionate hand on its victims. And I think it is true for all the people who have ever confused a moral wrong with a criminal wrong, whose self-defense against unethical behavior is: "I did nothing illegal."

The American system of laws and suits allows us to get retribution, even justice, for some crimes. But it seems to work against that process of confession and forgiveness that heals wounds as it rights wrongs. It even makes it harder for adversaries to explain themselves and to understand each other.

You don't have to go to Prince William Sound or Bhopal to see this. Consider the kind of defensive medicine practiced routinely by hospitals. In any hospital over time, there are operations botched, accidents that "took place." Patients and families are left suffering.

But many a doctor is advised not to apologize, even speak to the family, because that human expression of regret could be used in court as an admission of guilt. In turn, people filing malpractice suits often express their greatest anger against the very doctors who "didn't even say they were sorry."

In addition to defensive business and defensive medicine, we also practice defensive politics. Politics by advice of attorney. Politicians who get in trouble usually answer questions about right and wrong with answers about legal guilt or innocence. This is surely the theme of Jim Wright's woes.

America is a pluralistic society. Unlike Japan, we can rarely apply the pressure of a moral consensus. We have different interests, different points of view. As the trial of Oliver North showed, it is easier for us to make decisions about specific legal trespasses than general ethical concerns.

So the motto of American disagreement is: Go ahead and sue me. And there are some 700,000 lawyers in America available to take sides, to keep us on sides. One lawyer for every 350 Americans.

The more we sue each other, the more we retreat, trying to protect ourselves. The closer to the top, the greater the protective barrier of lawyers.

Ultimately, under the rule of lawsuits, it has become far too easy to confuse moral and legal responsibility. We mix up the long words like "culpability" and "liability." And in that linguistic and ethical confusion, it becomes harder and harder to express something as simple as regrets, dismay, and sorrow.

MAY 12, 1989

Gays in the Military I

||||||||||||||||||||||||||||||||||||||||||||||||||||||||||||||||||||||||||||||||||||||||||||||||||||||||||||||||

After a string of grisly stories about sexual harassment and sexual assaults in the military, I ran into more than a few people eager to overhaul the entire Defense Department. With only the tip of tongue in cheek, they were ready to ban heterosexual men from the Army, Navy, and Air Force.

Saner heads prevailed. So did open minds. Not every naval officer turned into Tailhooker at the sight of a woman. In the Persian Gulf War only a handful of men got out of hand. Anyway, it wasn't sexual orientation that was the problem. It was sexual behavior.

All of this brings us to the current question about homosexuals in the military.

Over the past week, the armed forces have gotten messages from two branches of government, the judiciary and the executive, that the long-standing ban against gay and lesbian soldiers and sailors is coming down. First a federal district judge issued a temporary order making the Navy reinstate Keith Meinhold, a sailor discharged last August after revealing he is gay. The judge said it was likely that a trial would find the ban unconstitutional.

Then Bill Clinton reaffirmed his promise to lift the rule after he takes office. He can issue an executive order, the way Truman did when he integrated the Army racially in 1948. Clinton hopes to do so in a way that will mute the culture shock, though to describe this as culture shock is bit like calling a 9.0 earthquake a little rumble.

We are witnessing another confrontation between the military and the civilian worlds, between the culture of diversity and the culture of uniformity. Uniformity, as in uniform.

Anyone who has done time in the military can tell you that the armed forces are designed to stamp out differences in boot camp democracy. It is less interested in preaching individualism than in teaching order.

But anyone who has ever seen one of those World War II movies—with "Tex," "O'Malley," and "Brooklyn" fighting the Nazis—also knows that even in the 1940s, the military was dealing with diversity. In the 1950s, when the South was still segregated, the military was newly integrated. And in the 1990s it has been on the front lines as well as the rearguard of advancing women.

The pressure to accept homosexual soldiers presents another challenge in this long line. That doesn't make it easy.

The traditional hostility to gays—to gay men at least—comes straight from the playground taunt: "Sissy!" Prejudice linked gay men and all women in a sisterhood of weakness that disqualified them from fighting "like a man."

Homosexuals were exempt from the draft and, if discovered, driven out of service. In ten years, some 17,000 men and women —including top guns and top nurses—have been dismissed.

The difference is that today military leaders acknowledge that there are thousands of homosexuals in the military, fighting and leading. The image of gay men and lesbians as security risks has been debunked.

The last, tenuous but tenacious argument left is that removing the ban would somehow give permission for "openly homosexual" behavior. (Gay parade grounds?) And that it would undermine morale and discipline.

In a careful and tempered statement last year, General Colin

Powell put it this way: "It is difficult in a military setting where there is no privacy, where you don't get a choice of association, where you don't get a choice of where you live, to introduce a group of individuals who are proud, brave, loyal good Americans but who favor a homosexual lifestyle."

When you parse this thought, it consists of two ideas. One idea is that both prejudice and homophobia are so rampant that the mere presence of an acknowledged gay or lesbian is unacceptably disruptive. That, I am afraid, is what they said about mixing black soldiers with white.

The other idea is that homosexuals are sexual predators who put other soldiers sharing quarters and showers at risk. This seems to be a particular worry to men, yet there is no evidence that gay men are more sexually aggressive than straight men. This may be killing with faint praise, but it's true.

More to the point, at least the original point, the military has every right to make rules and regulations about behavior. There may be good reason for a military "incest taboo" among shipmates and prohibitions within platoons. There are rules against harassment. But it's still the sexual behavior that counts, not the sexual orientation.

This fall Canada dropped its ban. Now it's our turn. The military should worry about how its people make war, not love.

NOVEMBER 17, 1992

Gays in the Military II

If you want a hint of what the military is going to face when it lifts the ban on gays in the military, follow me. Come on over here and reach into my mailbag.

First, may I suggest that you put on a glove. Or grab a set of tongs. Some of the letters I've gotten about gays are too slimy for the naked touch.

But put aside those wonderful missiles which come regularly to every journalist from that far-flung family of foulmouthed misanthropes who share the same name—Anonymous. There's still some pretty interesting reading. "Interesting" is putting it mildly, and neutrally.

For openers, nine out of every ten letters I received on this subject when I last wrote about it came from men. Virtually all of the letters *from* men were *about* men. The relatively few people who wrote about gay women worried that they would get too high, but the legions who opposed gay men wanted to keep them from getting too close.

The specter of showers and barracks came up so often in my correspondence that I suspect the Army spends more time in the sack than in the trenches, more time under the water than under the gun.

A military man from Cape Coral, Florida, wrote: "This tells me, as a straight man showering in the barracks, that I have no choice but to expose myself to any gay men present."

A man from Apache Junction, Arizona, who spent three years overseas in World War II, remembers sleeping forty men to a barracks. "Now suppose," he writes, "that neighbor was a man with the sexual inclinations of a woman, i.e., a homosexual."

Yet another man, this one from Tobyhanna, Pennsylvania, asked us to "imagine putting a homosexual in a community shower with sixty or so naked men." Someone from Melbourne, Florida, used his imagination to suggest that "it would be like putting a mouse in a cheese factory or a mosquito in a nudist colony."

The fascinating thing to this—female—reader was that nearly all the letter writers shared the same perspective: that of straight men worrying about being victims of sexual assault, harassment, lusting, or just plain ogling. This garden variety homophobia—fear of homosexuals—was fear of becoming the object of unwanted sexual attention. Being the oglee instead of, say, the ogler.

It's the closest that most men may come, even in fantasy, to imagining the everyday real-life experiences of women. The closest they may come to imagining a trip past a construction site, unease in a fraternity house, fear that a date could become date rape. In short, the closest men come to worrying about male sexual aggression.

A writer from Idaho put it in this rather charming vernacular: "Some of the gays are not little pansy guys but big hulking guys and if a small man said no, what is to stop him?"

I am sure that gay men and women do make some wrong passes at Mr. or Ms. Straight. I suspect this happens more often in a closeted atmosphere when communication is reduced to a secretive system of readings and misreadings.

There are instances of assault and harassment by homosexuals. There are also daily assaults of homosexuals. Consider the alleged gay-bashing-to-death of Seaman Allen Schindler a month after he told the Navy he was gay.

But—back to the barracks—if showers are such a charged venue, barracks such a threatening situation, how come the problem hasn't already wrecked morale and created dissension in the ranks? How come it's come up so rarely?

After all, between 5 percent and 10 percent of the military is estimated to be gay right now. The lifting of the ten-year-old ban on homosexuality would allow these men and women to acknowledge that they are homosexual without being dismissed.

It wouldn't mean that a straight man would be showering with a gay for the first time. It might mean that he would *know* for the first time.

Finally, the military has every right to make rules about sexual behavior. They can enforce any sort of sexual prohibition or aggression, from a shipmate's "incest taboo" to harassment to ogling in the shower. There is and should be a clear distinction between sexual behavior and sexual orientation. A difference between what we do and what we are.

And by the way, dear writers, wouldn't it be something if the military finally cracked down on sexual misbehavior because men were worrying about men?

FEBRUARY 2, 1993

History: Whose story?

||||||||||||||||||||||||||||||||||||||||||||||||||||||||||||||||||||||||||||||||||||||||||||||||||||||

Certain members of my family—who shall remain nameless —have suggested a bumper sticker for my car: "I Brake for Antiques." This, of course, is something of an exaggeration. I prefer to think of the afternoons I've spent stopping along the back roads of New England as adventures in social history.

As I have patiently explained to this same family, what we call antiques are a record of the real lives that real people led. They are a kind of down-home proof of the fact that people beat eggs, drank out of cups, used cupboards.

But what I tend to bring home from my much-maligned jaunts are words. The words of other Americans, captured in magazines and books. And, occasionally, if I make a hit—not of the automobile variety—I even get some perspective on history.

This time, in the musty corner of a store on the old Route 1, I found an even mustier, hundred-year-old *Pictorial History of the United States*. The author of this popular book, one James D. McCabe, wrote when historians were unencumbered by what are now called the "storm troopers of political correctness."

So his text brought back a time when even a colorless and relatively straightforward writer would describe the American past unselfconsciously as "a grand history—a record of the highest achievements of humanity—the noblest, most thrilling and glorious story ever penned on earth." In such star-spangled praise, McCabe called this not only "a Christian nation" but one which was happily "secured for the language and free influences of the all-conquering Anglo-Saxon race."

To read this now, when Christopher Columbus—the man and the day—are being debated, is to see how attitudes and ideas become antique. Speaking in the 1890s, my treasured McCabe did refer to some wrongs the white man inflicted on the natives, but this is not, to put it mildly, *Dances with Wolves*. He tended to regard the "savages" as, uh, fairly uncooperative.

Women show up in this text rarely and African-Americans make cameo appearances as victims of slavery or subjects of policy. And though this author tipped his hat more than once to religious tolerance—coming out squarely against the Salem witch trials— he rather casually referred to Joseph Smith, the leader of the Mormons, as a "cunning imposter."

But what was most striking is what was most typical of my yellowed history. A century ago, the story of America was cast as an onward and upward tale of great men and their institutions and their battles. Our history was one of glory and progress, a parade of Presidents, each of whom came with a fine résumé and nearly all of whom did the right thing.

The text is vastly out-of-date with our sensibilities. We are more contentious now, even about our past. In the schools and colleges, dusty and dry discussions about curricula have turned into heated and highly political debates that were unheard of a hundred years ago: What should be taught and learned about our country? Who has been excluded? What should be included?

They are questions that get to the soul of who we are as a people and what we will think about our country. The debate is often framed now as an attack on the excesses of multiculturalism and increasingly there is an angry edge to it.

The attempt to open up the worldview contained in the writing of men like McCabe is now seen as fragmenting, trivializing, even distorting. Blacks, women, Native Americans, who once criticized history as "his story"—a record of "dead white men"—are now being criticized in turn.

I feel no nostalgia in my antique-reading for the comfort and coherence that came from this limited view of the Great Men's March of Time. But what is typical of our present is the difficulty in agreeing on our past, writing *an* American history. What is typical of our era is the cacophony of voices, once left out, now scrapping for a piece of the historic pie to call their own.

If a historic sense is important, if we define ourselves by our past, then the task now is to find a way to hear the voices of the frontier women, and the Indians at the Little Bighorn, and the people who did not make laws. To include more voices without losing a connecting thread of shared values and ideals that make us part of something recognizably American.

It's a task that resonates in politics as well as education, in contemporary life as well as history. Can we have diversity and unity in these united states? What antique arguments will cause our descendants to smile smugly when they find them in a country store on a future afternoon?

SEPTEMBER 24, 1991

FAMILY VALUES

||||||||||||||||||||||||||||||||||||||||||||||||||||||||||||||||||||||||||||||||||||||||||||||||||||||||||

|||||| *In 1943, when Norman
Rockwell finished his classic painting,
the turkey was the centerpiece of
Thanksgiving. He drew an homage to
Freedom from Want. In the nineties,
when our own eyes focus on that scene,
family is the centerpiece. It's the
family that we want.*

Family Counterculture

||||||||||||||||||||||||||||||||||||||||||||||||||||||||||||||||||||||||||||||||||||||||||||

Sooner or later, most Americans become card-carrying members of the counterculture. This is not an underground holdout of hippies. No beads are required. All you need to join is a child.

At some point between Lamaze and the PTA, it becomes clear that one of your main jobs as a parent is to counter the culture. What the media delivers to children by the masses, you are expected to rebut one at a time.

The latest evidence of this frustrating piece of the parenting job description came from pediatricians. This summer, the American Academy of Pediatrics called for a ban on television food ads. Their plea was hard on the heels of a study showing that one Saturday morning of TV cartoons contained 202 junk-food ads.

The kids see, want, and nag. That is, after all, the theory behind advertising to children, since few six-year-olds have their own trust funds. The end result, said the pediatricians, is obesity and high cholesterol.

Their call for a ban was predictably attacked by the grocers' association. But it was also attacked by people assembled under the umbrella marked "parental responsibility." We don't need bans, said these "PR" people, we need parents who know how to say "no."

Well, I bow to no one in my capacity for naysaying. I agree that it's a well-honed skill of child raising. By the time my daughter was seven, she qualified as a media critic.

But it occurs to me now that the call for "parental responsibility" is increasing in direct proportion to the irresponsibility of the marketplace. Parents are expected to protect their children from an increasingly hostile environment.

Are the kids being sold junk food? Just say no. Is TV bad? Turn it off. Are there messages about sex, drugs, violence all around? Counter the culture.

Mothers and fathers are expected to screen virtually every aspect of their children's lives. To check the ratings on the movies, to read the labels on the CDs, to find out if there's MTV in the house next door. All the while keeping in touch with school and, in their free time, earning a living.

In real life, most parents do a great deal of this monitoring and just-say-no-ing. Any trip to the supermarket produces at least one scene of a child grabbing for something only to have it returned to the shelf by a frazzled parent. An extraordinary number of the family arguments are over the goodies—sneakers, clothes, games—that the young know about only because of ads.

But at times it seems that the media have become the mainstream culture in children's lives. Parents have become the alternative.

Barbara Dafoe Whitehead, a research associate at the Institute for American Values, found this out in interviews with middle-class parents. "A common complaint I heard from parents was their sense of being overwhelmed by the culture. They felt their voice was a lot weaker. And they felt relatively more helpless than their parents.

"Parents," she notes, "see themselves in a struggle for the hearts and minds of their own children." It isn't that they can't say no. It's that there's so much more to say no to.

Without wallowing in false nostalgia, there has been a fundamental shift. Americans once expected parents to raise their children in accordance with the dominant cultural messages. Today they are expected to raise their children in opposition.

Once the chorus of cultural values was full of ministers, teachers, neighbors, leaders. They demanded more conformity, but offered more support. Now the messengers are Ninja Turtles, Madonna, rap groups, and celebrities pushing sneakers. Parents are considered "responsible" only if they are successful in their resistance.

It's what makes child raising harder. It's why parents feel more isolated. It's not just that American families have less time with their kids, it's that we have to spend more of this time doing battle with our own culture.

It's rather like trying to get your kids to eat their green beans after they've been told all day about the wonders of Milky Way. Come to think of it, it's exactly like that.

AUGUST 16, 1991

The Problem of Twosomeness

||||||||||||||||||||||||||||||||||||||||||||||||||||||||||||||||||||||||||||||||||||||||||||||||||||||||||||||||

We have been to weddings this season, a flight of them. The children of friends are getting married. The churches that we visit ring out with words about union, togetherness, two people becoming one.

At times, it sounds as if the style of marriage is still as rooted in tradition as the bridal gowns. A costume of lace and pearls appropriate for exactly one day.

Sitting in my place, a veteran witness of marriages—both first and second—I have come to wonder how much even our fantasies about perfect marriages have changed.

Once, the dream of an ideal union meant that a wife would follow her husband in obedient contentment. A successful marriage rested, or so it was said, on her willingness to fold her life into and under his.

A generation ago, the fantasy of marriage was rather like that of simultaneous orgasm. The marital achievement manuals said that a husband and wife should be in such perfect harmony that their bodies reached mutual pleasure whenever they touched.

Today, we don't approach relationships quite the same way. We leave more room for reality and for differences. Two people may become one couple but, even for those who stay attached, the coupling is looser than it once was.

Our new version of the fantasy is that two people can lead lives that are both separate and together, independent and synchronized.

With a proper sense of timing, we want to believe that each of us can have whatever we individually want out of life—including each other.

Our daydreams, if we have them, conjure up scenes in which his chance to work in Oregon will be just what she dreamed about in her office in Missouri. That what they would choose for themselves is also happily best for each other. That no one will have to be selfish and no one will have to be sacrificed.

Wasn't this the marital success story that Michael and Hope left behind on the last episode of *thirtysomething?* The centrifuge of modern life threatened even this "perfect couple." They were spinning out of control—he to California, she to Washington, their marriage to divorce.

But at the last moment, the crash was averted. Magically, her need to work folded symbiotically with his need to break from work. The happy ending came without conflict or compromise.

Real life doesn't always wrap up in the nick of time. The seams in our lives tend to show, stretch, and rip even the very models of seamless unions.

We face what Alva Myrdal, that remarkable Swedish woman of the world, called "the problem of twosomeness."

A central theme in the stunning memoir that ethicist Sissela Bok has written about her mother, *Alva Myrdal*, touches on this: how difficult it is to lead a questing and individual life in context with another.

Alva and Gunnar Myrdal were in their lifetime the most heroic version of a contemporary marriage. Separately each had a brilliant career, indeed each a Nobel Prize. Together they had three children and a marriage that spanned sixty years, until her death in 1984.

They were defined publicly and often as a perfect modern couple. Yet Alva Myrdal, who began her marriage under the ideal of oneness in work and love, came to doubt that possibility. A writer, ambassador, cabinet minister, who focused her formidable intellect on dilemmas ranging from family to disarmament, she came to describe herself and Gunnar more like "consort battleships, crisscrossing the world but stronger together."

Yet the question Myrdal repeatedly pondered was: "How do I become myself?" Her pursuit of "self" struggled within marriage and strained its bounds. Here is how her daughter describes the dilemma: "This problem arises each time two persons join their lives together: To what extent does each one then remain a separate person while also becoming part and parcel of the other's existence?"

These are not words that I have heard this season or any other in a marriage ceremony. Weddings celebrate union. Today, the bride and groom are told, two people become one.

Well, not exactly.

It seems to me that sometime before the fifth or tenth or twentieth anniversary, "couples" come to see themselves as fellow strugglers. And the best of them try hard to keep the seams from splitting under the pressures and pleasures of "twosomeness."

JUNE 4, 1991

A   F a t h e r   L o s t   a n d   F o u n d

||||||||||||||||||||||||||||||||||||||||||||||||||||||||||||||||||||||||||||||||||||||||||||||||||||

This began as a story about "granny dumping."

An old man had been left at a racetrack in Idaho holding a teddy bear, seated in a wheelchair, and wearing a baseball hat with the deadly ironic message: "Proud to be an American."

John Kingery, a resident of Oregon and a victim of Alzheimer's, came to represent the modern American elder sent off on the modern American ice floe.

But then the news story took one of those odd twists. The spotlight turned from one daughter who presumably deserted her father to another daughter who discovered him.

In Tennessee, Nancy Kingery Myatt caught this man's picture in the paper. He was the father she had not seen in twenty-eight years. He was the father who "just slipped away from us," after divorce, after remarriage. The father who just slipped away from five children.

The pathos in their nursing home reunion is hard to overstate. A fifty-five-year-old woman tearfully and gratefully greeting an eighty-two-year-old father who could no longer recognize her. "I didn't have a dad for all those years," she said. "Now I have one." One who does not know his own name. Or hers. But a father all the same.

What a mix of family dramas in this sad tale. Granny dumping and kiddie dumping. Children who abandon their parents and parents who abandon their children. But what my ear picked up in Nancy Myatt's words was the simple, endless hunger of a child of any age for the father who disappeared.

Some 70,000 elderly Americans are abandoned by their families each year. But that figure is overwhelmed by the numbers of deserted children.

Today, about one-third of all American children—19 million —live away from their father. Among the children of divorce, half have never visited their father's home. In a typical year, 40 percent of them don't see their father. One out of five haven't seen their father in five years. There are millions of adults like Nancy Myatt and her four siblings who simply graduate to the next stage of fatherless life.

It is no wonder that the search for a man missing in the action of parenthood is such a recurrent theme in our culture and conversation these days.

In Nora Ephron's wonderfully funny and emotionally rich film *This Is My Life*, two daughters go off to find their father. They do not find the father of their fantasies but, rather, a man of disinterested and limited emotional means. A man who was not looking for his daughters.

In Mona Simpson's new novel, *The Lost Father*, a medical student in her late twenties, living a life filled with her father's absence, embarks on an obsessive search for him. She finds him and discovers neither the best she imagined nor the worst.

"He was only a man with his own troubles who didn't manage to keep track of his wife and child. After all those years, I was wrong about him. He was only a man."

The search for father, the longing for father is at the root of Robert Bly's *Iron John* and at the heart of *Boyz N the Hood*. It's on the mind of nearly every child whose father simply "slipped away."

Today's favorite image may be that of the "new father," says David Blankenhorn of the Institute for American Values, but "the real direction is toward fatherless children." He cites this absence as "the most socially consequential fact of our era."

It is not simply an economic matter, though the public conversation about missing fathers revolves around money. We speak less about the missing man than about the missing child-support payment. We call them deadbeat dads.

But the children who talk about their missing fathers are less calculating than yearning. In both fiction and real life, they speak about the "disappeared" in the language of emotional loss, not financial. One thought burns a hole in Mona Simpson's central character, the thought of a deserted child: "Why you are unwanted: that is the only question."

A sense of longing carries over to Nancy Myatt's reunion with her father, who is now present but literally absentminded. "The more I see him," she says, "the more I want to see him and talk to him."

There is an unhappy symmetry to the Kingery story of loss and reunion. A father abandoned by one daughter. A father discovered by the daughter he abandoned. How many ways are there to destroy a family? How many portraits as sad as the one of a woman "finding" her father only after he is lost.

APRIL 10, 1992

The Guilt Gap
||||||||||||||||||||||||||||||||||||||||||||||||||||||||||||||||||||||||||||||||||||||||||||||||||||

The woman doesn't want perfume for Mother's Day. Nor lingerie. Nor jewelry. She is too practical for the peignoir that graces the newspaper ad that lies between us as we fly from west to east, from work to home.

What she would like for Mother's Day, she says, is a bridge. Something sturdy to span the gap that has eroded between herself and her husband, the mother and father of their children. A bridge for what she has come to call the guilt gap.

Just ten years ago, the couple had a relationship built on the most up-to-date principles of marital engineering. They had schooled together, worked together, shared housekeeping, or non-housekeeping, together. They were also of the generation that went to birthing classes and used words like "parenting" instead of "mothering."

But ten years and two children later, the infrastructure of their partnership showed some wear and tear. One of the things they prized, a kind of rough equality between them, had shifted in ways she never predicted. The gap had opened, not just over what they did, but what they felt.

When it came time to leave their first baby with a sitter, she was the one who was more anxious. When they went looking for day care, she was the one with more expectations, more misgivings. When the teacher in second grade was incompetent and the kids in fourth grade unkind, she was the one who felt it. Acutely. And when it seemed the children needed more—more attention, more time—she was the one who gave it.

My companion says that in many ways the differences between her and her husband are personal. He regards the children as sturdy. She regards them as fragile. He sees their problems as potholes they will ride around or bounce over. She sees them as early-warning signs of a possible collapse.

But she also calculates that these personal differences run along gender lines, and I agree. The guilt gap, the worry chasm, may be narrower than before. But it most often has mothers on one side and fathers on the other.

Mothering and parenting are not yet, not quite, the same. Indeed, the parent who reads the children most closely, who feels their needs most directly, often finds herself faced with dozens of small choices that add up. Each seemed to present some conflict between the easy assumed equality of their early marriage and the needs of their children.

In the case of my companion, one of these choices was the task that took her away from home and deposited her beside me on this flight. Another was the job she declined because it meant nights. A third and fourth and fifth were decisions about how to spend time as a couple or a family. None of them was easy.

So for this, her tenth Mother's Day, she would like that bridge over the guilt gap, or at least some gravel to cover over their double standard of worrying. She wants them on the same track.

But which track would she choose? I ask my fellow traveler: Does she worry too much about the children or he too little? Does she want to cross to his side or get him to cross to hers? She isn't certain. But as we talk, it seems to both of us, two veterans of motherhood, that in these past decades mothers have gone the furthest in the movement from a double standard to a single standard.

In households with double standards of cleanliness, she says, it is easier to drift to an equal standard of messiness. In households with his and her standards of what children need, I reply, it is easier to drift to a single standard of letting go.

The result, we both calculate, has been a net loss in housework and a net loss in caretaking. But there is a difference between kids and dust balls. You cannot do an occasional full-tilt spring parenting job and then let it slide.

So the question is how "parents" can become more like mothers. How to raise awareness about what's missing, what's needed, what's important in children's lives. Teaching guilt, that goad to caring, may be as hard as training someone to see dirt on the windowsill.

But this is what many mothers want for their day and for their life. They want men to pick up more than the laundry. To pick up more of the anxiety and stretch it across the gap that still separates husbands and wives, mothers and fathers. We have finally come to that bridge. Now, to cross it.

MAY 11, 1989

The   Sins   of   the   Parents

|||||||||||||||||||||||||||||||||||||||||||||||||||||||||||||||||||||||||||||||||||||||||||||||||||||||||

A parent was arrested in Los Angeles last week. It happens every day, but not quite like this. Gloria Williams, you see, was arrested for being a parent.

More precisely, the thirty-seven-year-old mother of three became the first person accused under a new California law that holds parents responsible when their kids go bad. She is charged with "failing to exercise reasonable care, supervision, protection and control" of a child.

The child in question is seventeen years old and an alleged member of a street gang called the Crips. This son is accused of being among those who raped a twelve-year-old girl.

Mind you, if the police are right, Mrs. Williams is no candidate for the Mother's Day Hall of Fame. When they entered her apartment to talk about her son, they found walls covered with gang graffiti instead of rock posters. The photo albums showed members of the family pointing guns. The birthday cake for the eight-year-old was decorated with the gang name.

To this day, the mother, who works for an electronics firm not far from home, insists that her son is no gang member.

Perhaps she is blind or blindly loyal or chooses to believe that the Crips are a local Boy Scout troop and the guns are merit badges on the way to becoming an Eagle Scout. Perhaps she does condone her son's gang membership, as the city attorney charges.

But the crime she is accused of is a lack of parental control. Let me put it this way: It's ten o'clock at night. Do you know where your seventeen-year-old son is? Sure about that?

The California law was created and passed in the current desperate mood about street gangs and youth, about violence and drugs.

In the sociological search for a cause of all these woes, Americans buy one generic label these days. We blame it all on "the breakdown of the family."

If the cause is the breakdown of the family, then surely the cure is the repair of the family. Our search for a fix has taken us to many family mechanics. The favorites these days are the ones who believe that the breakdown is caused by a loss of parental authority.

Their special low-cost repair would put parents back in the driver's seat. Those who won't take the wheel must be forced into it.

This is the fix-it behind the law that threatens California parents of kids involved in criminal activities with a year in jail and a $2,500 fine. It's the thinking as well behind a Wisconsin law that makes parents financially responsible for the offspring of their teenage children. And it is in part as well the support for laws that require parental consent for abortion.

We are now seeing various attempts to put parents in charge, to shore up authority, to foster at least the image and maybe the reality of a traditional family unit. They are, mostly, efforts to control the behaviors that worry society the most: teenage violence and teenage sex, the yin and yang, the male and female of dangers.

I find this a notable pattern. After all, parents have always been held responsible for the care of their children. They've been held liable for child neglect, for child abuse, for child support. We have always drawn connections between behavior and background. Where did they, we, go wrong?

But this current society that knows little about how to restore relationships, that has done less to help parents trying to raise their children in safety and health, has now turned to punishing the failures.

More and more responsibility is passed to parents, even as we worry about their willingness to exercise it. We allow violence on the screen and tell parents to control the dial. We allow drugs on the streets and tell parents to monitor usage.

We offer few alternatives to street life and expect parents to keep their kids indoors. We remove communal supports and tell parents to make up the difference.

I don't know about Mrs. Williams's culpability, although if

they arrested the mother for her "failure to exercise supervision," why not the absent father? But for every Fagin figure of a parent, there is another who hasn't given up but, rather, has lost control of a teenager.

For everyone who is truly irresponsible, there is another who is overwhelmed, a third who is afraid for her child, a fourth who is afraid of her child. Is that parent now a criminal?

They say that California is the leading edge, the social trendsetter. Now the Golden State has turned the Bible on its head. They've decided that the sins of the sons shall be visited upon their parents.

MAY 9, 1989

Divorcing Your Parents
||||||||||||||||||||||||||||||||||||||||||||||||||||||||||||||||||||||||||||||||||||||||||||||||||||||

This is what passes for a happy ending after a sequence of family disasters. A twelve-year-old boy has gotten what he wants.

Gregory Kingsley, sturdy and unshakable in the face of courtroom lawyers in Florida, has a new family, a new name, and a new life. The boy who went from mother to father to pillar to post in the foster-care system is now permanently home as Shawn Russ.

More to the point, the child who will be forever known as the son who "divorced" his parents has grabbed a chance to reach his own goal: "I'm doing this for me so I can be happy."

Happiness is not guaranteed, of course, and happy endings do not always stay that way. It doesn't take a seer to wonder how he will wrestle over his lifetime with his new-old identity and new-old families.

But in its extended form, this was a story ripe enough for a Dickensian novel. There was enough family pathos to make the term "dysfunctional family" sound like an antiseptic label in the dictionary of psychobabble. And everything has changed.

Now George Russ—a man neglected by his own father, a lawyer with eight children who met Gregory at a home for abused and neglected boys—has a new adopted son.

Now Rachel Kingsley—a high school dropout who gave birth at nineteen to a premature Gregory, a divorced mother, poor, perhaps abused, certainly neglectful—has been legally severed from her son.

And now Jeremiah and Zachariah Kingsley—who also did time in foster care and live with the mother whom the court ruled neglectful—no longer have a brother named Gregory.

The importance of the case is not that it granted one boy a so-called divorce. It's that, for once, the sound of a child's voice was heard above the din of adult concerns. For once, when the family and the state both miserably failed him, a child was allowed to sue and speak for his own best interests.

The case, even more than the judgment, cast light on some hard dilemmas about families that fall apart and about a child welfare system with so many cracks that it lets the kids keep on falling.

It raised questions about when to support biological families and when to give up on them. About how much time a troubled parent may need to get his or her life together again, and how little time a child has. About the damage done when the state prematurely severs the ties between parent and child and the damage done when it takes too long.

These are not new issues. When Rachel Kingsley portrayed herself as a mother whose chief crime was poverty, it struck a chord. She is not the first parent to express bewildered anger that the state would pay money for foster care when she could have used it for parent care.

When a stream of witnesses described her as a woman who drank and smoked marijuana, slept with men for money, and left the kids for days on end, it struck a nerve. They are not the first neighbors, friends, or family members who want to rescue children.

When the state workers described the rock and hard place of their foster-care mandate, it had a dismal familiarity. On the one hand, they are supposed to give priorities to biological families, allow parents time to restore their ties. On the other hand, they are told that children should not languish in foster families.

But this time, the deciding voice belonged to the one person who was an expert on his life. It was Gregory who cut through the debate about neglect.

Whatever his mother's troubles or intentions, for eighteen months of foster care, he testified, she never phoned or wrote: "I thought she forgot about me. I thought she didn't care about me." Whatever the pros and cons about biological families and adoption, he said with remarkably emotional clarity: "I just want a place to be."

I don't know how much of a legal precedent he has set. There are some 420,000 children in foster care. How many of those children can wend their way to or through the legal system? How many adults want to adopt them?

In some ways Gregory's story is a foster child's favorite fantasy. But it may have a greater impact on our national consciousness than our law.

We live now in a time of renewed emphasis on the importance of the traditional family, the biological family, parental authority. Children's rights are often dismissed as the dangerous and disruptive tools of people who want to destroy families.

In Florida, however, we met a boy who wanted the right to create a family. He reminded us that every family story is different. What matters most is not biology, but belonging. This time, it was the child who knew best. Just call him Shawn.

OCTOBER 2, 1992

Family Feast
||||||||||||||||||||||||||||||||||||||||||||||||||||||||||||||||||||||||||||||||||||||||

The cousins from California have shown up just in time to help with the annual roundup and delivery of my late grandmother's china. Over the river and through the woods to granddaughter's house it comes.

The younger generation is here as well. They have wended their way out of area codes that stretch all the way from 310 to 212. We brought them in like sheaves from their assorted airports and highways.

Now, for the moment, I am standing alone in the kitchen that will soon be transformed into Thanksgiving Central, checking off the list of ingredients for Thursday's extravaganza. The wooden bridge chairs. The matching—well, mostly matching—glasses. The turkey platter that always shows up sooner or later. The thirty-cup coffeepot that is the collective property of this extended family.

This is what I, the modern nonfarm wife, am harvesting from the crop at our local market: three pans of sweet potatoes, two bowls and one cavity of stuffing, apples and onions, salad goodies, the makings for the dreaded and beloved string-bean casserole, and a twenty-five-pound turkey.

But as I survey the future foodscape, it isn't the feast that impresses me. A middle-class child of twentieth-century America, I am no longer amazed by a twenty-five-pound turkey. What seems more rare is the family that will come to share it.

After all, this is what we have learned about our country, isn't it? That in America, food is plentiful but family is scarce.

That in America, Thanksgiving was once a day to be grateful for the good luck of the land. That now we celebrate something that seems every bit as subject to weather patterns and disasters: our endangered families. That the holiday is less about food and more about that scarcer source of human sustenance.

In 1943, when Norman Rockwell finished his classic painting, the turkey was the centerpiece of Thanksgiving. He drew an homage to Freedom from Want. In the nineties, when our own eyes focus on that scene, family is the centerpiece. It's the family that we want.

There is more than a little truth in all this. At the supermarket, that urban acre that I work with a shopping cart, goods are sold in single servings. For most of the year, the turkey in the freezer comes packaged in parts for solitary eating.

In the wider world, we live more and more alone. Single-person households are the fastest-growing part of our population. A single-person household is not a family.

But, setting the table for nineteen people who come together from eight different households to one family gathering, I wonder if we haven't exaggerated the weakness of our family ties. Do we have an unrealistic portrait in our minds and memories of a Rockwell family? Does that image cloud the strengths of our own?

A series of surveys have been released, like season's greetings, in the past week. They show that Americans feel intensely the stresses of family life. But also the satisfactions.

By huge margins, we think relationships with our own children are good or excellent, but that family values are weaker than they used to be. We find our own families the most satisfying parts of our lives, but think that it's harder to be a parent "than it used to be." In one of these surveys 80 percent of Americans said they wouldn't give up Thanksgiving dinner with their families for even $1,000.

Well, I will not test this last theory with thousand-dollar options at my door. But I wonder at the internal conflicts that one pollster described as the "I'm okay, but you're not" syndrome. Why do we believe that our own family attachments and strengths are an exception in a sea of dissolution?

When the airports and highways are clogged, Americans are not just going home for the giblets. When we pull up a million bridge chairs to tables laden with one cousin's pumpkin pie and another's turkey dressing, it isn't just to debate the merits of gravy. It's to reaffirm our belonging.

So it is here as well. Soon this house will be filled with lemon pie and stories. It will echo with people bound together by blood, affection, time, shared pride, even common tragedies, and the collective terror that someone will break one of Grandma Celia's dishes. On such a day, not so rare after all, it is the harvest of family that marks my sense of good fortune.

NOVEMBER 26, 1991

Love and Law

||||||||||||||||||||||||||||||||||||||||||||||||||||||||||||||||||||||||||||||||||||||||||||||||||||||||||

San Francisco — Harry Britt, the ruddy and ebullient president of the Board of Supervisors, rushes into his book-lined cubbyhole of an office in city hall and immediately defines the subject at hand. "We're talking about love here!"

What we are actually talking about when we're talking about love(!) is the Domestic Partners Bill. The ordinance Britt wrote has just been signed. It sets up a new nonmarried, nonsingle category of relations called "domestic partners."

Any couples who want to enter into the earthly state of partnership will now be allowed an official ceremony called registration. They will sign a Declaration of Domestic Partnership. Once duly registered by the county clerk or notary public, those partners who are also city employees will be eligible for some of the same benefits as married employees.

Britt, a Methodist minister in his former life, waxes romantic over the prospects of domestic partnership. "The goal is to free human beings to develop their needs for affection and sharing." But in a more sober moment, he says, "We are trying to create a model for a pluralistic culture."

In San Francisco, the "pluralistic culture" includes homosexuals and heterosexuals, and so the so-called partners law has been hailed and reviled as an official recognition of gay couples. Gay couples, who can't legally marry anywhere outside of Denmark, are likely to be the first candidates for partnership.

But the potential pool is more extensive. In the words of the new ordinance, it includes any "two who have chosen to share one another's lives in an intimate and committed relationship of mutual caring, who live together." Indeed, since neighboring Berkeley began allowing city workers to sign up their partners for health benefits, straight couples who take advantage of this have far outnumbered gays.

What is going on here, besides love(!), is a series of experiments in which society is being asked or pushed to respond to a much wider range of human relationships. It's happening in pockets of lifestyle-liberal communities like San Francisco, Los Angeles, Berkeley, and it's happening in the courts.

Until fairly recently, Americans were either married or single. Straight couples who chose to cohabit but remain unmarried were, after time, considered married by government fiat. We called that common-law marriage.

One of the hidden effects of the so-called palimony case between Lee and Michelle Marvin ten years ago was that society stepped back from the view that a long-term cohabition was the legal equivalent of marriage. Michelle didn't get palimony because cohabiting isn't the same as marrying.

There are now more than five million heterosexual Americans who live together before, after, or between marriages. They have deliberately chosen to remain outside the "institution." At the same time there are a number of long-term gay couples who would like to, and cannot, marry.

As Pepper Schwartz, sociologist and co-author of *American Couples*, notes, "There are gay couples committed to each other who yearn for the acknowledgment of marriage. There are also heterosexual couples who feel that the [marital] set of rules would be detrimental to their relationship or their values."

How does or should society adjust to these conflicting interests for structure and freedom that go to the heart of love(!) and public policy making? Should we make new legal rules for the nonmarried, nonsingle?

The state itself has a double set of interests. It has an interest in stability. In an AIDS epidemic, that may also include an interest in long-term committed relationships among gays. And it has an interest in upholding the values of individual freedom.

It may be in both of those interests to allow unmarried couples to have some of the benefits of marriage. But working this out is sure to be messy and controversial, with effects on everything from health-plan costs to the tax structure to family law. If you can become domestic partners, how do you become ex-partners? In San Francisco, those who register can deregister. No-fault deregistration?

Americans live in a variety of relationships still so unacknowledged, so new, that we struggle to name them let alone structure them. Significant others? Roommates? Lovers? Now it's Domestic Partners. In small and uncertain experiments, the law is being pushed like a reluctant and dubious parent to catch up with love. Ah, love(!).

JUNE 13, 1989

A Family and a Spare Part

||||||||||||||||||||||||||||||||||||||||||||||||||||||||||||||||||||||||||||||||||||||||||||||||||||||||

When the Prince and Princess of Wales did their royal duty and begat two children, a British colleague of mine referred to their little boys in a poetic fashion. He called them "the Heir and the Spare."

It was a phrase that rang wildly off-key in the American ears of this second child. A spare? In the unroyal Western world, we don't have children for the sake of the crown. We don't set out to conceive a little regal understudy.

What then are we to think about the couple in California who conceived a child in hopes of providing their older daughter with a bone-marrow donor? Is this a new family designation: "the Heir and the Spare Part"?

Abe and Mary Ayala didn't plan to have a another child until their seventeen-year-old daughter Anissa came down with leukemia, a cancer of the blood cells that can sometimes be cured by transplanting bone marrow cells from a compatible donor. After a futile search for such a donor, the Ayalas decided to create a child, taking a one-in-four chance that it would be compatible.

Abe had his vasectomy reversed, Mary was impregnated, and seven months later their gamble may be paying off. Testing has suggested that the female fetus is compatible with the sister. At birth, they may be able to use the cells from her umbilical cord. At six months, they may be able to use her bone marrow.

This is a birthday tale that raises all sorts of ethical hackles. Is it right to conceive one person to serve the needs of another? Can parents distribute one child's bodily parts to save another child? Are there moral and immoral motives for creating life?

Not long ago, when fetal tissue was first used in treating Parkinson's disease, a woman considered deliberately conceiving and aborting a fetus to donate the tissue to her father. The ethicists' response was unanimous horror.

Last year, a medical journal reported the case of a couple prepared to conceive and abort any fetuses that were incompatible, until they got what they wanted: a marrow donor for their first child. The creation of human life as a means to an end rather than an end in itself was also regarded as horrific.

The Ayala case isn't that simple. No, it is true, this couple wouldn't have decided on another child if Anissa hadn't needed a donor. But they also determined to raise and love this child for itself whether it was compatible or not. As the mother said, "If it's not a match we'll love our baby just the same."

If we accept the parents' intentions, then, there are a variety of good intentions in this act. The desire to save their older daughter. The decision to lovingly raise another child. The hope that one can help the other.

Calculated carefully, these goods don't add up to a bad. The Ayalas have skated across the thin ethical ice to safety. But the ice is indeed very thin. I don't know how many other couples could negotiate the passage.

Bone-marrow transplants are relatively risk-free and pretty successful. The decision might look quite different if this baby were created to be a kidney donor or a liver donor. Parents don't have an unfettered right to sacrifice one child for another, or to give a piece of a child to another.

Even in this case, if Anissa goes into some medical crisis that could rush the need for a transplant, there should be safeguards to make sure that the baby's health is a matter of equal concern. I will leave it to the parents to ensure the baby's mental health. How do you explain to a child that she was created for her sister? What if that sister dies anyway?

The entire story raises a long-dormant set of questions about motives for having children. Throughout human history, people had children for all sorts of reasons. And mostly for no reason at all. We had children to be our farm workers and children to take care of us in old age. We had one child as a sibling for another or even, like the royals, as an insurance policy.

It's only since children began to survive longer, and since birth control, and since the family as an economic unit was replaced by its role as an emotional unit, that we have devised a list of right and wrong reasons to have children. Today, the one reason we admit to in public is an altruistic desire to raise and nourish and love human beings for themselves.

Now the new world of medical choices has offered us another entry onto the wrong side of the ledger. It is wrong to create a child only for its spare parts. Wrong to regard a person exclusively as something to be used.

But the Ayalas present us with a case of mixed motives, and mixed motives are more common than we allow. It is possible to decide to have a child for one reason and love it for other reasons. If this family is very, very, very lucky, they will have reason to be grateful for all their children.

FEBRUARY 23, 1990

The Father on the Lam

Lately, I've had Jake on my mind.

It's because of Father's Day, I'm sure. The warm and wiggly

cards and messages and ads are all over the place. Any gal's mind could wander to thoughts of a man like Jake.

It's because of Dan Quayle too. The man is running for President—oops, Vice President—against a "cultural elite" that says "fathers are dispensable." He reminds me that Jake dispensed of himself.

But mostly it's because of rerun season. Just last week, television went back to the beginning of Murphy Brown's now-mythic pregnancy to the wonderful moment when Jake discovered he was going to be a dad. Did he faint in a dead heap, 1950s style, when Murphy broke the news flash from her pregnancy testing kits? Did he blush with pleasure and run out to buy her pickles?

No, Murphy's ex-husband, who had lobbied to become Murphy's second husband, told her that he had to go and save the world. Good luck and goodbye.

So, I have had Jake on my mind.

I hope that he found some new and rare species of insects while trying to preserve the rain forest. I hope that they bit him badly. That sort of thing.

But I have also been thinking that when the controversy erupted over Murphy Brown, it missed the mark. Jake was the juicier target.

Last week, Quayle said, "The elite's culture is a guilt-free culture. It avoids responsibility and flees consequences." If he was thinking of Murphy, he was one lap outside the mainstream. You're looking for a villain? I give you the unwed and unwilling-to-wed father. Looking for a consequence fleer? I give you Jake.

In the last decade we've mapped all sorts of gaps that have grown in America between the haves and the have-nots. Of these, the widest is between children who have and have not fathers in their lives.

Out of this gap has come our two favorite Father's Day images: the New Father and the Deadbeat Dad. On the one hand, we have a picture of a father who is as involved emotionally with his kids as he is economically. On the other hand, we have a father who is only seen when his state posts his picture on the Ten Most Wanted list for child-support payments.

If Americans ever harbored the notion that "fathers are dispensable," it's long gone. From *Iron John* to *Boyz N the Hood* to the latest documentary on the family to the latest study of welfare policy, the focus is on the importance of fathers as a presence and an absence.

It may be that we have exaggerated the number of New Fathers in this process. But the Deadbeat Dad may also have become too generic a villain. Jake has become as much of a stereotype as Murphy.

The father on the lam, the seed-and-leave man on either end of the socioeconomic ladder, is only part of a very complicated story that we are just beginning to hear and tell. As Frank Furstenberg, one of the few to listen to and chronicle the vanishing father, is quick to say, "There is no single reason why men disengage from their children."

At one extreme, says the University of Pennsylvania researcher, are men who have little more than fleeting contact with the biological mother. At the other extreme are men who lived with their children over many years until the relationship broke apart.

All unmarried fathers are not, as the state would sometimes have us believe, deadbeats. All divorced fathers are not, as the men dragged into court would have us believe, broke. All fathers are not, as some men's groups would have us believe, kept from their kids by ex-wives who use the child-support checks for themselves. Though some, agrees Furstenberg, are all of these things.

What we know so far is that many men see marriage and children as a package deal, and when the package unravels, they may return it all. The fear about the fraying of fatherhood has limited public debate this way to marriage or money. Restore one, go after the other.

Indeed the wish that we could put together the Humpty Dumpty of many marriages, hope our way back to a society with one nuclear family model, can, in Furstenberg's words, "prevent us from focusing on the ties between fathers and children." The truth is that we have paid little attention to why some men remain in their children's lives and others fade away.

But if we cannot put together the traditional cultural package with rhetoric or will, we have a lot to learn about strategies that foster connections between men and their children.

Someday even baby boy Brown is going to want to meet a guy named Jake.

JUNE 19, 1992

The Price of Sneakers

||||||||||||||||||||||||||||||||||||||||||||||||||||||||||||||||||||||||||||||||||||||||||||||||||||||||||

We are talking about sneakers. Big sneakers. Size 12 sneakers. The new ones that are currently located on my friend's son's feet which are currently located on a high school floor.

The sneakers, which loom even larger than a size 12 in her mind's eye, came into her life all pumped up with hostility. Parent and child had wrangled over them for weeks.

This woman did not approve of the purchase. She and her husband regard $150 sneakers as proof of warped values, rip-off materialism, not to mention the decline and fall of Western civilization. Her son regards them as a necessity, an object of desire, proof of his need to make his own choices.

At the end of the family wrangling, the boy played his trump card or, more specifically, his paycheck. This is what he said: "I'll use my own money." He went into the store with a portion of his summer earnings and walked out with scientifically designed, engineered, and marketed ego-building shoes.

The woman and her husband were silenced by his declaration. And bothered by it.

This is what we talk about in the shadow of these sneakers, this woman and I: Our parents, ourselves, our children. Money and independence and family.

Our parents, who were young during the Depression, used to bring money home, put money on the table. Those were the expressions they used. The assumption was that whatever they earned went into the family pot for distribution. Little went directly to their own pockets.

Now, half a century later, teenagers earn "their own money."

They are much less likely to "bring it home." In some families, that money may ease pressure on the family budget. In others it may be designated for college as well as compact discs and sneakers. But it is usually described and circumscribed as "theirs." To do with as they will.

Immigrant families still seem to pool their resources. But American parents who depend on a teenager's earnings for groceries or rent are more likely to feel ashamed of themselves than proud of their children.

Is this an economic piece of the heralded breakdown of the American family? My friend thinks so.

We count the many ways in which the marketplace treats us as individuals rather than members of families. Most adults are employed on their own as workers who now earn single wages, not family wages. We are subdivided as consumers with separate wants—sneakers and Walkmans—not shared needs. Even preschoolers have their Saturday-morning TV market.

Increasingly each generation is on its own, liberated and isolated in and by the economy. We appear less like a permanent family unit than like temporarily connected individuals, currently cohabiting.

It happens up and down the age spectrum. On the turnpike this summer, I passed an elderly couple in a car decorated with a bumper sticker that read: "If you don't go first class, your children will." My friend remembers laughing at a boat named *My Children's Inheritance*.

We both know parents of our age wrestling with the costs of college. Should they borrow money on their house or have their children borrow? Should they invest in their children's future or their old age? Will helping their dependents leave them dependent?

What do they want/expect of their children later in life? The assumptions of family—I will raise you and you will care for me —have been replaced by the assumptions of independence. A reluctance to ask, a fear of needing.

Even divorce laws are now infused by the idea that husband and wife are separate economic units. The goal is to achieve independence, self-sufficiency as quickly as possible.

My friend's paycheck is, of course, not entirely her own, nor is her husband's. It is owned by the bank, the supermarket, credit card companies—the whole catastrophe, as Zorba might describe it. They don't ask their children to pay room and board, although in rancorous wrangling over these shoes, an ugly reference was made to this expense.

But in the aftermath of the Sneaker Affair, her family has done a great deal of thinking about money earned and shared. The pros and cons of our famed American self-reliance. About economic rights that belong to an individual and responsibilities that belong to a family.

This is not a simple talk. The mess of economics and emotions do not lend themselves to a bottom line. But this is what my friend has learned: It has become far too easy to run away from family in a pair of $150 sneakers.

NOVEMBER 8, 1991

A World for the Children

||||||||||||||||||||||||||||||||||||||||||||||||||||||||||||||||||||||||||||||||||||||||||||||||||||||

My young friend will celebrate her first Mother's Day a little ahead of schedule, or at least a little ahead of her due date. It is going to be a prenatal event. Her table will be decorated with a sonogram, and her labors toasted with something decaffeinated.

Like many women her age, thirty, and this age, 1992, she has planned this parenthood, although "planned" is far too lame a word. My friend has nested with more attention to detail than the robins on my walnut tree. Her child will come genetically tested, gender-known, prenamed, untouched by a drop of alcohol or single pesticide-infested piece of fruit.

She and her husband have readied their son's first environment with the same degree of attention. They have been through an entire

EPA list of dangers. They have tested the house for radon and the nursery for lead paint and checked with *Consumer Reports* for the ranking of cribs and high chairs. They have installed an intercom and read up on everything from breast feeding to the safest sleeping position for infants.

I watch their attention to the details of this birth with affection and memories. They are creating a world in which their boy will be both safe and central. Soon enough, my friend will be wearing the dazed look of new motherhood, honed to every cry of the child now housed happily in its own contained unit.

We are programmed to pay such attention to our newborns. In our species, it isn't so much the survival of the fittest as the survival of those with the fittest parents. We are expected to circumscribe our adult world to the space within earshot of our infant. As a society, we give new mothers some dispensation from the wider world, some maternity leave from worldly concerns.

But my Mother's Day carries different thoughts. I am on the other end of motherhood, beyond the nursery, the finger-painted hand pictures, the sticky trays of breakfast in bed.

My daughter is now a young woman on the other side of the continent and the other end of the phone line. I cannot design the world she sees from her window in Los Angeles, a view of a city gone up in smoke and rage and alienation.

We talk this past week on our AT&T intercom as two adults. Incredulous at the Rodney King verdict, dismayed at the violence, conscious of the painful irony of being at risk from people whose sense of injustice we share.

I remember I was pregnant when Martin Luther King, Jr., was killed and the streets erupted. Nothing has changed, she replies. I tell her what is different. She tells me what is not. We do not disagree much.

In our conversation, I think about how much time and energy in life is focused on the private venture of child raising. The dirty little secret of motherhood is that if you gave us—me too—a choice between saving a building full of people or saving our own, we would walk away holding our own child's hand and breathing a sigh of relief.

Most of us start out like my pre-mother friend, with the central illusion that we can raise our children in the womb of family life. They are our private property. We will protect them, raise them according to our values, fully formed and ready to install. We believe that if everyone raised their own child right—lit just one little candle—we could change the world.

But we also learn, the hard way, as our children leave the consumer-tested crib one by one, that we have to follow them. It isn't enough to worry about grades if the schools are falling apart. It isn't enough to feed our children vitamins if hazardous waste is dumped in the ground. We can't build a fence high enough to protect them from the stench of racism or the reach of war.

The central paradox of motherhood is that while our children become the absolute center of our lives, they must also push us back out into the world. Today's much-heralded return to the pleasures and pressures of family life sometimes seems like a retreat. But motherhood that can narrow our lives can also broaden them. It can make us focus intensely on the moment and invest heavily in the future.

And this Mother's Day I want to tell my friend, the pre-mother, as she puts the very last elaborate touches on her son's nursery: Don't forget the world. Before you know it—take my word for this—it will be his world.

MAY 8, 1992

AT LARGE

||||||||||||||||||||||||||||||||||||||||||||||||||||||||||||||||||||||||||||||||||||||||||||||||||||||||||||||||

|||||| *It may be that certain questions are universal. In every culture, human beings ask, "Is this all?" There may be something in our nature that—given a chance—churns, seeks new ground, struggles to make a life. If so, that something extends all the way from Poland to polo and from samurai to salaryman.*

People Pollution

||||||||||||||||||||||||||||||||||||||||||||||||||||||||||||||||||||||||||||||||||||||||||||||||||||||||||||||||||||||||||||||

The darkest tales of the environment usually come to us in neatly labeled scientific packages. The Greenhouse Effect. The Hole in the Ozone. The Destruction of the Rain Forest. Air Pollution. Water Pollution. These headlines reek of chemistry and technology.

But rarely do we see one entitled the People Problem. People, the growing number of us, seem at times mysteriously absent from the public discussion of the state of the earth. It's as if we talked about carbon-spewing cars without any drivers.

The "environmental President" himself has managed to speak about global warming more than once without mentioning the role of our own multiplying species. He leaves behind the odd impression that the culprits of the rain forest are gibbons or perhaps mosquitoes.

This peculiar split between environmental worries and population growth began a decade ago when birth control became a political issue. Family-planning money was cut. References to population were taken out of reports. Politicians were intimidated.

Even environmental groups concerned with endangered species shied away from emphasizing the dangers of our own burgeoning species. Those who did talk about population, like the Audubon Society, were accused by pro-life logicians of making room for birds by getting rid of people. The desire of women across the world for access to birth control got lost in the shuffle.

But the days when Presidents, politicians, or citizens could cast themselves as advocates of the environment without also being advocates of population limits are gone. Family planners and environmentalists both talk about the "carrying capacity" of the earth today, as if the planet were a camel and people its straws.

Earth-breaking population growth was the subject of a new report this week from the Population Crisis Committee. They took the United Nations' warning—today's 5.3 billion people could be 10 billion by 2025 and 14 billion in a century—and called it "a preventable disaster." And they wrote a prescription.

Vice president Dr. Sharon Camp said that during this decade we have a chance, perhaps the last, to stabilize population before government coercion—the China solution—or environmental devastation. The committee figures it will cost international governments $10.5 billion a year to make birth control universally available and raise its use worldwide from about 50 to 75 percent. That's a world-class price tag for what is literally a Whole Earth problem.

It takes no mathematician or economist to see the collision course between the earth's resources and the numbers of people sharing them. To put it in the simplest terms, the more people there are, the more wood is gathered, the more land is cleared, the more soil is eroded. Each year the world's farmers are trying to feed 90 million more people on 24 billion fewer tons of topsoil. It is the story of countries from Kenya to India. Countries where families are caught between feeding their children today and saving the land for tomorrow.

The Third World is not the chief culprit of pollution, nor are people the only environmental danger. In industrial countries each of us annually dumps five tons of carbon into the air; in the developing world, it is one ton. But as Worldwatch Institute's Alan Durning says, "Underneath it all, the basic question is how many people are consuming how much stuff."

Children are born, one by one, to a family and culture as well as a world. Slowing the birth rate takes more than money and contraceptives. But we know from experiences in Thailand and Mexico and Zimbabwe how to make a difference. We know that poor women want choices. We know it can't be done without funds.

The Population Crisis Committee wants the United States to contribute $1 billion a year to international family planning, a huge chunk of money. Yet we spend five times as much on military aid for foreign countries. Call this another peace dividend, another defense policy.

During the past decade, families lost choices and the world lost time. Now there is a renewed recognition that we are on this rather fragile place, this earth, together. Three more of us every second. And counting.

MARCH 2, 1990

Post- Cold War

||||||||||||||||||||||||||||||||||||||||||||||||||||||||||||||||||||||||||||||||||||||||||||||||||||||||||||||||

The woman was pleased as punch or maybe as eggnog. The timing, she told the television reporter, was just perfect. Imagine, the wall had come down on schedule for the Christmas season.

This joyful commentator was not thinking about peace on earth or goodwill toward all. Her St. Louis company had apparently gotten hold of three concrete slabs of the Berlin Wall. It had shipped them to America, chopped them into pieces, and packaged them in little gift boxes. In short, with a bit of help from Erich Honecker it had the pet wall of the 1989 Christmas season.

Here we have another heartwarming international holiday tale about people who are beating the Cold War into stocking stuffers. They are proving the victory of capitalism over Communism, of private over public enterprise. It's all part of the story.

These days, we wake up to discover another government has fallen. The television set is full of young Germans, Hungarians, Poles, and Czechs wearing headbands fashioned after Tiananmen Square, raising their hands in victory signs imported from the American sixties via Winston Churchill's forties, and uttering sentiments that resonate of the French Revolution.

The international pursuit of freedom of expression and government is ripe with the sense of fresh possibilities. But sometimes it seems there is a smaller, shabbier piece to this new international style. Along with the best of the West that is winning in the East, we are also seeing the worst. We are witnessing the takeover of the truly tacky.

It's not just this *perestroika* of pet walls, although the Germans may one day ask us to glue it all back together for their museums. It's what's happening in Moscow and its Warsaw Pact pals. There is a case of kreeping kultural kitsch.

Until recently the only Communist-approved symbols of Western culture were American jazz and Pepsi. Then along came *glasnost* and right behind it came a Miss Moscow contest. It was the first post-*glasnost* meat market in the city.

Next came Bloomingdale's. Remember when the Russian musician in *Moscow on the Hudson* entered the Manhattan store, took one look at the goodies, and defected? Well, now the Soviets are importing the total consumer concept. They're negotiating to bring Bloomie's to Moscow.

Even when the Soviets buy ideas, something happens on the way to the cash register. *Glasnost* has brought more fresh air to the pages of Soviet press. It's also brought some fairly spacey reporting. This fall they printed, deadpan, a story about a three-eyed alien with a robot sidekick who landed by spaceship and made a boy vanish by zapping him with a pistol. From the censored Truth to the *National Enquirer* in less than five years.

As for the newly emancipated Soviet colonies, Hungary has just opened up to those harbingers of Western culture, *Playboy* and *Penthouse*. The first issue of *Playboy* reportedly on the stands now brings a "pictorial" of LaToya Jackson to the freedom-starved souls of Budapest.

Some of this is just the allure of the different. We buy klunky Soviet watches; they buy underpants with Bloomie's written on them. More of it is the inexplicable allure of the lowest common denominator of Americana: McDonald's food and *Dallas* TV are sweeping the world.

But in the case of East following West, something else is going on. Americans may purchase pieces of the wall as history; Soviets are setting up beauty pageants as hip. Their present is our past; their trend is our rerun.

It's as if the folks from the Eastern Bloc were trapped in a time warp of Soviet Realism and mimeograph machines. They had four decades of the 1940s, while the rest of us went through the 1950s, 1960s, 1970s, and 1980s. Now they want to catch up by reliving our Oldies but Baddies.

In America, beauty pageants have become camp, the tabloids are read for the laughs, *Playboy* has lost its youthful lust, and Bloomingdale's, the citadel of consumerism, is up for sale. But in Eastern Europe, in a host of ways, people seem to be longing for what we are losing or leaving behind.

The talk is about the future over there. Funny, how in some ways that future looks an awful lot like our past.

DECEMBER 8, 1989

Leisure   Suits   Us
||||||||||||||||||||||||||||||||||||||||||||||||||||||||||||||||||||||||||||||||||||||||||||||||||

Occasionally, when he saw a man from the old neighborhood who had moved so far above his roots that he would barely acknowledge them, my father would shake his head and say with a humorous edge, "From Poland to polo in three generations."

It was his stock commentary on assimilation, on making it in America, on the immigrant experience. But it was also a commentary on the nature of success in a country whose economic ladder extended from the working class to the leisure class. In theory at least, we Americans worked our way up and out. Of work.

In reality, of course, we have always been ambivalent about leisure. On the one hand, it's the pot of gold at the end of the rainbow. On the other hand, it's lazy, immoral.

Our Horatio Alger stories stop at precisely the moment the national hero became rich. They don't tell us what he did with the wealth or what happened to Horatio Jr. Was Alger the Elder one of the parents who struggled to give his children everything he never had. And then ended up wondering why the son wasn't motivated to work hard?

I ask these questions because we're in a time when many are worrying about the American work ethic. Has it disappeared from our continent and reappeared as the Asian work ethic or, most especially, the Japanese work ethic?

Consider the strange story of international trade. When the government announces our trade enemies next week, one country will be conspicuously absent from the list: Japan.

To avoid a trade war, we made a kind of preemptive peace treaty. Among the items in the treaty, the Japanese agreed—as a concession to us!—that they would shorten their workweek. They would reduce the hours for government employees and encourage the private sector to do the same.

What this suggests is that working hard is somehow an unfair labor practice. According to a University of Michigan study, Japanese men work about eight hours more a week than Americans. We don't have to catch up; they have to slow down.

This is the sort of reasoning that says Americans don't really have to start saving money; the Japanese have to start spending it. Next year, we may demand that their children study less.

I have my doubts about putting cultural values on the international trade table. If we're going to start rearranging other cultures to match economies, why not mandate that Japanese salarymen, as they are called, do their share of housework? At the moment they do about three hours a week, or ten hours less around the house than their American counterparts.

The notion that the Japanese need pressures to *make* them work fewer hours, to force them into leisure, fits neatly into our stereotype of their society: hardworking and workaholic, unified and closed, disciplined and rigid.

But it discounts the reality that countries, like families, may go through generational changes. One generation picks itself up by its bootstraps, the next generation makes it, the next wonders what "it" is all about.

It is a familiar progression for one family to go from the shopkeeper to professional to artist. People go through these stages in one life as well, from the search for safety and security to what psychiatrists call "self-actualization." Having wondered about their next meal, then their next year, they eventually pause to wonder about the meaning of their life.

It's what the mid-life crisis is all about. It's behind the cliché of executive life: "Nobody ever died wishing they'd spent more time at the office."

Japan may also be at the cusp of this change. Many Japanese are asking what rewards they should have from their international success story. They also are worrying about their own "younger generation," not sure they need to work so hard and afraid that they might not.

It may be that certain questions are universal. In every culture, human beings ask, "Is this all?" There may be something in our nature that—given a chance—churns, seeks new ground, struggles to make a life. If so, that something goes all the way from Poland to polo and from samurai to salaryman.

APRIL 27, 1990

Women and War

||||||||||||||||||||||||||||||||||||||||||||||||||||||||||||||||||||||||||||||||||||||||||||||||||||

My friend has called to deliver season's greetings and second thoughts. The greetings come seriously, deliberately. A Happy New Year is nothing to be assumed as the odds against it amass in the desert. The second thoughts come more haltingly.

This is what she has seen on her television set over the holidays. Men and women in uniform saying, "Hi, Mom," to the television camera. Men and women in uniform saying, "Hi, kids," to the children they've left behind.

At least once she heard a small boy talk proudly and sadly about his parents, who were both overseas. The boy was at his grandmother's. One other time she saw a husband holding up a baby to the camera to wave to "Mommy."

My friend considers herself rational, even tough-minded. When others sympathized with soldiers who signed up for school and ended up at war, she did not. Joining the Army, she said, is like joining the fire department. You have to expect a blaze.

More to the point, she is among the legion of women who heartily applauded the integration of the military, who saw a coed Army as inevitable, as right. The mother of a son and a daughter, she did not agree that there was anything less horrible about a boy in a body bag. If the thought of women dying in combat was too chilling, she said, let it chill the passion for war altogether.

But that was theory. The second thoughts she is having these days, as images bounce off satellites from half a world away, are not as tough as her usual style. It is the mothers at war—especially the mothers of young children—who have touched her heart if not her mind. Did we—women, she means—get more equality than we bargained for?

This is not the first time I have heard unease these days, even from the most egalitarian quarters. Women wonder if somehow it wasn't their pressure for equal rights that landed these younger women in the desert. Their concern isn't unlike the second thoughts about young mothers struggling with infant care and work, with two jobs or one income. Second thoughts about whether life is more challenging or just harder now.

I know what my friend is feeling, have shared her second thoughts. But today, I tell her at first what she already knows. War does not respect motherhood, whether military or civilian. In all the wars of the 1980s, three out of every four people killed were civilians. Women and their children were not "protected" in Kuwait. Nor will they be protected in Baghdad or Riyadh if war comes.

A truly just war, I argue, a war of self-defense, of survival, is worthy of sacrifice. A war any less moral, a war confused in its purpose, is unworthy of any lost life. To say a conflict is worth the sacrifice of men but not women, fathers but not mothers, is to plea-bargain with the gods.

But this does not counter her second thoughts. Remember, she says, when women first supported the idea that mothers were like fathers? Most of us assumed that working beside men, fighting beside them, was part of a trade-off. In return, men would father more and women would become decision makers. It was a deal we were making.

Now, in the lopsidedness of change, fewer women have made it to the top than have filled in the bottom. More women are on the front lines than in the inner circle. What happened to the deal?

My friend draws a border around the photograph in the paper of George Bush and the fabulous Baker boy. She says in a word, "Suits." The men in suits are still making the policy moves. Only now they have military pawns of both genders.

We are too realistic to think that everything would be different if women had titles of power. But we cannot believe they would be exactly the same.

So these images—"suits" drawing lines in the sand and babies waving to "mommy" soldiers—become second thoughts. If this is what equality looks like, were we better off before?

Only, of course, this is not what equality looks like. This is what it looks like in the middle of lopsided change, in the uneven, unsettling process, on a path that looks more rugged and more circuitous than we knew at the beginning.

In the desert, the mother-soldiers waving to their children are not a reminder that women have gotten more than we bargained for. But that we have gotten so much less.

JANUARY 4, 1991

A Front-Row Seat at the
Pit of Hell

||||||||||||||||||||||||||||||||||||||||||||||||||||||||||||||||||||||||||||||||||||||||||||||||||||||||||||||

This is how the war began. Live on television with voices from
Baghdad: "Something is happening outside."

There wasn't so much as a split-second lapse in time between
the moment the bombs began to drop and the moment that the
whole world knew. The words that will be remembered are not
those of the President—unblessed by eloquence—but those of the
reporters with their unscripted eyewitness accounts from a hotel
window.

"Ladies and gentlemen," said Bernard Shaw, looking over the
city of Baghdad, "I've never been there, but it feels like we're in
the pit of hell."

For once, all the sports metaphors that have so offensively colored the talk of war took on a TV reality. We were able to watch
and hear the outbreak of war, play by play. We knew when the
planes had taken off in Saudi Arabia and when they attacked
Baghdad.

We even had the first instant interview with the first pilot who
had downed an enemy aircraft. He was questioned as he stepped
out of his plane, dare I say, off the playing field. What will come
next, the instant replays? How will we cope with the injured players?

This instant war, this "you are there" sense, is not entirely new.
We have crept up to it slowly, by technological increments. From
Edward R. Murrow's radio broadcasts of bombs falling on Britain
to the videotapes from Vietnam and Tiananmen Square. If there
are fewer elegiac poems about war and more sober documentaries,
it is because of what we have literally seen and heard.

This time, however, we have witnessed in the early hours the next leap, the full array of communication technology that now unites the world with shared information. We are able to know the same things at the same time. And this impressive unifying technology is used to show just how disastrously splintered, fractured, literally warring that world can be.

The contrast is astonishing. We have now the most remarkable high-tech methods of war and communication with which we can accomplish, and then record, our most primitive aims.

There is a cliché about space uttered by every cosmonaut and astronaut: The earth as viewed from a shuttle or capsule shows no borders between countries. The satellites, telephones, fax machines of modern life that link us to sons and daughters in Saudi Arabia or an air strike in Baghdad tell us the same thing.

It has become commonplace as well to talk about how technology has outstripped our human capacity to cope with it. We think about this duality mostly in medicine, where machinery can keep us "alive." We are able to do much more than we may want to do—than we can even contemplate with the same tools of mind and feeling.

But in wartime especially, the rich array of technological advances stands in ever-starker contrast to human limits. We seem in many ways as overarmed by science as a child with an AK-47.

Information races ahead. Understanding creeps at its same pace. We are one world, courtesy of television, able to see what's happening anywhere. But the one world we see is wracked by tribalism. And what is happening is another round of murderous rivalries.

Like army ants seen under those astronauts' space microscope, we fight over turf. It seems that the end result of all of our technology is the faster expression of hate and the universal, instant, simultaneous transmission of conflict.

There is more than the usual dose of wartime ironies in this age of high-tech communications. For all the minicams and satellites, we are no more sophisticated at resolving conflict than in the age of the Marathon courier. What we have is a front-row seat, a minute-by-minute ticket to events at the edge of Bernie Shaw's "pit of hell."

JANUARY 22, 1991

What We Remember
||||||||||||||||||||||||||||||||||||||||||||||||||||||||||||||||||||||||||||||||||||||||||||||||||||||||||

We are getting ready to celebrate the golden anniversary of a dark day and images of the past are already oozing up like oil from the hulk of the U.S.S. *Arizona*.

The Movietone news shots of Zeros and subs and ships in flames are out of storage. There are interviews with survivors. A grandfather remembers a friend who died on the deck beside him and cries as if he were nineteen and not sixty-nine.

The elders who were at home tell about the day the world exploded into their America-first living rooms. Where were you when you heard?

It looks like December 7, 1991, is going to be a day to relive the infamy.

But there are other snapshots as well for this fiftieth anniversary. At Pearl Harbor, a former Navy aircraft mechanic who survived the attack guides visitors around the memorial. These people come from Tokyo as well as Toledo. "It was a long time ago," he tells a reporter. "Too long for hate to linger."

On the mainland, those who remember the war and their grand-children watch the reruns of this grim "opening day" on Japanese-made television sets with Japanese-made cars in the garage. And while some grumble—"who won the war?"—few think of the Japanese as enemies.

As an American born too late for such memories, I hear all sorts of mixed messages in this orgy of history. But the ones that resonate the most in our world are about the moral costs of both forgetting and remembering the past. History is alive, not just in the Pacific, but in Eastern Europe and the Middle East and everywhere people wrangle over wrongs.

Remember "Remember Pearl Harbor"? The price of forgetting any searing moment is the fear that we'll do some injustice to innocent lives that were lost or forever changed. Making bygones into bygones can weaken the claim victims have on our collective sympathy. One cataclysm settles back into what we call historic perspective . . . that endless sequence of cataclysms.

But remembering with an intensity that remains undiminished over time and generations destines people to live in the past. We become the curators of our ancestors' grievances.

What was the George Santayana line? Those who cannot remember the past are condemned to repeat it. Well, those who remember too well are also condemned to repeat it. To be stuck in feuds far more ancient than the Hatfields and McCoys.

In this, the year of our fiftieth anniversary, the Serbs and Croats are murdering each other, calling up ancient hostilities from as long ago as eight hundred years. In the rest of Eastern Europe, where history itself was occupied by the Soviets, ethnic hostilities have reemerged, dangling their roots. And those are modern memories compared to the biblical datelines over land disputes in the Middle East.

There is no excuse for sending the past down the memory hole. The final assault of the Holocaust is the "revisionists'" denial of the Holocaust. Even a Toyota-driving American is uneasy hearing that the young Japanese know more about Hiroshima than about Pearl Harbor. Not long ago, a Japanese professor told of a junior high school student who thought Pearl Harbor was where her countrymen dive for Mikimoto pearls. But how do any of us acknowledge the past and honor it without being trapped in it?

Historian Carol Gluck at Columbia University makes the case for three R's: remembrance, reflection, and responsibility. "We don't want to transmit all the burdens of the past," she says. "We're not looking for a constant open wound. What we need is remembrance for those who died and the 'day that will live in infamy.' We need reflection for understanding how it really happened. We need to take responsibility for the past and therefore the present and future."

This is especially true on this anniversary. In all likelihood, this President will be the last to have fought in World War II. Pearl

Harbor is becoming a geriatric memory now, on its way to history.

It may be the veterans who pass the best message about history to the next generations. Like the guide on the *Arizona*, most of them have passed through the fourth R, reconciliation.

In the past half-century the Japanese and the Americans, separately and together, have filled a new memory bank. Not always an easy task, but without amnesia or vengeance. So this week we remember Pearl Harbor, but in its proper place: the past.

DECEMBER 3, 1991

Down to Earth

||||||||||||||||||||||||||||||||||||||||||||||||||||||||||||||||||||||||||||||||||||||||||||||||||||||||||||

Casco Bay, Maine — The tomatoes are in the ground at last. I step back and look at the neat rows, each small green plant set in its own mound of earth, waving slightly in the warm breeze, like a fragile banner to summer.

By July, I will tie them to stakes or encase them in their metal cages. But to do so now would be absurd, like tucking an infant into a king-size bed.

In the next few hours, the temperature will dive by forty degrees, and on Sunday it will rain solidly. The weatherman on the television set will banter with the anchors, apologizing for this inconvenient bout of bad weather, as if it were a flaw in his radar equipment.

In our human world, rain is an uninvited weekend guest, an affront to the tourist bureau, a spoil to the sport. Even a meteorologist, speaking on behalf of his viewers and his species, regrets the rain's inconsiderate timing.

From my window, holding a cup of tea in my hand and wrapped in sweaters, I will watch with a different perspective. Lovely weather for an infant tomato.

For most of the year, I confess, the relationship between such things as food and weather is as far from my consciousness as a report of fog holding up an airplane full of lettuce from California or apples from Australia. Winter is an obstacle to harvest if it keeps me from the supermarket. Food that is "out of season" doesn't disappear, it just costs more.

Like most Americans, I spend my life in what is called the built environment. Built by people for people. Weeks go by when I am officially "outdoors" for only minutes between home and parking spaces and man-made structures. My climate is controlled and in my vocabulary the word "nature" is usually preceded by the adjective "human."

Then summer comes and with it a long-dormant appetite for "real" tomatoes. My deep abiding prejudice against any of the red fruit that comes by plane or train from some factory farm, my suspicion of any produce bioengineered for its shelf life, drives me back to the earth.

Maybe this is what it means to garden—even in the small and amateurish way that has produced vegetables on my fraction of an acre. Digging out New England's most abundant crop—rocks— from dirt that is not dirty, I experience a different sort of belonging.

I can feel my sense of the human place in the scheme of things shift a degree or two from the center of the universe. The weather isn't here for us. The world isn't here for us. However great and personal is my greed for sliced tomatoes, I know that I am essentially playing by nature's rules, on nature's home turf.

As Bill McKibben writes in *The Age of Missing Information*, his book comparing the world of nature and that of television, "Even the dullest farmer quickly learns, for instance, a deep sense of limits . . . some sense that the world as a whole has limits, a piece of information we've largely forgotten."

In the next weeks, my plants will, with luck, take root and begin their miraculous ascent. At the same time, a group of world leaders will arrive in Brazil at what is billed as the Earth Summit.

They will be greeted with much fanfare. Much attention will be paid to politics and the environment, the politics of the environment. The television cameras, which, as McKibben notes, cannot film the destruction of the ozone or the greenhouse effect, will focus perfectly on people.

But I wonder how many of these people traveling by plane and limo and expense account from one cabinet room to another will put aside ego for environment. How many have been outside of human nature long enough, recently enough, to recognize that while we can destroy the world, it isn't just "ours."

"Human beings—any one of us and our species as a whole— are not all-important, not at the center of the world," writes McKibben. "That is one essential piece of information, the one great secret, offered by any encounter with the woods or the mountains or the ocean or any wilderness or chunk of nature or patch of night sky. . . ."

It's this information that grows in the garden as well, though in a modest domesticated version. It's in the land that measures time by seasons, not clocks or calendars. It's in the soil that reaches into the past and future beyond the brief egocentric moment that I call it "mine." It's there as well in the lesson that the rainy weather this day may be bad for tennis, but it's good for a patch of infant tomatoes.

MAY 29, 1992

Thinking about Tomorrow
|||||||||||||||||||||||||||||||||||||||||||||||||||||||||||||||||||||||||||||||||||||||||||||||||||||||||||||||||

The children are missing from the streets of Rio de Janeiro. The street urchins, the homeless kids who roam the city by the thousands, were apparently removed like so much debris when the Brazilian government cleaned up for the Earth Summit.

What a shame. Instead of taking them out of the city, the officials should have brought them right to the center of the pomp and circumstance. They should have left them where they belong, smack in the middle of this pin-striped meeting of world leaders.

After all, this Earth Summit is about children. No matter how you couch the concerns of this gathering in long words and simultaneously translated speeches, it's about children, generations of them.

Population, poverty, pollution. A changing climate and disappearing species. Some say the conflict in Rio pits one hemisphere against another. A Southern Hemisphere damaging the last of the world's natural resources against a Northern Hemisphere spewing spoilage from its overconsumption machines.

Some say it's between the economy and the ecology, growth and preservation. The standoff between spotted owls and loggers' jobs multiplied by millions of species and billions of people.

But the deeper conflict is between a long-term and a short-term perspective. It's about how people think about the year 2030 and how we don't think about it.

From my post in the Northern Hemisphere, it seems to me that in my lifetime we have not only darkened the natural horizons, we have shortened the human horizons. Our own country, rich by any standard, has somehow stopped paying attention to the future.

How else can we explain the casual neglect and impoverishment of our own children? One of every five children in America is poor. We spend $11,000 for every senior and $1,000 for every child. We borrow a billion dollars every day to pay for the national debt which will add to our children's debt.

How else can we explain a business world that thinks only as far ahead as the next quarterly estimate, if that? A year ago, one corporation promised and paid its executives huge bonuses to pump the stock up to $100 a share for just ten days.

And how else to explain a President who only thinks as far as November? Or an electorate that has yet to push the future to the top of the agenda.

Nearsightedness is hardly a new or uniquely American condition. Throughout history people living hand to mouth have never had much time to look ahead. If the children of Rio were invited to the conference, surely they would ask, first of all, for lunch.

But today the comfortable and middle-class, the leaders as well as followers, have also had their vision crimped. As Al Gore, the Tennessean heading the Senate delegation to Rio, worries, "We have had the idea that we can exploit the earth for our own short-term desires and designs."

Gore, a thoughtful leader in environmental politics, says that our attitude toward the future has been crippled first by denial and now by despair. "Denial is a barrier to recognition," he says. "Despair is a barrier to grief and all the related feelings that people have to experience in order to understand the necessity for significant changes."

During the Cold War, it was the nuclear bomb and the dooms-day scenario that made people doubt a future. The bomb shifted the equation between today and tomorrow.

Now we enter the post-Cold War world and the threat is less from a falling bomb than from a rising thermostat. It's from too many cars and too many babies. The threat grows with each cleared acre of rain forest at a time. We may suffer less from future shock than future phobia.

Go into any schoolroom, says Gore, who has done it dozens of times. Ask the kids the most important issue and they will say the global environment. Ask them if they care more than their parents and they will say yes. Ask them why and they'll say it's because kids will be around longer and because they know more.

"But they really do not understand how we could be so paralyzed," says Gore. More adults are also finding it hard to understand.

So, in the midst of all the posturing and wrangling in Rio, there are signs of movement, even if they are only small stretches, careful warm-up exercises. A good antidote to despair.

The children are not to be seen on the streets of Rio these days. Nor are they to be heard in the conference hall. But sooner or later, they're the ones we have to answer to.

JUNE 9, 1992

HE SAID,
SHE SAID

||||||||||||||||||||||||||||||||||||||||||||||||||||||||||||||||||||||||||||||||||||||||||||||||||||||||||||||||||||||||||||||||||||

|||||| *Okay, boys and girls, back to your corners. Can we talk? Can we hear?*

Clarence Thomas and Anita Hill I

|||||||||||||||||||||||||||||||||||||||||||||||||||||||||||||||||||||||||||||||||||||||||||||||||||||

It was her word versus his. Just a he-said, she-said sort of thing, as Senator John Danforth had put it, dismissing the "October Surprise," the "smear campaign," the "eleventh hour" accusation of sexual harassment that had thrown Clarence Thomas's sure thing into full disarray.

Who was this "she" anyway? The senators who found her "credible" called her Professor Anita Hill. The others called her "the woman," or "this lady," or even, in the strange case of Senator Alan Simpson, "the lady who was lured."

Before Anita Hill stepped into her televised Oklahoma classroom, measured and earnest, dignified and strained, the Senate's Judiciary Committee had simply dismissed her. Before Professor Hill said, "It is an unpleasant issue. It is an ugly issue," they had decided to deal with her charges the old-fashioned way. Among themselves.

Any way you cut it, some of these men had known since mid-September that the former head of the civil rights enforcement agency was accused of violating a woman's civil rights. Any way you run the sequence of events, they had known before the committee vote that a Supreme Court nominee had been accused of sexual harassment as defined by that court.

But like businessmen running a private corporation, they handled this "delicate matter" discreetly, among their own kind. Why, Arlen Specter, the very model of judiciousness, had gone to Clarence Thomas in person, eyeball to eyeball, and gotten a forceful denial. Dennis DeConcini had "made the judgment, right or wrong, that he was credible to me."

It was her word versus his. They took his without hearing hers. They didn't tell the rest of us.

Would it have been better if Hill had gone public earlier? Sure, although anyone who wonders why she was reluctant can listen to the messages on her telephone tape. Did the senators have any legitimate reason for protecting Thomas's privacy? Sure, FBI files are full of scurrilous attacks.

But anyone with half an investigative eye open could have discovered that Anita Hill was "no kook," as Senator Paul Simon put it. And anyone doing his job should have understood that this is a subject that deserved as much attention as Douglas Ginsburg's tokes of marijuana.

This portrait of men in power is not very pretty. Capitol Hill is not just a place where you can bounce checks with impunity and discriminate without fear of the law. (Civil rights laws don't apply there.) It's a place where men can listen to Clarence Thomas's straight-faced claim that he had no opinion on abortion and then question Anita Hill's credibility.

If these men kept the lid on the charges of sexual harassment, however, it was not just to protect Clarence Thomas. To many, Anita Hill is their worst nightmare. The woman who could come riding out of the past waving a charge. False, of course, or maybe true.

Women have always lived with a sense of vulnerability. They have been vulnerable to rape, to harassment, to abuse; on the street, at work, even at home. Slowly, they have won some tools of self-defense. In the shouting match of his word against hers, it is not always or only his that is heard.

Date rape, battered women's defense, sexual assault. With each modest change in attitude and law, there has been a stunning overreaction on the part of many men. Where women feel vulnerable to male assault, men feel vulnerable to a woman's accusation.

Rape is still vastly underreported. Twice as many men kill their wives as wives kill husbands. Sexual harassment remains as widespread as it is hard to prove.

Yet when a Willie Smith is arrested, how many men think: Any woman could accuse me. When a battered wife who killed her husband is granted clemency, how many think: It's open season on husbands. And when Clarence Thomas is hit with a charge, how many think: You can't even ask a girl out anymore.

In real life, false accusations are few, maybe even fewer than false acquittals. But in fantasy life, they are the "reverse discrimination" story lines of the time, the female pit bull attack on the ankle of an innocent man.

Her word is not always the right one. The chore of proving in public what happened in private remains as difficult as ever. There is no assurance that airing Anita Hill's charges and Clarence Thomas's countercharges would lead to a crisp clean-cut winner.

But it was not for the all-male Senate committee to silence "her word" before it was spoken in public. At the eleventh hour and the fifty-ninth minute these senators finally heard, loud and clear, the voices of women. The women they represent.

His word, her word. This is our word to Congress: Listen up.
OCTOBER 11, 1991

Clarence Thomas and Anita Hill II

Since the volatile mix of sex and harassment exploded under the Capitol dome, it hasn't just been senators scurrying for cover. The case of the Professor and the Judge has left a gender gap that looks more like a crater.

We have discovered that men and women see this issue differently. Stop the presses.

On the *Today* show, Bryant Gumbel asks something about a man's right to have a pinup on the wall and Katie Couric says what she thinks of that. On the normally sober *MacNeil/Lehrer NewsHour* the usual panel of legal experts doesn't break down between left and right but between male and female.

On a hundred radio talk shows, women are sharing experiences and men are asking for proof. In ten thousand offices, the order of the day is the nervous joke. One boss asks his secretary if he can still say "good morning," or is that sexual harassment? Heh, heh. The women aren't laughing.

Okay, boys and girls, back to your corners. Can we talk? Can we hear?

The good news is that women have stopped rolling their eyes at each other and started speaking out. The bad news is that we may each assume the other gender not only doesn't understand but can't understand. "They don't get it" becomes "they can't get it."

Let's start with the fact that sexual harassment is a concept as new as date rape. Date rape, that should-be oxymoron, assumes a different perspective on the part of the man and the woman. His date, her rape. Sexual harassment comes with some of the same assumptions. What he labels sexual, she labels harassment.

This produces what many men tend to darkly call a "murky" area of the law. Murky, however, is a step in the right direction. When everything was clear, it was clearly biased. The old single standard was male standard. The only options a working woman had were to grin, bear it, or quit.

Sexual harassment rules are based on the point of view of the victim, nearly always a woman. The rules ask, not just whether she has been physically assaulted, but whether the environment in which she works is intimidating or coercive. Whether she feels harassed. It says that her feelings matter.

This, of course, raises all sorts of hackles about women's *feelings*, women's *sensitivity*. How can you judge the sensitivity level of every single woman you work with? What's a poor man to do?

But the law isn't psychiatry. It doesn't adapt to individual sensitivity levels. There is a standard emerging by which the courts can judge these cases and by which people can judge them as well. It's called "the reasonable woman standard." How would a reasonable woman interpret this? How would a reasonable woman behave?

This is not an entirely new idea, although perhaps the law's belief in the reasonableness of women is. There has long been a "reasonable man" in the law, not to mention a "reasonable pilot," a "reasonable innkeeper," a "reasonable train operator."

Now the law is admitting that a reasonable woman may see

these situations differently than a man. That truth—available in your senator's mailbag—is also apparent in research. We tend to see sexualized situations from our own gender's perspective. Kim Lane Scheppele, a political science and law professor at the University of Michigan, summarizes the miscues this way: "Men see the sex first and miss the coercion. Women see the coercion and miss the sex."

Does that mean that we are genetically doomed to our double vision? Scheppele is quick to say no. Our justice system rests on the belief that one person can get in another's head, walk in her shoes, see things from another perspective. And so does our hope for change.

If a jury of car drivers can understand how a "reasonable pilot" would see one situation, a jury of men can see how a reasonable woman would see another event. The crucial ingredient is empathy.

Check it out in the office tomorrow. He's coming on, she's backing off, he keeps coming. Read the body language. There's a *Playboy* calendar on the wall and a PMS joke in the boardroom and the boss is just being friendly. How would a reasonable woman feel?

At this moment, when the air is crackling with hostility and consciousness raising has the hair sticking up on the back of many necks, guess what? Men can "get it." Reasonable men.

OCTOBER 15, 1991

Clarence Thomas and
Anita Hill III

||||||||||||||||||||||||||||||||||||||||||||||||||||||||||||||||||||||||||||||||||||||||||||||||||||

Athens, Ohio — There is no joy in this. No backslapping, high-five cry of victory will accompany Clarence Thomas as he limps to the Supreme Court.

The sorry spectacle that ended Tuesday night bore all the earmarks of an American tragedy, something that might have been scripted by Theodore Dreiser. A man reaches for the gold ring, wraps his fingers around it, and a door from the past opens under his feet. A woman is called forward out of anonymity to tell her story and is slapped back to her place.

Before the lie detector registered one opinion and the Senate another, I had formed my own. To accept Anita Hill's story, you only had to believe that Clarence Thomas would lie to salvage his honor in front of the country and his family. To accept Thomas's denial, you had to believe that Hill was a psychopath.

This is what I saw at the hearings. A man who believes, deeply, fiercely, passionately, that he is not the sort of person who would ever do . . . what he did.

It was widely said that the American sense of fairness would be outraged had Clarence Thomas's fate turned on a ten-year-old charge. But what will happen to our sense of fairness as court decisions come tainted with doubts about the youngest, newest Justice?

These senators gave him much, much more than the benefit of the doubt. They gave him a seat for life on the highest court in the land. But this drama had more than two characters. What will happen on the wider stage? Last week, a decade of obituaries for the women's movement were declared premature. Women—not women's groups, but women—found their voices and each other.

This was never a female vendetta against the judge. There was no get-Thomas fever. Just fury that the men in the Senate "didn't take it seriously." If they could ignore Anita Hill, a law professor, a conservative—dear gawd, a Bork supporter—what chance did any woman have? If not her, who? If not now, when?

The old women's movement slogan, the personal is political, came out of mothballs. Sexual harassment became sexual politics. That great click of recognition was heard across the country: "I'm not the only one."

In thousands of homes, men asked their wives if this had happened to them and asked themselves what they might have done. Even the women who testified for Thomas had stories to tell. The willful ignorance about sexual harassment was exploded in one spontaneous combustion.

The reality is that sexual harassment—like rape, like abuse, like pornography—unites women. Today more women feel their freedom is more constricted by fear and intimidation than by any formal rules that bar their entry to the inner circles of power.

Can the instant protest that forced this issue to the Senate floor be harnessed to the nuts and bolts of politics, to win family and medical leave, to change some of the faces on the Senate Judiciary Committee? Or will it be deflated in the cold morning light of the Senate vote?

Tuesday night, after the Senate vote was counted, a dozen young women here on the Ohio University campus asked me with dismay, "How could they not have believed her?" The polls said that Americans, men and women, found him more believable. Less than half took her side.

Well, how do you explain to these young women the cynical historical truth: There's progress in the numbers. How many would have believed Professor Hill fifteen years ago. Ten percent? Would she have believed it herself?

Her treatment at the prosecutorial hands of Arlen Specter and Orrin Hatch gave women a taste of what happens when you lodge a complaint. But this outcry gave men a taste of how women judge these acts. If I were forced to pick between making the world easier for sexual harassment lawsuits or making such suits less necessary, I know which one I'd take.

One of the witnesses for Thomas called Anita Hill, disdainfully, the Rosa Parks of sexual harassment. Not a bad label to live with. If someone will print up a bumper sticker—"Honk If You Believe Anita"—I'll take two.

When the FBI came, when the reporter called, when the senators summoned, this woman had a choice between telling the truth or ducking. That's the mundane way that courage gets tested.

Maybe the last words belong to Eleanor Roosevelt. On a wall poster that hangs on Professor Hill's wall are these words: "You gain strength, courage and confidence by every experience in which you really stop to look fear in the face. . . . You must do the thing you think you cannot do."

OCTOBER 18, 1991

Gender
||||||||||||||||||||||||||||||||||||||||||||||||||||||||||||||||||||||||||||||||||||||||||||||||||||||

Los Angeles — The man leans across the table and asks the question again, as if I had not heard him the first time. "Where is the line?"

It is mid-morning and we are sitting over coffee—the West Coast's drug of choice—talking ostensibly about national politics. But the subject gravitates naturally toward sexual politics. He wants to know: "Where is the line?"

Ever since Anita Hill's story exploded all over his office, spewing its uneasy debris, he has been searching for an E-Z marker to separate flirtation from harassment, a threshold between attention that is welcome and unwelcome. At times, he says, the line is as hard to find as Waldo in one of those elaborate drawings.

My coffee companion is young, single, and sincere. He is not whining about being victimized or misunderstood. He recognizes that the map of the male-female domain is changing and the line he is searching for is a safe path.

You see, the office, he says to me earnestly, is his workaholic generation's version of dating bar and matchmaker. The hours are long, work life and social life intermingle. It has become the primary meeting ground for men and women.

In this world, men are expected to pursue women, he says. Men are supposed to initiate relationships, take the first step, make the opening gambit, risk the first call. But when does the attention a woman may want from one man become harassment from another, less welcome "suitor"? He wants something to follow as a Triptik through the land mines.

As we talk, I find something refreshing and familiar in his

uncertainty. If men are suddenly walking a fine line and searching for a solid one, isn't that what women have always done?

Women who were not born yesterday have had to learn to negotiate tricky territory. How do you turn a boss off without losing your job? How do you end the behavior of the men you work with—the sex jokes, the too friendly hand on the shoulder—without ending the camaraderie. Where is the line between encouraging him and offending him?

If men were expected—boys will be boys—to be aggressive, women were expected to be the gatekeepers of male sexuality, even at work. Indeed, women share this expectation of each other, even of Anita Hill.

When the overnight polls, those indications of knee-jerk responses, found that a majority of women were not on her side, I was not all that surprised. The very universality of her experience seemed to work against her as well as for her.

At some level, many women looking at the poised law professor thought that she should have been able to "handle it." After all, they had, every woman had.

Now, however, in this shift, men are being told to "handle it." They are being given a mirror-image task. To express interest without being seen as a "lech." To ask for a date, once, twice, thrice, without being labeled or even sued. When does one man's claim that he is "socially awkward" at this task become a woman's belief that he is sexually harassing her. As my table companion asks: "Where is the line?"

Of course, there are many ways to change this unsettled topography. Some women can become more assertive both about asking men and about refusing them.

But it seems to me that at last we have raised the expectation that men will read something more important than maps. They will read women.

We are insisting that they learn the clues, the body language, the verbal signs that differ with every human interaction. They will have to receive as well as deliver messages. To know what she heard, not just what he meant. That's not such a bad thing. Not such a bad set of skills to have in the world.

When women first got into the man's world, they were expected to abide by its rules. They were supposed to deal with the world on its own rough-and-tumble terms, to swap stories with the boys and not blush, to handle it rather than fight it. Now women are trying to balance the lopsidedness of this change. They are saying, wait a minute. How about trying it my way?

I tell all this to my young companion as we finish both the coffee and the conversation. No, sorry, I have no set of instructions in my pocket to hand him. There is no crib sheet for changing relationships at work, no shortcut for negotiating the delicate landscape of male and female relationships.

Even if I had a Magic Marker, I would draw a very different line than the one he wants. It would be a time line.

This is going to take a while.

OCTOBER 25, 1991

Click!

||||||||||||||||||||||||||||||||||||||||||||||||||||||||||||||||||||||||||||||||||||||||||||||||||||||||

Never mind the backlash, that instrument widely used for whipping women back into their place. Forget about the double shift, the glass ceiling, and the mommy track.

We here at the Institute for Happily Ever After Living (HEAL) have finally identified the most reactionary implement currently used to undermine equality in modern marriage. This is the small innocent-looking rectangle known as a television remote control. The clicker.

HEALers have spent long months researching this subject. We have visited many homes filled with egalitarian ideals. We have talked to many couples who share child raising and toilet-bowl cleaning. We have interviewed New Men who "just DO understand" and New Fathers who have never once in their lives cried helplessly, "Honey, I think the baby's diaper is wet."

Nevertheless, we must now report that even among the most liberated subset of spouses, somewhere between 84 percent and 93 percent of the remote controls are found in the hands of men. Indeed, it could be said that the clicker has become the last remaining scepter, the last power-wielding symbol of the former male dominion. The once head of the household has taken his last stand as Head of the Household TV.

This would not be an inordinate source of concern for HEAL. After all, power struggles are waged over lesser household implements, like, for example, thermostats. But there is another gender gap in this activity that adds to our concern for the future of marriage.

The average man switches channels approximately eight times more often per quarter hour than would the average woman. She is thus subject to an endless series of mind-numbing television flash cards. We encountered one man, a champion channel-surfer in an extensive cable area, who watched no one station longer than nine seconds. The clicker was named as a co-respondent in his wife's divorce action and her subsequent mental health claim.

So in hopes of HEALing, our researchers have tried to get to the root of this. One of our number, an urban anthropologist with a background in singles studies, ties it into courtship behavior. Men are playing the field. Women are looking for a commitment.

Men's relationship to television thus mirrors the famous commitment phobia. A man with a remote control cruises the cable world, romantically searching for what lurks just beyond the Rainbow or the Shopping Channel.

A woman, on the other hand, is more willing to give the program on the screen a chance. It just might grow on her. Besides, there's no guarantee the next one will be any better.

Another in our think tank, a linguist, says that the essence of the problem can be found in the language itself. Some words have a particular appeal to men. Remote. Control. Need we say more?

The biologists on our staff, of course, prefer to tie the male compulsion to the old right brain, left brain thing. The man with a clicker has the same anatomy as the boy who once clicked in and out of second-grade math class. The cable system with its hundred opportunities has become a smorgasbord for his short attention span. The remote control is the fork.

Our sociologists, however, prefer to blame nurture over nature. Consider a boy raised on a visual diet of sporting events. There is no narrative in these games, but merely a series of brief plays. Click. A girl raised on soap operas? The action is glacial, lingering, emotional. Stay tuned.

None of this, however, solves the essential dilemma that we wish to HEAL: the visually dysfunctional couple. What to do when you are intimate with a remote-control freak?

There is the old standby recommended by therapists. This is known as taking turns. He gets one hour or night. She the next. There is the compromise. He would click every nine seconds, she every nine minutes. Together they can click every four minutes twenty-five and one-half seconds.

There is the separate but equal solution: two TVs, not two remotes for one TV. (Two remotes mean civil war.) Then there is the "ditch the problem" solution. Hide the clicker.

But in the spirit of true HEALing, we ask couples to consider whether the issue is just male chauvinism or television chasm. If he is surfing and she is suffering, it may be because there is nothing worth watching.

Click.

MAY 19, 1992

The 3 Percent Difference

|||||||||||||||||||||||||||||||||||||||||||||||||||||||||||||||||||||||||||||||||||||||||||||||||||||||||

Toward the very end of his book about mythology and men, Robert Bly finally turns to math. The genetic difference between men and women, he notes, amounts to just over 3 percent.

Nevertheless, he says, "I think that for this century and this moment it is important to emphasize the 3 percent difference that makes a person masculine, while not losing sight of the 97 percent that men and women have in common."

His mathematical observation is something of an apologia to a book that is unabashedly about differences. And Bly is not alone.

Wending my way through the pages, it occurred to me that *Iron John* has any number of counterparts in current books and research about women. It made me wonder why many are staking out this "3 percent difference" as the old-but-new turf.

Is it important, as Bly says, "for this century and this moment," to talk about gender differences? Do we still even believe that men and women have 97 percent in common?

Over the past year or two, Robert Bly has become something of a phenomenon. In this best-selling reverie about masculinity, in his poetry readings, in his interview with Bill Moyers, in his gatherings of men, the white-haired Bly has become a father figure or elder figure for a psychic men's movement.

This is not the men's movement of the seventies, which often seemed scripted by the women in men's lives. Nor is it about watching less football and doing more dishes. It is about what is lacking in men's lives today, which Bly sums up in one phrase: "There is not enough father."

Bly goes after maleness, using Grimm's fairy tale of Iron John as a text. A storyteller around the campfire, he leads men down through confusion, through grieving, through myth and culture to an ancient/modern idea of manhood.

I am not, I confess, much for myth-speak. The story of Iron John is far more abstract, even obscure, than my brief description allows. But Bly's post-chauvinist search for maleness has a counterpart to the post-feminist search for femaleness. It's as if Iron Man and Earth Mother had become separate archetypes for our time.

For most of history, woman was "other" and "other" was lesser. It is no wonder that, in the women's movement, equality was defined roughly as "sameness."

In the late 1960s, men and women were no longer opposites that attract. Men and women became, rather, persons. Mothers and fathers became parents. In the 1970s, differences were drowned by a wave of androgyny.

But in the past several years, they have reemerged. The 3 percent has come to occupy a larger place in our minds. We talk easily about women's values, women's ways of managing and of seeing the world as if they were obviously distinct from men's.

From Carol Gilligan's first work to far-less-grounded research, it is again fair game to explore the psychic gender gap. In law and public policy, questions have recycled about whether we want maternity leave or parenting leave: unisex legislation. After decades of integrating male schools, there is again a feminist argument in favor of educating adolescent girls separately: single-sex education.

Bly himself believes that only men can make men. He tells a story, approvingly, about a tribe in which boys live with their mothers until the men come and—with the complicity of the women—kidnap the children and turn them into men. He says there is not enough "father," as distinct from "parent."

For my own part, I would like to believe that the current fascination with differences is indeed "post-feminist," "post-chauvinist." That we are now so comfortable with equality that we are no longer threatened by differences. That the age of androgyny has simply passed like massive shoulder pads on the old power suits. Something softer will do.

Maybe it's the military music in the air these days, the sounds of war, which, despite our coed Army, have a masculine beat to them. But Bly's differences seem less like harbingers of a new men's movement than of the old. Bly's descriptions of women, and of relationships, are often more reminiscent of the 1950s than the 1990s. His search for the male reminds me a touch too much of the days when the tom-toms sounded and the women were kept from the ceremonies.

Is it important, as he says, to emphasize the 3 percent? Differences may make it easier to understand ourselves, or harder to understand each other. But sometimes this new interest in gender resonates with the slight snap of a backlash.

FEBRUARY 5, 1991

Money and Marriage

|||||||||||||||||||||||||||||||||||||||||||||||||||||||||||||||||||||||||||||||||||||||||||||||||||||||||||||||||||

A few years ago, a friend of mine published a book bearing the standard spousal acknowledgment. She wrote: To my husband, without whom this book would never have been written.

Twelve months later, the book was headed for paperback, the marriage was headed for divorce court, and the author wanted to change the inscription. She wanted to write: To my husband, without whom this book would have been written ten years earlier.

Since then, I have been aware of how thoroughly people rewrite the scripts of their marriage after the book has slammed shut. The wife who earns her PHT—Putting Hubby Through school—may get gratitude at graduation. But when the bloom is off the marriage, he has a better memory of her hampering his studies than paying his bills.

A husband who stands by his wife while she climbs the corporate ladder is dutifully dubbed "supportive." But when she jumps out of the marriage, she remembers him as the ball and chain rather than the helium of her ascent.

All sorts of story lines change when the happily ever after is abruptly ended. Did her dinner parties help his promotion or did her fallen soufflé nearly ruin his career? Was he the savvy manager of her career or merely a hanger-on? Ask their lawyers.

This reevaluation of marriage has been a running joke of rich and famous men and their ex-wives. In the postscript to divorce, the pampered wife becomes the money-grubbing ex-wife.

But what is different now is that it's happening to rich and famous women as well. Man bites dog. Or, rather, husband sues for alimony and half the estate.

This variation on the theme dropped into the tabloid consciousness early this summer when *Good Morning America*'s Joan Lunden
was ordered to pay her husband of fourteen years $18,000 a month
in alimony. Lunden, who is said to earn some $2 million a year,
called it "a deplorable and shameful statement on how working
women are treated today. Why the courts don't tell a husband who
has been living off his wife to go get a job is beyond my compre-
hension."

Her and other howls of protest have reappeared everywhere from
People magazine to the latest *Redbook* to your friendly neighborhood
dinner party. Whether it's actress Jane Seymour or Seema (the ex-
Mrs. Ivan) Boesky, the women have money and the men want it.

According to my own sample of conversations about these men
and money, attitudes divide into three parts. Pre-feminist Consciousness I says simply that no self-respecting man should take
money from a woman. Feminist Consciousness II says that what is
sauce for the gander is sauce for the goose. Post-feminist Consciousness III laments that equal rights works better for men than
for women: As soon as women go to work, they get taken to the
cleaners.

But our outlook may have less to do with changing consciousness
than with the constant of emotional cost accounting. As Pepper
Schwartz, a sociologist at the University of Washington who has
been studying marriage for decades, says, "People don't like the
economic side to marriage and pretend it isn't there." Basically,
she says, "people still want the economic contract to be tied to
sentiment. They think they shouldn't have to pay for something
they don't like."

The economic worth of a husband or wife, she says, "is a very
hypocritical, unexamined, and always dangerous topic in a marriage." If you want to know what people really want to give each
other, she adds with a clear, even cynical eye, look at the terms in
prenuptial agreements: "There's a notable lack of generosity." The
message of these contracts is: "I will keep you in the style in which
I want to live but only while I feel good about you."

If such premarital agreements are still relatively rare, Schwartz
says, "it's because they can't get the person they love under those

conditions. So they promise, 'Everything I have is yours.' But they really mean what's in the agreements.''

Compared to Schwartz, I may be a hopeless romantic. I do belong resolutely to Consciousness II. Either spouse can get a prenuptial agreement and either can sue for support. But that's only partially out of a belief in equality. It's mostly out of a belief in— blush—marriage.

It seems to me that most married couples already belong to two competing economic systems. We work as individuals. There's one name on a paycheck. On the other hand, we think of marriage as a partnership. Family life is the one thing we still try to separate from the values of the marketplace.

When marriage succeeds, it's by muting the relationship between money and power. Indeed, if marriage is to work, it must operate more like a mutual fund.

But from the front lines of divorce, we are learning a dirty little secret: Many husbands and wives were keeping book on each other all along.

AUGUST 14, 1992

Palm Beach I: Date and Rape

||||||||||||||||||||||||||||||||||||||||||||||||||||||||||||||||||||||||||||||||||||||||

I am told by those who can find the silver lining in a cloud of squid ink that there is some good news in the media storm centered over Palm Beach. It has focused attention on date rape.

Maybe so, but not every spotlight is truly enlightening. Date rape is the should-be oxymoron that we use to distinguish rapes committed by acquaintances from those committed by strangers. But it is also a phrase that glues together the two sides of the story. His date and her rape.

Which story is the truth this time? What really happened in the Kennedy compound on Easter weekend? If this case gets to trial, I will bet big money on the courtroom scenario. The man will portray steamy sexual intercourse in the grass with just a spicy soupçon of rough stuff. The woman will describe sexual assault and a piercing violation of her will.

Moreover, if both of these parties go to the polygraph machine, it is entirely possible that they will separately and equally pass their lie detector tests with flying colors. Male and female alike may make equally convincing witnesses. Because in fact both may believe what they say.

This is what is so unsettling about this so-called gray area of sexual assault. Two people leave the scene of a sexual encounter, one remembering pleasure, the other pain.

In the most often cited 1985 study of 6,000 college students, University of Arizona professor Mary Koss found that over 25 percent of college women had experienced a completed or attempted rape since their fourteenth birthday. Four out of five of these encounters were with men they knew. But among college men, only 8 percent admitted to behavior that fit these definitions.

It isn't that the same 8 percent of the men are assaulting 25 percent of the women. Nor are they necessarily lying. The kernel of the research suggests, rather, that many men simply don't believe they have used force. Not really. Nor do they believe that the women have resisted. Not really.

In alleging date rape, Koss says, "the women reported that they had said 'no' forcefully and repeatedly. The men held out the possibility that 'no' meant 'yes.'

"The women considered the amount of force as moderately severe. The men, though they noticed a degree of resistance, believed it could be consistent with seduction. They believed women enjoyed being roughed up to a certain extent."

How is it possible that there is such a perceptual gap about "consent" for sex? It is, in part, the *Gone with the Wind* fantasy: Scarlett O'Hara carried to bed kicking and screaming, only to wake up humming and singing. It is the bodice-ripping gothic novel, rock-and-rape cultural messages. It is the ancient script of the mating game—he persists, she resists—that passes for "normal" sexual relationships.

All of this leaves the burden of proof on a woman that she didn't really want it or didn't at least accede to it. But Koss asks mischievously and seriously what would happen if the burden of proof were turned around.

"How could a man convince us that he went into the sexual encounter with the intention of a satisfying sexual experience?" she asks. "Did he try to determine whether she liked sex outdoors, liked it on the ground. What did he find out about disease and pregnancy prevention? Do you see the difference I am trying to suggest?"

What if a woman's pleasure were the standard of consent? And why is that the sort of question only asked by female stand-up comics?

There are women who like "being roughed up." There are women who make false accusations. Probably in similar numbers. The FBI estimates that 2 to 4 percent of all reported rapes are false and only a small percentage of rapes are reported.

When date rape reaches the courtroom, as it rarely does, says Koss, picking her words carefully, "the only way to convince a jury that his force went beyond the 'normal' male assertiveness in pursuing his sexual agenda, and that her resistance went beyond the 'normal' female reticence in the interest of protecting her purity or inexperience, is if she sustained a lot of injury."

Without such an injury, without a witness, we have only the two and opposing views of a man and a woman. Without a legal recourse, the hope lies on "crime prevention" and that means closing the gap in sexual perceptions.

So, I am told, the Palm Beach story has focused attention on date rape. But I'm afraid that all we are likely to learn from this celebrated story is that we still live in a culture in which he says date and she says rape. And each fervently calls the other a liar.

MAY 3, 1991

Palm Beach II: Sexual Mores and Sexual Violence

||||||||||||||||||||||||||||||||||||||||||||||||||||||||||||||||||||||||||||||||||||||||||||

The women in this case fill a Rolodex of roles. Presiding over the courtroom: a woman judge. Prosecuting for the state: a woman lawyer. Testifying as an expert witness: a woman emergency-room physician.

On the front bench, a phalanx of females named Kennedy: mother, aunt, family defender. And looming over them all, the accuser: woman as victim or vixen. Old roles, new ones, traditional, and even post-feminist—how many female images can fit into a courtroom? What do they say about how much life has changed for women, and how little?

I will not attempt to scoop some redeeming social message from the hazardous waste oozing out of Palm Beach. The trial of William Kennedy Smith has been stripped of any such pretense. Neither CNN—the station that gave us the war in the Gulf—nor the print media even attempt any longer to flavor this story with any greater issues. The people who line up for seats have come not for social insight but for a glimpse of her undies and his uncle.

But what of the women who read about this case . . . despite themselves? What of the young women who were glued to the strange, talking gray spot on their television sets—the spot that blocked out the accuser's face, turning her into Everywoman or Nowoman? What about their body language as they watched and listened and thought about rape, violence, consent, sex, and their own vulnerability and responsibility?

In the months since this story first emerged, and in the days since the trial opened, I have talked with a number of young women about the complexity of their own changed lives. They have grown up being told that they can be the judge, the lawyer, the doctor, *and* the rape victim. Why, they can have it all.

If there is one thing that unites these women in an era when much of sisterhood has been shattered by success, it is the fear of sexual violence. This is the chill in the campus air, the threat in the garage late at night, the tension on their faces as they listen to this woman's story.

But there is also enormous confusion around the words that infiltrate their single lives with less terror than the word "rape": words like "sexuality," "sexiness," and the nature of "consensual sex." It is as if another huge gray spot has covered up these topics too, making it hard to see clearly.

Any woman under forty has grown up with the disintegration of the double sexual standard. That double standard didn't evolve into a single standard but into a thousand smaller ones. Cultural cues are no longer universal and the likelihood that two people who meet will share the same assumptions isn't as high as it once was.

Today, one woman gives her daughter black lace underwear to lift her spirits. Another considers this underwear proof that this daughter was looking for love in all the wrong places.

One woman feels free to sit in a bar past midnight or go home with a man if she wants. Another woman, man, or jury asks, "What was she doing there at three o'clock in the morning?"

We have increased exponentially the number of messages hand-delivered to women. Be free and safe. Be sexually attractive—but careful. Be sexually active if-you-must—and more careful. Even Disney's updated heroine, Beauty, is given the contemporary mythic task of fending off one overbearing man's attention while turning another, a Beast, into a prince.

In Palm Beach, the jury is being asked to determine if this was rape or consensual sex. But I hear young—and not so young— women talk about the contour of consent, the nature of not-saying-no in their own experience.

They hear of a woman being "tackled" on the lawn, of a brief encounter in which the standard of pleasure was his own, and another woman left worried about pregnancy. They talk about the times they did not say no and the men who didn't notice that they didn't say yes. Even now and future doctors, lawyers, and judges talk about the difficulty of setting their own sexual standard in such uncertain times.

There is no crime for sexual mis-manners, for thoughtlessness or the absence of tenderness. But there are personal penalties we hear about every day. In a time of fewer norms the only way to bridge the gaps of changing sexual mores is through public and private conversation.

So we have the case with a giant gray spot. In this year's ongoing dialogue about men and women, the Palm Beach trial has become another unhappy, unseemly, and riveting conversation piece.

DECEMBER 10, 1991

Playing with Pain

||||||||||||||||||||||||||||||||||||||||||||||||||||||||||||||||||||||||||||||||||||||||||||||||||||||||||

It was an average week. A separated shoulder or two, a few broken bones in one hand, ligament damage to a couple of knees. The football coverage sounded like Grand Rounds on the orthopedic ward. Your average scoreboard of injuries.

Then Jeff Fuller barreled his 49ers' helmet into an opponent on the 29-yard line. It was what the commentators call "a possible career-ending injury." It was also a possible walk-ending injury, a possible move-his-body-ending injury, but nobody put it that way at first. Was his neck broken? The game went on. Round up the usual casualties.

I am no football fan. I do not share the allure of this alleged sport. Thousands of pounds of human flesh and armor pound more thousands across the turf, Astro and real, Saturdays, Sundays, Monday nights. But watching Fuller being carefully carted off the field, I know why I am hooked on the dynamics of the thing.

Somewhere in the middle of every game, the same thing happens. A man is knocked down and writhes in pain. The team plays on. A man is carted off on a stretcher and replaced. The game goes on. As I watch it now, I have come to wonder: Is this what men mean when they talk about teammates and team players?

All my life, I have heard about the disadvantage women have in business because most don't play team sports. It is said that we don't know what it is like to be turf buddies together, to get muddied together, to win together. Togetherness.

The ultimate model is, I am told, this all-American, only-American sport called football. It is true that on this turf men work together for victory. But on this same turf, they are trained to block a teammate's injury out of their minds. Also trained to be carried out of the way.

This is the image of a team we take from football: a group of people strong and close enough to go for it together, but not intimate enough to stop and take care of each other.

Not long ago, I talked with Harvard's Carol Gilligan, who has studied moral development in children. She has observed the different ways grade school boys and girls generally deal with sports. When a boy is injured, he is taken off the field while the others continue. When a girl is injured, the game stops while they gather around the one who was hurt.

When does that break occur? Most children, even the littlest boys and girls, express compassion when another of their kind is hurt. Is it taught out of boys on the playing fields? Is it how they are prepared for war or business or just manhood?

Recently, an open and friendly eighteen-year-old high school football star, Brett Law, unselfconsciously told a *People* magazine reporter, "Mostly I like knocking people over." When do people learn that to be a "pro" in many worlds you have to equip yourself with blinders against the weak and the injured? Do they have to learn first to ignore their own feelings?

I don't think every game should halt while a splinter is removed or that every business deal should be sidetracked by injured feelings. Indeed, there are times when people, especially women, get paralyzed by the opposite problem: their fear of causing pain or even making others angry.

But it occurs to me that this image of teamwork may be all

too successful a training for business in an era of takeovers and lean, mean strategies. Today, "competitiveness" is the key word. Those who would be winners often learn not to care when colleagues are cut from the "team." The bottom line may indeed reward those who aren't distracted by bodies on the field.

What would happen in America if just once the pros stopped playing ball until they found out if a teammate had indeed broken his neck? The producers, the coaches, the advertisers would scream.

But they just might send abroad a startling new image of a team player: not an interchangeable digit on a shirt, not a group of men united by an external goal. Somewhere down in the Pop Warner Leagues and in the living room there would be a small flash of understanding: "Pros" also take care of each other.

In time, with this radical sort of teamwork, they might even make the field a less dangerous place. And in time, on more than one turf, in more than one office, we might learn to play the serious games with much less pain.

OCTOBER 27, 1989

The Champ and the Woman

||||||||||||||||||||||||||||||||||||||||||||||||||||||||||||||||||||||||||||||||||||||||||||||||||||||||||||||||||||||

Few of the reporters could resist the boxing metaphors. Mike Tyson, conqueror of so many men, had been brought down by a teenage woman. Iron Mike, who had fought his way to the heavyweight championship, lost the biggest decision of his life, 12–0, to a beauty queen.

Even after the Indianapolis jury had labeled these two clearly as the Rapist and the Victim, there was an undertone to this story that would forever describe them in another way. The Champ and the Woman Who Brought Him Down.

It has been that sort of a year. Not just a year of he-said, she-said, not just a year of sexual politics, but a year in which the one female power on display—or in the ring, if you must—is the power to bring a man down.

The judge and the professor. The Kennedy and the nobody. The candidate and the cabaret singer. The champ and the beauty queen. Right or wrong, innocent or guilty, the stories are all different, but the public sex roles have remained constant. In each one there is a man on top and a woman who tries to topple him.

Even the hit movie of the month seems to imitate life. *The Hand That Rocks the Cradle* is a horror story about a nanny from hell, but there is another subtle scare tactic. The good mother, after all, sets into motion the terrible events that almost destroy her own family when she accuses a doctor of sexual assault.

Plots of male and female power have a special resonance when they are played out in the black community. Most especially when they appear at opposite ends of the black success spectrum: the Supreme Court and the Boxing Ring.

When Anita Hill spoke up last fall, opponents focused their rage on the idea that she was out to sully Clarence Thomas's success. The judge rode into that nomination on an African-American tale of triumph. His was a story of rags to robes. Hill dipped the hems of those robes in sleaze.

Just this month, one woman wrote to *Glamour* magazine, "If Anita Hill is a Woman of the Year, then an appropriate Man of the Year might be Charles Manson. Both are known for destroying lives."

In turn, when Clarence Thomas talked about a "high-tech lynching" he wasn't just accusing the Senate committee of imitating a Ku Klux Klan meeting. He was painting Anita Hill white. By virtue of testifying against a black man, he implied she had become a traitor to her race.

There were similar themes of race and gender in the Tyson story. During the trial the crowds cheered the champ. There were more than a few in public, though not on the jury, who saw him as a star and her as the villain.

At a black church rally for the boxer, one woman preached,

"We're here tonight because a brother is in the fight for his life." What of the eighteen-year-old woman? Was she drummed out of the sisterhood because she accused a brother?

After the verdict, a rumble of remarks about racism was heard in between the boxing metaphors. Some people pointed to a jury of ten whites and two blacks. Others talked about how this case promoted stereotypes of black rapists. At its extreme, there was the hint that the accuser had fed the fans of racism, not the rapist.

Such issues run deep in the black community, which shares a long history and a concern about the future of young men. There are few male role models in the lives of children and none to waste. Tied into this complicated knot is the notion that if only black women were more supportive—less independent—black men might be stronger. A black woman standing up for herself is easily charged with bringing a black man down.

The Tyson trial made the news because of the fighter's life story, not the victim's. Tyson was a fatherless child with an alcoholic mother. He was an orphaned teenage thug "saved" from the violence of the streets and trained for the violence of the ring. He became the champ.

Only the success story was never that pretty. Mike Tyson was an assault waiting to happen. Without boxing, he once said, he would have been "in jail—or dead. One of those." In the end boxing was just a detour on his way to jail.

But this was not a woman out to pull down a man, to wipe stardust off his gloves. She was a victim of violence, a victim of sexual assault. Only the saddest twist of roles, the strangest rewrite of Samson and Delilah, can read her as a woman out to beat the big guy.

Spare me the metaphors about boxing rings and KO punches and female contenders. In the end she was a young woman with courage. The real kind.

FEBRUARY 14, 1992

CHARACTER AND
CARICATURE

||||||||||||||||||||||||||||||||||||||||||||||||||||||||||||||||||||||||||||||||||||||||||||||||||||||||||||||||||||||||||||||||||||||||

|||||| *We hold two very different sets of moral attitudes in America. One is essentially about obeying commandments. The other is about relationships. The first is as straightforward as sin. The second is as complicated as human feelings.*

Wait a Minute

||||||||||||||||||||||||||||||||||||||||||||||||||||||||||||||||||||||||||||||||||||||||||||||||||||||||||

The cop and the rap singer went on the air together last Wednesday. It's the American way. One minute you're arresting a guy and the next minute you're in the greenroom with him. One day he's putting cuffs on you, the next day he's your co-guest.

When the lights went on at *Geraldo*, the Florida sheriff, Nick Navarro, and the leader of 2 Live Crew, Luther Campbell, played their parts like polished performers assigned the role of enemies. Navarro portrayed himself as a lawman and Campbell as his obscene lawbreaker. Campbell cast himself as the rap singer and Navarro as his "Communist and racist."

Then the two parted company and Campbell went on to *Donahue* and then to *Live at Five*. Another opening, another show. That's entertainment.

The scene wasn't much more heartening in Congress, where the players are feeling the dramatic heat of flag burning. Those who were for and against a constitutional amendment to ban the desecration of the flag were worrying about the reviews. Some, like Nebraska senator Bob Kerrey, imagined bleakly how they would look: "Bob Kerrey votes for gun control and he won't vote to protect the flag. It's a great thirty-second spot."

These days, it seems every issue becomes instant theater. Every advocate worries about how his act will play. Every conflict becomes a Punch and Judy show. Are you in favor of Robert Mapplethorpe's photographs? Are you against censors?

In public, people swing beliefs at each other like fists. The audience is expected to identify a hero and a villain. Which do you prefer: the First Amendment or pornography, the Bill of Rights or the flag, freedom of speech or obscenity?

What is so appalling about these one-acts is that they lead the audience to assume that every issue must be equally polarized. Like guests on a talk show, we either have to buy *Me So Horny* or ban it. We must favor the flag or the flag burners. We have to choose between license and crackdown. Now.

Indeed, at the ends of the American spectrum there are people who can only scream at each other across a stage. Americans do feel differently about symbols and speech.

Over the years, the passion to crack down on dissent or on speech has come from those who believe there's a natural human drift down to the lowest common denominator of behavior. Unchecked, they say, the human heart of darkness grows.

Those who have defended free speech have put their faith in reason, persuasion, what was once called enlightenment. In the free marketplace of ideas, they wager, the 2 Live Crew will lose and the flag burners will simmer down.

Over the course of American history, the value of free speech has outlasted both its abusers and its attackers. Over time, the Bill of Rights has been shielded from those who want to express their outrage by repressing outrageousness. But I wonder if these days, we have the time.

Out of the limelight, most Americans are not as certain as talk-show guests or as polarized as attack ads. There are First Amendment absolutists who would like to throttle Andrew Dice Clay and be there when Luther Campbell's daughter asks him to explain his work. There are people who neither want a Mapplethorpe on their wall nor want to dine with his censors.

But today public debate has been pared down to its speed-racing form, a sleek and simplistic shape. Even the Senate now pushes for an amendment with the urgency of a television host trying to wrap things up before the political commercial break.

When asked about the flag amendment, Arkansas senator Dale Bumpers said, "I belong to the wait-just-a-minute club." It's a club with a shrinking membership.

I don't think we need to imprison a rap singer to express our abhorrence of sexual assault songs. Like profanity on *Geraldo*, 2 Live Crew is a bleep in time. Nor do I think we need to singe the

Constitution to punish the few who torch a symbol. Flag burning isn't even a fad.

How do you defend a two-hundred-year-old principle in the era of the thirty-second spot? How do you wait-a-minute, and listen-a-while, in the passionate and polarizing ethic of the moment?

The Bill of Rights is on the political entertainment schedule now. And, it appears, the producers are only worried about today's show.

JUNE 19, 1990

Playing the Sex Card

||||||||||||||||||||||||||||||||||||||||||||||||||||||||||||||||||||||||||||||||||||||||||||||||||||||||||||||||||||||

The segue from the Super Bowl to 60 *Minutes* was ominous. As the credits to the largest male-bonding, testosterone-loading sporting event of the year rolled by, there was Prince singing: "Cuz I'm ready, willing and able / Gonna lay my cards on the table."

Minutes later, there was Bill Clinton, willing and able to place the pack on the table, but not about to turn over any Queen of Hearts for public inspection. The candidate admitted to wrongdoing but spared the details. Asked the A-word, he said what he has said before: "I'm not prepared tonight to say that any married couple should ever discuss that with anyone but themselves." And I suspect that the public, queasy after Long Dong Silver and Talking Gray Dots from Palm Beach, felt more relief than disappointment.

This is not *Monkey Business* in 1988. It is private business in 1992. Bill Clinton is no Gary Hart, the *National Star* is no *Miami Herald*, and Hillary Clinton is neither Lee Hart in '88, Joan Kennedy in '80, nor, as she put it, Tammy Wynette.

"You know, I'm not sitting here like some little woman, standing by my man like Tammy Wynette," said the feisty lawyer and gritty wife. "I'm sitting here because I love him, and I respect him and I honor what he's been through and what we've been through together. And you know, if that's not enough for people, then heck—don't vote for him."

Clinton's own best minute in the twelve minutes of 60 *Minutes* was his unrehearsed reaction to Steve Kroft's suggestion that the couple had an arrangement. "Hey, wait a minute," he said. "You're looking at two people who love each other. This is not an arrangement or an understanding. This is a marriage." At least Bill Clinton would not call for an international conference—forgive me, Michael—if his wife were raped.

I don't know if this interview will de-Flower the Clinton campaign and get the issue behind him. But in the lengthy American seminar about sexual morality, about the private lives of public figures, about the press and privacy, it looked a lot like a clarifying moment.

After all, I never thought the Gary Hart debacle was a story of character assassination but rather one of character suicide. It is not coy to say that many of us were less concerned with sex than with stupidity, hubris, dishonesty, exploitation, carelessness, even compulsive risk taking—any of the above—and what these characteristics would mean in the Oval Office.

But there was, and often is in sexual matters, an uncomfortable alliance between people who arrive at the same point of view from wholly different directions. In the Gary Hart case it wasn't just the sleazoid and the serious media who became strange bedfellows. So did the religious right and the secular left, puritans and feminists, those who condemned him for breaking his vows to God and those who condemned him for the look in Lee's eyes.

We hold two very different sets of moral attitudes in America. One is essentially about obeying commandments. The other is about relationships. The first is as straightforward as sin. The second is as complicated as human feelings. The first asks God for forgiveness. The second asks his wife.

These differences may seem too stark. Many Americans go back and forth between the polls. But the differences are real. One moral view is focused on heaven's wrath, the other on human pain. One holds a single judgment about the meaning of adultery in every life. The other is sure that adultery says something about a person. But when asked what, they are likely to say: It depends.

The union that held these cultural opposites together in dumping Gary Hart splits in two when faced with the Clintons' story. This is a husband endangering his marriage, not his eternal soul. This is a wife who is not a victim but a partner. Together they ask a valid question whether the public allows second acts in first marriages. Whether the public should judge what the couple has resolved.

The CBS poll said that 14 percent of the public wouldn't vote for anyone who committed adultery. That 14 percent wouldn't vote for Jerry Brown, who went around with Linda Ronstadt, or for Bob Kerrey, who dallied with Debra Winger. They might think Paul Tsongas's cancer was God's judgment and Tom Harkin is the liberal from hell. Not much to lose there.

But a 60 *Minutes* performance is not an election. You can approve of the marriage without voting for the man. This isn't a referendum on the press but a campaign for the Presidency. Loyalty to any of these candidates is still very shallow.

The Clintons played their hand as well as possible. For some he's simply and irrevocably cast as a knave. But in the vast and ongoing debate over private lives, most Americans can put the sex card back into the full deck.

JANUARY 31, 1992

Joe Camel: A Cartoon Character

||||||||||||||||||||||||||||||||||||||||||||||||||||||||||||||||||||||||||||||||||||||||||||||

In a year when political ad watching has become a media special, I am not surprised at the fate of Joe Camel. He's getting the truth-in-advertising treatment. At this rate, the old smoothie may not even make it through the primaries.

Old Joe was just another cartoon character when he immigrated here from European ads. He ended up in the hands of consultants and message marketers who decided he was the candidate to grab the hearts, minds, and lungs of Americans.

Soon, his name recognition became the envy of the entire field of competitors. Among certain segments of the population today, Old Joe Camel is as well known as Mickey Mouse. Why, 91.3 percent of six-year-olds not only know Old Joe but also know what he stands for. That's more than can be said for Old George Bush.

Joe's image is fixed in the public mind as a Smooth Character. He is known far and wide for shooting pool, scuba diving, and, of course, smoking.

He also has an acknowledged sex appeal. There is first and foremost his, uh, nose, prominently displayed—or dare I say hung?—on thousands of billboards. Then there are the girls who surround him at the Oasis, and the T-shirts, and the promotion of Hump Day.

But now, despite all the efforts of campaign consultants and media experts, the Camel Cigarettes candidate may finally have met his match. This Super week, Surgeon General Antonia Novello, along with the American Medical Association, called on RJR Nabisco to dump the dromedary. And they asked magazines and retailers to ban the cartoon cigarette pusher from their premises.

The opposition has finally proved that Old Joe's campaign message is directed at citizens too young to smoke. A growing body of research shows that this commercial creature has been deliberately directed by his handlers to get children sold on smoking. He's working the underage nicotine beat.

An assortment of studies in last December's *Journal of the American Medical Association* showed that Old Joe was extremely effective in delivering his $75 million-a-year message. Young children found the cartoon more appealing than adults did and they acted on it. Camel's share of the illegal children's cigarette market jumped from 0.5 percent to 32.8 percent in three years.

The cigarette makers, who make your average politician look

like a paragon of straight-talking virtue, insist there's no proof that advertising leads to smoking among children. They advertise merely to increase their share of the adult market.

But you do the math. In any given year only some 10 percent of smokers switch brands, while two million quit—400,000 of them quit the hard way, by dying from tobacco-related illness. About 90 percent of the people who smoke started before they were twenty years old. The only source of new customers is kids.

The Camel campaign is so blatant, so pernicious a pitch to hook the young that even *Advertising Age* editorialized against the ads. But it has to be that blatant and that pernicious before a public made passive by smoking reacts.

The last time enough ire was raised to throw the cigarette rascals out was in 1990 when RJR test-marketed a cigarette targeted directly at African-American lungs. "Uptown" went down.

In fairness, the Marlboro Man is not far behind the front-runner Old Joe in his pitch for the kiddie vote. The assorted ads associating slimness and smoking may do as much damage to teenage girls as the Smooth Character.

Cigarettes simply remain the renegade of the American system. Lethal but legal, lawful but unregulated.

If cigarettes were invented today, they'd never get on the market. But because they are on the market, we can't get them off without creating a huge underground of lawbreaking addicts. Tobacco is exempt from every federal health and safety act. The Surgeon General can only ask RJR to give Joe the heave and use moral suasion against the magazine ad directors.

The only way to reduce the enormous health risks of smoking is to encourage quitting and discourage starting. But every year some 1.8 million Americans start smoking. Which brings us back to the tobacco industry's $3.6 billion-a-year ad budget—enough money to send *any* cartoon figure to the White House.

My own view is that cigarette advertising is intrinsically false except for the little rectangles carrying the Surgeon General's warnings. But the worst of the pitchmen are those who stick their noses under the children's tent. So we begin with candidate Camel.

If the issue of the year is character, Old Joe is the first to go.

MARCH 13, 1992

The Culture of Personality

||||||||||||||||||||||||||||||||||||||||||||||||||||||||||||||||||||||||||||||||||||||||||||||||||||||||||||||||||||||||||||

Not that I have anything against Socrates. I agree with the wise Greek who said that the unexamined life is not worth living. But he came up with that one-liner before the invention of film and videotape, all the paraphernalia of electronic recording.

Now I wonder if it's the overexamined life that isn't worth living. Or the inner life that is suffering from overexposure.

This highly un-Socratic notion first occurred to me at *Eating*, a kind of docudrama about female eating disorders in which some L. A. women endlessly obsess about food at a birthday party. Midway through this movie—which could serve as aversion therapy for the weight-fixated—I wanted to scream: "Shut up and send the cake to Bangladesh!"

The impulse recurred—bigger and better—during a scene in *Truth or Dare*. The camera which had been tracking Madonna day and night through her tour, plumbing her depths and shallows, now accompanied her to the throat doctor. And filmed everything but her larynx.

Until then, the audience had seen Madonna at her best with all her in-your-face outrageousness. They'd seen her at her worst with all her "I have to protect my artistic integrity" banality. But suddenly the voice of reason and sanity passed to none other than Warren Beatty.

The older star gasped at the younger's exhibitionism in its most literal form. In the line that's been snatched and repeated most from this movie, he offered a footnote of bewilderment: "She doesn't want to be seen off camera, much less talk. Why would you say something off camera? What point is there in existing?"

But poor Warren was dating himself. There he was, tagged forever, as a member of a generation that actually draws a line, however often violated, however egotistically crossed, between life and art, between the private and the public self.

Madonna, it seems from myriad interviews, regards life backstage and onstage as parts of the same body of work, which is herself. Her allegedly real life is actually and also a piece of her performance art.

She is always expressing and examining herself. And since that is true, even a throat exam is something to be captured for posterity. It is Madonna, therefore it is art.

The superstar may well be blazing the current high-tech route to immortality. It's all rather like the postmortem trial in *Defending Your Life* when Albert Brooks discovers that the ultimate Jury has every minute of his life on tape. Such a conceit could only have been conjured up in post-video Los Angeles.

Shakespeare, Rembrandt, and the boys wanted to beat oblivion in their days, I am sure. Plays and paints were the tools of their legacy. Only now, you don't have to leave work behind. You can leave yourself. Indeed, if you can find a filmmaker, you can deposit every day in the collective memory bank.

Most of us remember our great-grandparents through family stories, photographs, letters, or snippets of memories. Our great-grandchildren will have us, live and in color, on reams of America's not so funny home videos. We won't have to worry about disappearing, though we may worry about getting erased.

I admit to a certain bias in my thinking. Writers too strut their stuff, but by and large their stuff is ideas. But with the camera, docu and drama, we enter the culture of personality. Personality becomes our most important product. It spills over the edges of everything else, even the page.

What was it the author Amy Tan said at a recent book convention? "Publishing is getting more like the entertainment world. You have to manufacture a personality." She added impishly, "The person talking to you is not the person I am. In real life I wear glasses, I look different."

In *Truth or Dare*, the director makes a visual line between person and performer. He uses black-and-white film for backstage, color for onstage. But Madonna crosses that line performing her role, playacting real life. In the strikingly narrow world that she rules as a superstar, the projection of her personality is her greatest artistic achievement.

What a tool the camera is. We can examine a life from the psyche to the larynx. What would Socrates say about this? Fast-forward and pass the hemlock.

JUNE 11, 1991

Magic, Morals, and Medicine

|||||||||||||||||||||||||||||||||||||||||||||||||||||||||||||||||||||||||||||||||||||||||||||||||||||||||||||||||

The stories all begin the same way, as if they were marking days on a chart after a life-changing cataclysm:

"In the three days since Magic Johnson . . ."
"In the ten days since Magic Johnson . . ."
"In the two weeks since Magic Johnson . . ."

On November 7, the superstar with the smile announced that he tested positive on an exam everyone wants to flunk. We now know he is carrying the HIV virus and some of his stardust is illuminating the corners of the disease we call AIDS.

In the SM (Since Magic) Era, we are talking about condoms, and the heterosexual epidemic, about penises and vaginas in their anatomically correct terminology. But in all of this matter-of-factness, we are still having trouble talking about the Psyche and Sex. To be specific, about promiscuity, values, and value judgments.

On Day 12 of the SM Era, on my way to work, I listen to two men arguing on the car radio. One offers thinly veiled suspicions that Magic "caught it" from men, not women. The other angrily rebuts this attack by citing Magic's reputation as a "womanizer." I walk into the office shaking my head over this character defense.

At lunch, a doctor talks about the luck of having Magic as a spokesperson for AIDS. He's a man of kindness, a role model for teenagers. Something good, says the doctor, may yet come from something god-awful.

But over coffee our conversation shifts from the medical to the personal. The doctor recalls Magic's description of the life he once led: "Before I was married, I truly lived the bachelor's life. . . . I was never at a loss for female companionship. . . . I did my best to accommodate as many women as I could. . . ." What kind of life was that? the doctor asks, sheepish and bewildered. But it is not a question she asks in public.

Later in the day, I spot a story in the paper about a high school student in Texas who asked his teacher why someone as smart and successful as Johnson led that "lifestyle." The teacher told him that Magic came from a generation that didn't know the dangers.

I wonder if the teacher who answers in such measured classroom tones thinks about these things differently at home. Does she try to imagine Cookie Johnson's thoughts about the nameless women her husband knew in the years they were "just" dating?

At times it seems that AIDS has made it easier to talk about sex in technical terms and harder to talk about sex in emotional terms. It's polarized some of us and silenced the rest.

When AIDS first came into our consciousness, "the Gay Plague" seemed to splinter off groups of moral and medical absolutists. The moralists talked about sin and the medicalists talked about disease. The moralists preached about human behavior. The medicalists, in reaction, lectured about viruses.

This split has come down to us in different forms. In the debate about condoms in schools, the moralists talk about abstinence and the medicalists about safer sex. In the debate about passing out needles to drug addicts, the moralists focus on drug use and the medicalists on safer shooting up.

Now, in the SM Era, the moralists have captured the market on monogamy while the medicalists have adopted Johnson as a heterosexual poster child. The rest of us are rather quiet about the sex in this sexual disease.

The silence is partially out of sympathy toward Johnson himself.

Who among us would yell at a paraplegic because he didn't wear his seat belt? He knows, he knows. It's out of the sense that sex is private even when someone goes public. And out of the knowledge that you can get AIDS from one partner.

But the poverty of this dialogue about human behavior comes largely out of the choices that we see. In the wake of the sexual revolution we are pressured to be either prudish or approving. To follow the Seventh Commandment or none.

These either/ors are laid over the traditional male talk about "the bachelor's life" or "scoring." Wilt Chamberlain, after all, boasts a lifetime record of 20,000 women.

It may be easier to find a cure for AIDS than to find our bearings. But the outlines of a consensus are there. After all, few of us believe that protection makes a virtue out of promiscuity. Most of us recognize that premarital sex is here to stay. On the whole, we are happier with the vision of sex as an intimate exchange, not a sporting event.

Instead of choosing a prefabricated value, we can begin to clarify our values. We can approve both condoms and caution. We can hold some single standard of medical and emotional care-ful-ness. And in the third week of the SM Era, we can be grateful for the strengths of the man who has spoken out, without ignoring his weaknesses.

NOVEMBER 22, 1991

Martin Luther King, Jr.:
No Stick Figure
||||||||||||||||||||||||||||||||||||||||||||||||||||||||||||||||||||||||||||||||||||||||||

At the beginning, the subject was so touchy that the scholars were asked not to even use the word. For over a year, those working with Martin Luther King, Jr.'s papers called it, cynically and sadly, "the P-word."

Now the revelation that King appropriated the words of others throughout his graduate career is common knowledge. Great passages of his Ph.D. thesis weren't his.

Again, a P-word has tarnished the bright heroism of this leader. Last time it was promiscuity. Today it is plagiarism.

Once, Martin Luther King, Jr., talked about a time when his children would live in a "nation where they will not be judged by the color of their skin but by the content of their character." Today, he is being judged by the complex content of his own character.

The country is learning of the flaws that their owner felt so intensely. King was no stick figure, appropriate for holiday framing, no object for the school lessons we offer up to our holiday heroes. George Washington fathered the country. Abraham Lincoln freed the slaves. Martin Luther King championed civil rights. Class dismissed for the long weekend.

This person of great courage and vision had wide fissures in his moral makeup. The man who had a dream also had secrets, though not from himself.

By all accounts, King was mercilessly self-critical, often insecure, wounded by guilt, and nagged by a sense of unworthiness. Once he preached, "There is a schizophrenia . . . within all of us. There are times that all of us know somehow there is a Mr. Hyde and a Dr. Jekyll in us."

While he was far and away his own harshest judge, King was also wisest perhaps in calculating the distance between a hero and a human. It is something the rest of us find difficult.

To be sure, promiscuity is not a felony, nor is plagiarism. It matters little to the world what King might have written on the Ph.D. subject of "A Comparison of the Conceptions of God in the Thinking of Paul Tillich and Henry Nelson Weiman."

It was what he did for, and said to, the country that crystallized our ideals as much as any Gettysburg Address. But where do we put the revelation that the man who took on the mantle of leadership in a moral cause also cheated? On his wife. In his scholarship.

In the time-honored tradition, King has gone through the transformation from ordinary person to leader to martyr to saint. The cause was personified and the personification was Martin Luther King, Jr.

The people who discovered his plagiary knew in their dismay that this would give aid, comfort, and ammunition to enemies. Not just the enemies of King, but to those of civil rights.

Now, as David Garrow, a King biographer deeply surprised by the evidence of plagiarism, says, "Using King as an inspirational symbol for children or teenagers is much, much more difficult now. There's no getting around that."

But maybe we have had too much of heroes manufactured and disassembled. As Clayborn Carson, the head of the King papers project, says, "I don't think it's healthy in a democracy to believe that there are some people who were born great and not without human flaws and limitations. To me an heroic figure is someone who recognizes his or her own limitations and yet has the courage to respond to the demands of historical moments."

Perhaps it's time not just for a revisionist view of King but of hero worship itself. We have lived, after all, most familiarly with the notion that leaders make change. The Great Man school of history is taught to our children.

America doesn't celebrate National Founding of the United States Day or the War to End Slavery Day or Civil Rights Day. We give faces and names to our crises. Today, many talk about a lack of leaders as if the genetic strain had run thin. But it is moments and movements that produce greatness in people.

In one sermon, King said prophetically, "You don't need to go out this morning saying that Martin Luther King is a saint. I want you to know this morning that I am a sinner like all of God's children, but I want to be a good man and I want to hear a voice saying to me one day, 'I take you in and I bless you because you tried.' "

After all the P-words are placed in the alphabet of his character, this is the lesson for the children. Here was a man, an ordinary man, with human strengths and weaknesses. But when the time came and much was demanded of him, he found the greatness within himself. Martin Luther King, Jr., "tried"—and he changed the world we live in.

NOVEMBER 16, 1990

Decency and Exposure
||||||||||||||||||||||||||||||||||||||||||||||||||||||||||||||||||||||||||||||||||||||||||||||||||||||||||||||

From the sound of it, you would think that Demi Moore had posed for a Rorschach test rather than a cover photo. The image of the very pregnant star, naked but for her two strategically placed hands, has *Vanity Fair* being compared to everything from *National Geographic* to the *National Enquirer*.

The magazine has been banned from supermarkets in North Carolina and has flown off the newsstands in Harvard Square. Her photo is now an instant visual poll on the subjects of sexiness and pregnancy, prudery and discretion, the uterus and the ego.

Indeed, one amateur sociologist of my intimate acquaintance has been flashing Demi in the buff around her home and office. She has collected comments that range from "indecent exposure" to "it's about time."

One woman said that it was wonderful to see a woman who was big—with child—and beautiful. Another, in her "seventeenth month of pregnancy," groaned about this new role model. Having not looked like a movie star before pregnancy, she now knew for sure that she didn't look like a movie star during pregnancy. She would have preferred a close-up of varicose veins.

It is true that people feel free to offer their opinions about the behavior of pregnant women. Pregnancy seems to turn women into public property. Co-workers who wouldn't touch your shoulder are suddenly rubbing your stomach. Strangers are telling you what to eat and what happened to them in labor.

But this tempest in a Demi-tasse has a familiar edge to it. Remember last year when Deborah Norville was pictured in *People* magazine breast-feeding? Some said she was wonderfully natural, quintessentially maternal. Others said she should keep her blouse buttoned in public. Everybody said something.

Demi herself has posed nude before. It was, as they now say about Supreme Court nominees, a youthful indiscretion. But some of the same people who would criticize her for posing with a flat stomach exposed praise her for publicly protruding. Others seem to suggest that nudity is even worse for a mommy-to-be.

It seems that photographer Annie Leibovitz focused her lens on an especially fertile territory in contemporary life. The place where attitudes about sexuality and motherhood conflict.

When the questions started pouring in, Tina Brown, the editor of *Vanity Fair*, said that the pictures illustrated the beauty of maternity. "There is nothing more glorious than the sight of a woman carrying a child," she demurred, wrapping herself in the flag of motherhood.

But the pictures, as Brown knows, are far more ambiguous than that. This isn't a photo spread for the Lamaze class.

Inside the magazine are three more images. The most deliberately provocative is the one of Moore in a skimpy black bra, bikini undies, and spike heels. Mommy meets *Hustler*? Did she mean to reveal Victoria's Secret? Guess what, Victoria's gonna have a baby!

Frankly, I would not rush over to see Demi's baby in utero. Spare me the videotapes of her first childbirth during which she directed three cameramen to get all the right angles. She is far more fully and comfortably exposed on camera than in the dry, dull text that accompanies the pictures.

But the lens has captured and, uh, exposed a visual taboo. It walks the line that still ordinarily divides a woman's body as a source of pleasure and a source of reproduction. After all, a mother isn't supposed to be a sex object and a sex object isn't supposed to be a mother and where is Freud when you need him?

Remember the analysts who said that Western culture saw Woman as either a madonna (the original) or a whore? There are a lot more sexual options now but also a lot more opinions.

There's an ongoing argument about whether good girls wear garter belts, whether a centerfold is liberated or merely exploited, whether female nudity is sleazy or nature's way of staying cool. There's a talk-show, kitchen-table debate about good and bad sexiness that gets focused around Deborah Norville's breast-feeding and Demi Moore's pregnant poses.

Most of us harbor mixed feelings. Which is why this issue of *Vanity Fair* is selling . . . and why it's discreetly wrapped. Why the photos are getting a long look, but not on the subway.

Giving credit where it's due, I give it to Leibovitz more than Moore. She's taken a strong, unexpected image and thrown it on the national screen—a conflict wrapped in amniotic fluid. Some pictures are worth a thousand words. This one's a bargain.

JULY 19, 1991

When Good Guys Do Bad Things

||||||||||||||||||||||||||||||||||||||||||||||||||||||||||||||||||||||||||||||||||||||||||||||||

There are days when I want to stand on the edge of the great cultural divide and echo a phrase that's usually thrown at the other side. I just don't get it.

I don't understand how a senator like Bob Packwood, who used his power to help women succeed as equals in public life, apparently also used his power to take advantage of them in private life.

I don't understand how a man could work seriously with a lobbyist on women's rights issues and then, reportedly, take a run at the same woman. At the same meeting.

It's not that I'm naive. I've been around long enough to know that it happens. I can think of a dozen book titles to describe syndromes I've seen: Progressive on the Job, Neanderthal in the Home. Good Guy by Day, One of the Boys at Night.

I can even rattle off the historic list of men who had one moral posture in public and another in private. JFK, MLK, fill in the blanks. Nor is this disparity only over women and sex.

But I still don't get it.

I don't understand precisely *how* it happens. What synapse misfires in a character who make advances for women and then also makes "unwanted sexual advances" on women? What part of the electrical system simply disconnects?

Such questions have been running through my mind—and that of many others—since *The Washington Post* revealed a history of unwelcome encounters between the longtime senator and at least ten women who worked for him or with him.

These questions remain unanswered by the senator's not quite apology: "If any of my . . . actions have indeed been unwelcome . . . I am sincerely sorry." They remain unresolved by his admission this week to an alcohol abuse clinic. Alcohol is no more acceptable an explanation of sexual misconduct these days than it is of bad driving.

What unsettles many of us are these contradictions. The newly and barely reelected senator was a certified friend of feminism who took political risks for his beliefs. He stood up for abortion rights and family leave and even—ironies abound—voted against the confirmation of Justice Clarence Thomas.

Any number of women will attest to the fact that Packwood was genuinely supportive of their professional success. "His office was a place where Republican women had a chance to take on substantive work and move up," muses political consultant Ann Lewis, who adds, "But it was also a place where young women could find themselves harassed and beleaguered."

Maybe this is why all ten women described various degrees of shock in their stories of his sudden, unwanted advances. Maybe this is why one woman still says that the senator "genuinely respects the intelligence that women bring to their work."

This split or splintered character makes this allegation even more unsettling than those against other senators or even against Clarence Thomas. The closest comparison is to the tempest created by the accusation that a respected, even revered chief judge of the highest court in New York, Sol Wachtler, had harassed his former lover and sent lewd and threatening notes to her and her fourteen-year-old daughter.

Sol Wachtler? Bob Packwood? It's easier to think someone was mad—or drunk—than to acknowledge bad seeds in good guys.

Maybe there was something in our culture that allowed for such a compartmentalized life. Maybe there was something that allowed men in power particularly to disconnect their principles from their behavior. Especially their sexual behavior.

Constance Buchanan, the associate dean of the Harvard Divinity School, sees it that way. She says, with some degree of frustration, that "good guys do this all the time. That's the problem. We have to stop being stunned."

The difference, says Buchanan, is that once a "cloak of privacy surrounded male sexual behavior at work and at home." For a long time, she says, we only looked at what leaders did in public.

There was no dichotomy, no contradiction in our view, because we didn't really "see" the private side. It was shielded by institutions, the Senate, the corporation, or even the church. Maybe it was even shielded from the men themselves.

Now that cloak has been ripped off. The harsh public light that shines now into nooks and crannies of public lives isn't always comfortable, or always fair. It may illuminate the worst in one person and miss another person entirely. But this is the one way things change.

I still don't get it. Maybe you don't either. But then, maybe we shouldn't get it. The contradictions between public and private life, between principle and behavior, are just too glaring. The men in this public spotlight don't have to be understood. They have to change.

DECEMBER 4, 1992

Nannygate I

||||||||||||||||||||||||||||||||||||||||||||||||||||||||||||||||||||||||||||||||||||||||||||||||||||||

Washington — Just when everyone had finished poking through the carry-on baggage the baby boomers were bringing to Washington, just when we exhausted the subjects of the draft, sex, drugs, rock 'n' roll, along comes an extra steamer trunk full of generational issues. This one is labeled child care.

On Tuesday, the first mother of a preschool child ever nominated to the cabinet came up to Capitol Hill for hearings. And for the first time in American history, the central ethical question about her confirmation was child care. Never before has a group of prospective employers cared so deeply about one woman's babysitting arrangements.

For the past twenty years, the best-tracked aspect of social change has been the emergence of the two-worker family as the norm. The least publicized story is precisely how these families care for their children. What corners are cut, what compromises are made in attempts to take care of the kids while we are taking care of business?

In the early 1970s, feminists liked to say that every housewife was one man away from welfare. In the early 1990s, many a working mother of a small child is one babysitter away from unemployment.

So the tale of Zoë Baird struck at the baby boomers' Achilles' heel. On one level, the revelation that she and her husband had hired illegal aliens to care for their son produced one of those sinking feelings. Oh no, the next Attorney General broke the law?

On another level, it produced a separate sinking sensation. Oh no, a mother who earned half a million bucks a year still couldn't find child care?

In the years from my daughter's birth to her thirteenth birthday I had three and a half babysitters—the half is a story for another day—which puts me in line for the Guinness record for having the longest-lasting caregivers. Nevertheless, some of my life's worst moments of panic were "between" sitters.

I never hired an illegal alien, but I have more than a modicum of empathy for a woman like Baird, who had an eight-month-old baby, a new job, and a working husband when she finally found a couple who were trustworthy, maybe even caring. If my lawyer, as did Baird's, had called their immigration status a mere "technical violation," I would have attached myself to that thought like Velcro.

As Baird told the committee, "I was acting more as a mother than as someone who would be sitting here designated to be Attorney General."

In the underground child-care system in America, nannies-without-papers is just the upper crust. The other layers include the child caregivers paid off the books and under the table, the providers operating without a license, and the little kids being left home alone—not by parents vacationing in Mexico. Add them all together and you get a pretty good picture of child care in America. It's a mess for parents. It's a mess for caregivers who are underpaid, unprotected, and overworked.

This is not to say that what Zoë Baird did was as meaningless as a parking ticket. Moreover, the story adds to the perception that there are rules for the rich and rules for the rest.

As Baird said at the hearing, "People are fairly questioning whether there are classes of individuals who hold themselves above the law." She added, "And I assure you I do not."

Coming right after the announcement that Chelsea Clinton is headed for private school, it heightens the cynicism about yuppies among the new populists. It highlights class divisions within the ranks of the would-be sisterhood. Half-a-million-dollar insurance executives don't get many tears when they talk about their troubles with "help."

When all is said and done, this is another issue that comes with the new generation of two-worker families. We didn't see it in Senate hearing rooms before; we didn't see mothers of young children facing confirmation before. The men who held those offices had the sort of child care that came with the marriage license.

But hiring an illegal nanny in the 1990s is a crime on a par with smoking dope in the 1960s. The fact that she treated the couple well, filed papers for them, and sponsored them for citizenship reduces even that charge.

She is guilty, yes. But guilty of smoking without inhaling.

JANUARY 22, 1993

Nannygate II

||||||||||||||||||||||||||||||||||||||||||||||||||||||||||||||||||||||||||||||||||||||||||||||||||||||

When Zoë Baird streaked across the national sky from anonymity to ignominy in two weeks, I was one of her few defenders. I didn't think that hiring an undocumented nanny was a career-ending injury. Illegal child care is as common in the 1990s as smoking dope was in the 1960s.

Well, if Zoë Baird was judged and convicted of smoking without inhaling, Kimba Wood was just found guilty of getting a contact high. She didn't break any law, she was just standing around breathing in the atmospheric fumes.

Back in 1986, when Judge Wood and her husband—yes, yes, working hubbies too are involved in these decisions—hired a nanny from Trinidad whose papers had expired, it was legal for them to do so. They filed all the requisite papers and forms.

If the judge committed any misdemeanor at all, it was thinking like a lawyer instead of like a politician. When the Clinton team asked if she had a "Zoë Baird" problem, the answer was, technically, no. But she had the whiff of it in her hair.

The words "illegal alien" are now enough to make strong men and women run screaming in horror. They transform the most sedate

résumé into a tabloid headline: ALIENS INVADE EARTHLING—
DESTROYING FUTURE!

The administration was damned if they did appoint her. Déjà
Zoë all over again. And damned because they didn't. The judge
got a bad rap and working mothers got a bad vibe. But we are all
now damned to another chapter in the pursuit of perfection in public
life.

Over the weekend, the list of offenders began to grow. On the
equal opportunity circuit, Charles Ruff was apparently also disqualified on account of his household hiring. A squirming Ron
Brown admitted to paying taxes for his weekly cleaning lady as
soon as he found out that he should: last month. Stay tuned for
more late-breaking news.

The search through the household-help accounts is going to
make the search through Henry Kissinger's trash cans look relatively
clean. If you think there are a lot of illegal alien nannies and
housekeepers, you should see how many all-American neighbors
and relatives are being paid off the books.

One of the many things that make me squeamish about all this
is not just the way child care has become the whipping girl of the
moment. It's the way we get the ethical blemish of the moment.

We seem to deal with character issues as if they were a grab
bag. We reach in, pull out the latest one in no particular order,
and use it to judge anybody in public life. For a while, it's all that
we see of that person. It blots out everything in a person's life.

Consider what happened to Zoë Baird and Kimba Wood. In
one brief searing moment, Zoë Baird was reduced to one line: She
was the $500,000-a-year-lawyer-who-hired-illegal-aliens. It didn't
matter whether she was capable of the job or kind to her babysitter.
When life becomes a one-liner, nobody reads between the lines.

Now Kimba Wood, the judge who helped put Michael Milken
in jail, may go down in history for her household hiring practices,
not to mention her brief training as a Playboy bunny. A career
becomes a cartoon. Character becomes caricature.

I think that private ethics are important. How we behave in
our personal lives should count in public. It would be fascinating
if we decided to judge people's character by how they treat those

who work for them, whether the worker was a secretary, a hamburger flipper, or a housekeeper. Whether the issue was sexual harassment or economic exploitation.

That's not really what's happening. Rather, we lurch from one lethal "sin" to another. Wiping out one person after another. Every time we appear to come to some more balanced perspective on character and its flaws, life and its complexity, Clinton and infidelity, something else comes out of the grab bag.

On the night the judge withdrew her name from consideration, I was not the only one who found herself in the middle of an informal Kimba Wood seminar. A klatsch of good friends with decent résumés and serious moral convictions went through a joking-but-real review of our own personal histories.

We could find enough blemishes in our lives to make for a collective case of acne. Not one of us would be thrilled to see videotapes of the three worst moments and four worst decisions of our lives.

Is there a Zoë Baird problem? You bet. It's the problem you hear when people think about public service life and say, "Not me." It's the problem when they think about the spotlight and say, "It's not worth it."

Oh, by the way. Dear Kimba: I once played a Hot Box Girl in *Guys and Dolls*. If the White House ever calls, I'm out.

FEBRUARY 12, 1993

POLITICS '92

||||||||||||||||||||||||||||||||||||||||||||||||||||||||||||||||||||||||||||||||||||||||||||||||||||||

|||||| *It seemed that the baby-boom
generation had trouble coming into
power because they couldn't resolve
their own deep divisions. In a tough
and grueling way, this campaign did
some of the work of resolution. In
many ways this campaign was* about
generational change.

Game Time

||||||||||||||||||||||||||||||||||||||||||||||||||||||||||||||||||||||||||||||||||||||||||||||||||||

The crocuses are a-blooming, the Ides of March and the Ides of Super Tuesday are upon us. So, by all these portents, it must be time for my quadrennial plea against the use of sports metaphors in writing, speaking, and thinking about politics.

This has been a long, personal, and so far entirely futile attempt on my part to have an impact on the rhetoric of democracy. By my calculations, politics has been described as the great American sport ever since the first election was called a race and the candidate became a winner.

But sports reached a saturation point in the 1980s when politicians began to sound like *Wide World of Sports* and the media turned from analysis to play-by-play. One favorite mixed sports metaphor came in 1984 from Lawton Chiles, now the governor of Florida, who described the "game plan" for the Presidential debates this way: "It's like a football game. . . . Mondale can't get the ball back with one big play. But the American people love a horse race. I would advise him not to knock Reagan out."

Well, as expected, the 1992 campaign began with the usual assortment of slam dunks, knockout punches, end runs, and hardballs. But something happened after the campaign left New Hampshire and relative civility. While I was trying to get out of the locker room, we ended up in the trenches.

The metaphors switched from sports to war. The political coverage reads less like *Sports Illustrated* than *Soldier of Fortune*.

We have campaign "assaults" and "attacks." The Super Tuesday states are "battlegrounds." The candidates "snipe" and "take aim" at each other. Jerry Brown is accused of using "slash-and-burn" tactics. Paul Tsongas is "under fire." And Pat Buchanan is a man who will "take no prisoners."

How did this primary get off the playing field and onto the killing field? Kathleen Jamieson, political wordsmith and dean of the University of Pennsylvania's Annenberg School for Communication, says that war images creep in as a campaign gets, well, hostile.

"When you are playing fairly within the rules of the game, the sports metaphors fit. The war metaphor is much more negative. It doesn't assume fair play or a referee."

If words are the way we frame our ideas, the war metaphor is more than rhetoric. It forces us to talk and think about elections as if they were lethally combative events in which the object was to kill the enemy and declare victory. In the end, the war metaphor produces a victor or a commander in chief. But not necessarily a governor, or a leader, or a problem solver.

War talk doesn't allow the candidates to describe or stand on common ground. "It doesn't assume the goodwill and integrity of the other side," says Jamieson. "It doesn't talk about common good and collective ends. It assumes one person is right and the other's wrong."

As for the media and the metaphor, fighting words frame the campaign as a search-and-destroy mission. It is not a coincidence that attack ads make the headlines. Nor is it a coincidence, says Jamieson, that men are much more likely to talk like warriors and write like war correspondents.

Jamieson herself has been trying to elaborate a different political campaign language. She first played with a courtship metaphor since the candidates do woo the electorate and pledge forms of fidelity. That was, to put it mildly, fraught with sexual undertones.

In New Hampshire, a focus group came up with the metaphor of an orchestra. The government is, after all, a collective entity that needs a leader to keep things in harmony. This had a nice ring, but it didn't hit all the right notes.

Now Jamieson is toying with a metaphor that would picture the campaign as a quest. In the vernacular of the "quest" metaphor, the candidates would overcome "tests" that reveal their "character." The campaign would become a "search" for answers, not for the soft underbelly of an opponent.

The point is to shift the verbal focus from strategy—"Is he doing what's necessary to win?"—to problems—"Does he understand them, can he solve them?" Her own quest for this "quest" metaphor has just begun. Any ideas are welcome in our metaphor mailbag.

In the meantime, in the spirit of a peacemaker, may I suggest that candidates and those who cover them block that war metaphor. Tackle it if you must. There are already enough bodies on the combat field, careers blown to smithereens, and land mines planted for the fall election. All we have learned so far this election year is that politics is hell.

MARCH 10, 1992

The New Balance on the Ticket

||||||||||||||||||||||||||||||||||||||||||||||||||||||||||||||||||||||||||||||||||||||||||||||||||||||||||||

So much for the idea that geography is destiny. The old ironclad rule that a political ticket ought to look like a Triptik for a party that travels north to south, east to west, was just torn into as many pieces as a used airline stub.

When Bill Clinton picked Al Gore for the second spot, he barely stretched from one Southern state to another. It's not a lot of frequent-flier miles from Hope, Arkansas, to Carthage, Tennessee.

By the traditional political map, the Tennarkana ticket looks lopsided. We not only have two white guys, mid-forties and middle-of-the-road, but they were raised in two towns where, as Gore said, "people know about it when you're born and care about it when you die." A hub if there ever was one.

In many ways, though, this choice says something about the changing American reality. America is less divided by place than ever before.

We may still use geographic terms as if they had philosophical meaning. We may talk about the West, the South, the Midwest, the Northeast as if they were distinct nationalities. But we rarely even consider geography when we think about diversity.

Regionalism has gone the way of the local accent. In the older generation, Howell Heflin of Alabama was the Southern standard. Cabdrivers spoke linguistically pure Brooklynese. By comparison, today's accents carry a hint of origin and the spice of local color. But we rarely have trouble understanding each other.

People may root for the hometown boy, but they find it as hard to identify their hometowns as George Bush does. The average American moves twelve times in a lifetime. We reach out and touch our parents or kids by telephone. The most popular family policy in America this summer is the bargain air fares.

In Garry Wills's new book, *Lincoln at Gettysburg*, he says that the Civil War President deliberately encouraged citizens to think of the United States as a singular, not a plural name. People used to say the United States *are*, now they say the United States *is*. It took a while but it worked.

Today the electoral college counts us as residents of a state, but in Presidential elections we vote as individual Americans. Today each region has its own weather, history, traditions, establishment. But we are more likely to divide by class, age, race, zip code, and "lifestyle enclave" than by map.

We think of the country the way merchants do. Spangles sell in Dallas and black dresses are hot in Manhattan. But there are T-shirts and jeans in every mall in America.

The Democrats in essence are going for the T-shirts. If not the Gap market, the generation gap market. This flat-out baby-boom ticket is generational politics to the hilt.

As Gore said, "That time has come again—the time for a new generation of leaders." In fact, the old regionalism has been replaced by a lingering civil war over values with baby-boom roots in arguments over Vietnam, over drugs, over gender roles. The baby-boom generation has been fractured by its own internal divisions which have kept the best and the brightest of them out of power. What this team lacks in geographical balance it may make up for in a kind of intragenerational balance. Al Gore, the son of a senator, and Bill Clinton, maybe the last candidate to grow up with what he genteelly calls outdoor plumbing, both ran up against the issues of their generation.

One fought in Vietnam; one didn't. One inhaled; one didn't. Indeed, their wives provide a truly balanced ticket of gender roles. Tipper was mercilessly trashed by the left for proposing that records carry a label like the movies. Hillary was trashed by the right for stepping on a land mine in the mommy wars.

If these two couples travel these rocky trails and end up a team, it's not a bad sign. The distance this generation has to cross to common ground may be getting shorter.

Carthage to Hope, Hope to Carthage. This was the easy leg of the trip. The only geography that counts now is finding a way to Washington.

JULY 14, 1992

Not the Year of the Wife

|||||||||||||||||||||||||||||||||||||||||||||||||||||||||||||||||||||||||||||||||||||||||||||||||||

New York — It's the tail end of a killer day and Hillary Clinton settles into the sofa on the fourteenth floor of the Inter-Continental looking remarkably alert and limp-free, drinking spring water straight out of a plastic bottle.

The day broke some fifteen hours earlier with a sheaf of headlines declaring that the campaign was manufacturing a "gentler, kinder" Hillary. *Family Circle* featured a political bake-off between Hillary's and Barbara's chocolate-chip cookie recipes. More than one story talked about the "two sides" of the candidate's wife: heads up she's a lawyer, heads down she's a wife. And Republicans were comparing Hillary Clinton at the stove to Mike Dukakis in a tank.

The candidate's wife had spent the day at the Texas caucus, the Emily's List luncheon, a powwow for congressional wives (dubbed "power wives" on the schedule), and eight other stops, where she offered everything from a wave to a twenty-five-minute speech without notes. At the Women of Color reception, not surprisingly, a woman in my row offered this piece of high praise with a kicker: "Isn't she great!" Pause. "Gee, I wish she were running for the Senate."

Now, in Madison Square Garden, six female Democratic nominees for the Senate were speaking and everyone was talking about the Year of the Woman. Women have become the symbols of change in the political process. But what about wives?

Is it actually easier for a woman to be the candidate this year than the candidate's wife? Have we come that far? Or not so far?

Hillary answers that with a knowing but cautious "Maybe." We knew what it was to be a wife, she agrees. Over the past decades, we've learned what it is to be an independent woman. But we haven't yet figured out what it looks like to be strong, independent, and wifely—especially First Wifely—all at the same time.

"I thought I understood that before this race was under way," says Hillary Clinton, who comes across as comfortable and thoughtful. "That's what I was living. I thought that with some stops and starts and changes along the way trying to get it all straight, I was a very lucky person because I had a profession that I valued, a marriage that I thought was a partnership in the best sense of the word and gave me a lot of personal satisfaction.

"I thought I understood how to walk through that minefield of defining myself and striking the balance between my own needs and family needs that we all struggle with all the time."

Now this mother, wife, and lawyer finds the controversy that has followed her from conservative Arkansas to the national stage "surprising" and even "bewildering." Hillary had, to be sure, a rocky introduction to the American public. Her image was flanked by Flowers and cookies, Tammy Wynette and Betty Crocker.

But much of the Hillary Problem, she suspects, is another case study about men, women, change. And this time also marriage. As Hillary says, "I thought we [women] were beginning to develop a framework for that kind of life we could lead, still married, still committed to family, still engaged in the outside world. And I've just been surprised, I guess, by the assumptions that bear little resemblance to how all of us—not just me—make our way through this uncharted terrain."

Where do we still get lost in this terrain? At the White House door? In the territory marked partnership? At the women's caucus Tuesday morning, Bill Clinton tells the audience of women, "We have to say that building up women does not diminish men."

Harvard Business School's Rosabeth Kantor says our trouble is with teams as much as with mates: "We don't understand teams in America. We have this idea there has to be one leader, one CEO. So we can't help comparing couples. We can't see it as *both/and*. It's *either/or*."

But more acute is this disparity between our view of marriage as a merger—two people as one—and our view of what it means to be a successful individual. It's not easy for women to be seen or to feel both professional and coupled. Ask any woman who ever felt awkward bringing her husband to a work event. We have few models of "twosomeness," as Alva Myrdal once described it, relationships in which men and women remain two but together.

As Hillary Clinton knows well, "We're all trying to work this out. We're all trying to find our way and we don't have a common language." In the era of public partnership marriages, she says, "I may be on the front line."

Front lines are notoriously unsafe places. Cookies or not—the one I tasted could have used some more chocolate chips—there is no makeover in the making. A whole generation lives on these front lines now. Hillary Clinton has just become the most visible resident.

JULY 17, 1992

The Week of
the Woman

||||||||||||||||||||||||||||||||||||||||||||||||||||||||||||||||||||||||||||||||||||||||||||

New York — When Bill Clinton stopped in to the women's caucus it was more than a courtesy call. Standing in front of a line of women candidates, he said flat out, "I think we know where the energy of the Democratic Party in America is."

Women are, to put it mildly, the life of this party. The female candidates and officeholders have been feted and toasted, put up front and center stage at Madison Square Garden. They've been star attractions at a running list of receptions East Side, West Side, all around the town.

The most popular sticker at the convention reads: "When Women Run, Women Win." The most popular money raiser is Emily's List, the fund for electing Democratic women to the Senate. Even Nancy Reagan's old hairdresser has defected and is coiffing the Democratic women backstage.

As Barbara Mikulski, the shortest U.S. senator with the longest repertoire of sound bites, says when she introduces the Democratic class of '92 female candidates, "*This* is the new world order." Pat Schroeder describes them as a "tsunami of women getting ready to wash into Washington."

The enthusiasm is close to contagious even for those of us who have developed some immunity to the Year(s) of the Woman. We remember when 1972 was the year of the woman: Shirley Chisholm ran for President, Cissy Farenthold came in second for Vice President, a miniwave of women reporters were sent to their first political convention to cover the "women's story."

Then of course 1984 was the year of the woman when Geraldine Ferraro got on the ticket. And so were 1988 and 1990 . . . well, you get the idea. Change has been somewhere between glacial and gradual. It's tough to believe in breakthroughs.

Indeed, as Ruth Mandel, head of the Center for the American Woman in Politics, not to mention resident scorekeeper and sometime wet blanket, says, "I don't like this Year of the Woman business. We're turning history around and one year is not going to do it."

She cautions that even if six women are added to the U.S. Senate—the magic number bandied about here—that means only 8 percent will be female. Mandel would rather talk less about the year and more about "the era of our empowerment." But then, she's an academic.

Jane Danowitz, who runs the Women's Campaign Fund, also admits to a mild case of election-year jitters, the raised-expectations anxiety. She is more pleased than worried about the fact that "women are running these campaigns under a microscope." She believes that doubling the number of women in Congress is "as close to a sure thing as I've ever seen."

But she warns, "Women are used to running as underdogs. This year we're front-runners. I keep waiting for something to crumble and it doesn't."

The enthusiasm for and from women here may perversely reflect a lack of enthusiasm for the ticket. It's also easier for Democrats to get more excited about the first African-American woman in the Senate than about a New Industrial Policy.

At more than one caucus and fund raiser you meet some party regulars who are devoting time and money this year to Carol Moseley Braun and Lynn Yeakel instead of Bill Clinton and Al Gore. Clinton tacitly acknowledged the enthusiasm gap among voters when he said, "I'm glad to be on Dianne Feinstein's or Barbara Boxer's coattails any day."

Twenty years ago, at the McGovern convention, long lampooned as a hippie-radical-freak gathering of lefties, women could barely get their issues on the platform or get their voice in the hall. Now, at the gathering that's been stereotyped as centrist and moderate to the hilt, women are stars. My, how the center moves.

For the moment, then, women represent not only change but

the sweet smell of success. Even Mandel catches the fever: "When everyone says this is a special year, it means something. It reflects emotions that run high: anger, excitement, enthusiasm. No matter what happens, women will come out of this election with a lot of energy and the recognition that they can have an impact."

The Year of the Woman? It's been a pretty good week.

JULY 21, 1992

Family Night

||||||||||||||||||||||||||||||||||||||||||||||||||||||||||||||||||||||||||||||||||||||||||||||||||||||||||||||||

New York — They ended with Family Night in Madison Square Garden. Bill Clinton and Al Gore presented themselves to the American public Thursday as a governor and senator, would-be President and Vice President. But they also offered themselves as sons, as husbands, and, more than anything else, as fathers.

On the day that Ross Perot became a government school drop-out, the Democrats from the baby-boom generation made their case to the American public with family biography as well as policy.

Al Gore described himself first as the son of a woman born before suffrage who graduated from law school when it simply wasn't done. He was the son of man who was a teacher before he became a senator, and the husband of a woman who, in Gore's words, helped do more for children in the last dozen years than the entire Reagan and Bush administrations.

But he was also the father of a boy he'd seen hit by a car and thrown nearly lifeless to the pavement. It was a tale that brought this rambunctious hall of Democrats as close to silence as it ever gets.

Bill Clinton reintroduced himself earlier this week to an audience of women as the grandson of a working woman, the son of a single mother, the husband of a woman who'd earned more money than he did, and the father of a daughter who wanted to build colonies in space. On the final night of the convention he rounded out that family picture.

He was the child born after his father's death. The boy whose mother went off to nursing school so she could support him. The big brother who watched over the younger. The stepson who stood up to and for an alcoholic stepfather. And in the film that preceded his speech, the father who sat and watched the famous 60 *Minutes* interview on television with his daughter by his side.

If there were stories that people repeated over coffee the next morning, one was the tale of young Al Gore's brush with death. Another was the image of Clinton seeing what his own father had never lived to see, the birth of his child. A third was the tough moment when Chelsea Clinton, after watching her parents reveal the troubles in their marriage to a nation, reassured them that she still thought they were okay.

Call this the hearts and flowers, soap opera, Oprah Winfrey, New News part of the Democratic show-and-tell. Maybe we try to know too much of anyone asking to lead the country. We strip-search our candidates, looking for the moments when life reaches out, touches and toughens people.

But these biographies were important as well because the Democrats are trying to tell a family story of their own. A debate about "family values" is expected to track this campaign all the way to November. The Republicans are going to talk about Gennifer Flowers and Murphy Brown. They'll be selling Hillary Clinton as the Liberal Co-President with an Attitude.

We know where the Republicans stand. Traditional Families R Us. Any family that doesn't fit the mold is dysfunctional or pitiable or immoral. They divide families by moral fiber.

The Democrats are trying to create a politics of inclusion and a family portrait as diverse and complex and sometimes as hard as real family life in America. For the Democrats, families include not only, as Clinton said, "every traditional family and every extended family. Every two-parent family and every single-parent family and every foster family."

They also include imperfect homes in which there may be trouble *and* love; too much alcohol *and* forgiveness; infidelity *and* renewal. Where life can change as quickly as a kid can run in front of a car.

The family portrait painted by this Democratic Party is not permissive. "Governments don't raise children; parents do," said Clinton. "Hear me now, I am not pro-abortion. I am pro-choice." To any father who abandons his children and his child support he warned, "Take responsibility for your children or we will force you to do it." To any mother on welfare he said, "Welfare must be a second chance, not a way of life."

But to the children who don't have an easy life he said, "I *know* how you feel. . . . If the politicians who are lecturing you don't want you to be a part of their families, you can be a part of ours."

Republicans, like Ronald Reagan himself, also include the sons of alcoholics who've been over the coals of marriage and divorce. But Bill Clinton Democrats deal with it by talking about it.

For twelve years, we've been asked to see families through the wash of nostalgia and the harsh glare of moral judgment. What they offered at Family Night in Madison Square Garden looked a lot more like real life.

JULY 17, 1992

The GOP Goes
Wife Bashing

Houston — If they ever expand the laws against hate crimes, I want to file a suit against the Republican National Convention on behalf of one Hillary Rodham Clinton. We are talking hate speech here. We are talking Hate Hillary speech. And it's gotten out of hand.

Before they got to Houston, the Grand Old Party had begun this verbal assault on the would-be First Lady. Campaign director Rich Bond made a political pretzel out of her words, claiming that the lawyer believed that marriage was slavery and children should be liberated from parents. His deputy Mary Matalin had a photograph of Hillary posted on her office wall with the Wicked Witch of the West caption: "I will get you, my pretty, and your little dog too!"

But only at the convention did they dish out a poisonous brew of snide words and innuendo in gag-me proportions.

From Pat Buchanan to Pat Robertson, speakers described the Democratic ticket ominously as a Clinton-and-Clinton administration, with "radical feminism" on the agenda. Buttons appeared proclaiming "Another Cookie Baker for Bush." And in interviews, Liberal Hillary took more hits than Slick Willie.

The public excuse for wife bashing was that the Clintons described themselves as a two-fer, buy one get one free. The President used this as a disingenuous cover story to explain why Hillary bashing is acceptable.

And so, I regret to say, did his wife. After briefly criticizing the nastiness, Barbara then gave her stamp of approval, saying, "If it's a self-proclaimed co-President," it's legitimate.

Clearly, the Republicans would rather run Barbara against Hillary than George against Bill. But the most unpalatable of their attack-Hillary dogs was Marilyn Quayle—a woman whose age, ambitions, and options should have made her a sympathetic fellow traveler through the times, if not exactly a soul sister.

Remember Hillary's frustrated crack that she "could have stayed home and made cookies"? (Who will be allowed to forget it?) Well, when Dan was elected Vice President, guess who said, "I thought, man, it's going to be tea and crumpets and I would just go nuts."

Remember when Marilyn described giving up her law practice to help Dan run? Well, guess what Hillary just did.

If Hillary is a partner, what is Marilyn? "When Dan married me, he married a budding lawyer. He wanted a partner and he has one." A co-Vice President?

Yet on Ladies' Night at the convention—what would have

happened if Hillary had spoken in New York?—Marilyn gave a speech that was filled with jabs about the lawyer from Arkansas.

In my generation, she said, "not everyone believed that the family was so oppressive that women could only thrive apart from it."

She described unnamed-but-not-unknown liberals as angry. "They're disappointed because most women do not wish to be liberated from their essential natures as women. Most of us love being mothers or wives."

Make no mistake about it. The hate speech is not just directed at liberalism. It's aimed at uppityism.

Marilyn Quayle said that "frankly nothing offends me more than attempts to paint Republicans as looking to turn the clock back for women." Maybe so, but the Republican Party is tripping all over itself trying to figure out a way to defend traditional roles for women without offending the women whose lives have changed.

The updated, composite portrait looks something like this: Women like Quayle are praised, as she was in the introduction by "Major Dad" as "a woman of remarkable accomplishment for whom the family comes first." Working mothers are admirable as long as they have to work to put food on the table. And single mothers are "heroic" as long as they are struggling to bring up the kids in the wake of a deserting deadbeat dad.

Women are to be praised, in short, as long as they are dependents or victims or self-sacrificing. It's the too independent woman—the one choosing her own direction in life and happy about it—who is now cast as the alien, the other, the not-one-of-us. Hillary in a headband.

Ironically, the Democratic candidate's wife is currently a contender for the supportive spouse citation. She looks a good deal like any other woman struggling and juggling.

But the meanspirited, nasty edge to the Hate Hillary speech turns this into a class-action suit. This isn't just about politics. The Republicans are giving more than one woman a backlashing of the tongue. This time it may backfire.

AUGUST 25, 1992

The GOP, Woody, and the Kids

||||||||||||||||||||||||||||||||||||||||||||||||||||||||||||||||||||||||||||||||||||||||||||||||||||

Houston — The scene here is almost heady enough to make a captive of the Astrodome welcome one outrageous and clarifying family scandal: Thank you, Woody Allen—I think.

There have been more words about "family values" released into the atmosphere this week than balloons. The Republicans have joined the Democrats in a knockdown fight to prove that they deserve sole custody of the American family.

First, the GOP platform boasted that "Republicans trust parents," implying that the Democrats don't. Then the buttons at the God and Country rally proclaimed: "Dan's Right, Murphy's a Tramp."

On the first night, Pat Buchanan declared that a "cultural war" was being waged with the family at its epicenter. On the second, Newt Gingrich accused the Democrats of a "multicultural, nihilistic hedonism." Dan Quayle said the cultural elites are not just laughing at him but at "you . . . your families and your values."

The party devoted an entire night to "family values," which turned out to be Ladies' Night at the convention, or more accurately Wives' Night Out. And the President in his warm-up act made this distinction between the two parties: "On the one side, the Democrats have their liberal agenda. On the other side, the Republicans stand for those family values that we all share."

In the court of public opinion, each side is struggling for the role of family defender. They want to describe the other as family offender. But if the party rhetoric is growing, the party differences are actually shrinking.

The hard-core Republicans gathered here may still be more

concerned with family form than function. But the traditional model they favor now includes at least mothers who are working because they must and mothers who are single because they were left.

As for the Democrats, they are still more comfortable talking about economics than morals. But it was the Democratic platform that proclaimed this time: "Governments don't raise children, people do. People who bring children into this world have a responsibility to care for children and give them values, motivation and discipline."

It's hard to know the parties without the scorecard. People are also better at defending "family values" than defining them. But as was said of pornography, we know them when we see them. Or see them flouted, anyway.

Enter Woody Allen. Not laughing.

In the scandal that wiped the President off the tabloid covers this week, the fifty-seven-year-old Allen proclaimed his love for the twenty-one-year-old daughter of his former companion, Mia Farrow. Talk about defining moments.

There are now all sorts of charges flying back and forth. But the mother-daughter affair, the sexual liaison with the girl who was for all emotional purposes his stepdaughter, broke enough cultural taboos to qualify for an anthropological study.

"Regarding my love for Soon-Yi," he announced, "it's real and happily all true. She's a lovely, intelligent, sensitive woman who has and continues to turn around my life in a wonderfully positive way." After decades of much-heralded and much-filmed psychotherapy, Allen has escaped the clutches of guilt only to fall into the arms of narcissism.

The national gasp that followed this admission—how does this horrify me, let me count the ways—offers a bit of shock therapy in the "family values" debate. Guess what. We do have a common bottom line in this whole dicey business of values.

I won't make too much of one outlandish scenario that springs out of a Woody Allen movie past and future: Take the daughter and run. But this is one startling starting point that shows us how much more often Americans agree.

If nothing else, we agree that elders—parents, stepparents, or pseudo-parents—are there to take care of the young, not exploit them. If nothing else, we agree that the grown-ups are supposed to support family ties, not wreck them.

When you cut through the rhetoric, what matters most about family isn't its form but its human relationships. It's how we are to each other.

In our very collective value system, families are not just room-mates, or for that matter co-workers. They are, at root and at best, the web of intimate, trusting, personal relationships that form our designated haven in the heartless world. They may not always succeed, but they offer that ideal.

Family values mean a lot to people. And they mean a lot of different things. But in any debate, start with commitment and caring. All the rest is politics.

AUGUST 25, 1992

The Return of H. Ross Perot

So he's back. The Texan who fancies himself the thinking man's Rambo. The outsider who sees himself on a national rescue mission.

At his press conference in Dallas Thursday, H. Ross Perot said he would "accept the request" of his volunteers. "There's only one issue today. What's good for our country."

From the very beginning, Perot has talked about the country as if it were a POW, a prisoner of war held captive by the two parties. On Thursday he declared that "the issues" were still lan-guishing, gagged and bound in some hidden cell.

With his bells and whistles, his talk shows and 800 numbers, his volunteers and dollars, his straight talk and his ideas, he wants to single-handedly free democracy from the parties' old grasp. All we have to do is tie a yellow ribbon round the old Perot tree. Again.

Well, I didn't share the Perotphilia the first time around. I don't put stock in maverick billionaires with egos as large as their bank accounts. Especially when they deny those egos. Especially when they portray themselves as mere servants of the people.

Last July, though, I saw that Perot had injected something into this campaign. Call it energy if you want, call it excitement. He had engaged the disengaged, won the affection of the disaffected, gotten the jaded to be involved.

Maybe Perot was never more than a name for None of the Above. But the stamp-licking, petition-signing, grass-roots activism he incited hadn't been seen since 1968 when students shaved themselves "Clean for Gene" McCarthy.

So I was uneasy when my media mates came down on Perot with such a heavy hand. I think it showed how conservative we have become as professionals—too much a part of the system, too comfortable with the old names on our Rolodexes.

For all our overt passion for news, newness, change, some of us were hostile to the notion that a Ross Perot might really throw the whole process up for grabs. Reporters who had trudged through months of primaries, commentators who had nurtured all the right (and left) contacts in Washington, were not friendly to the new outsider, the nobody.

But when the guy upped and quit one day in July, without a word of warning or apologies to the people who believed in him, I agreed with the disgusted New Yorkers milling around outside Madison Square Garden during the Democratic convention. The city's in-your-face *New York Post* headline screamed: "What a Wimp!" I would have added, "What a Phony!"

There are moments in life when you learn a lot about a person's character. Across the country, people had left their jobs, upended their lives, to work for Perot. They had put Perot first. Unfortunately, so had Perot.

In a critical decision, he behaved like the most ruthless businessman who closes the factory, abruptly, when the bottom line starts to fall. Workers be damned. If he treated his own people that way, with such personal disregard, how would he treat the country? There is more than one way to be unfaithful.

Rationalizing his way back into the race, trying to erase the "quitter" image, Perot said that he was reentering the race only because the people want him to. Who can believe that? This is a man as unable to listen to detractors as is his 800 number. No matter what a caller wanted to say, the toll-free number only counted approval for his reentry.

He described himself again as the alternative to the "ego-driven, power-hungry people." But this description has as much credibility as "volunteers" on a payroll.

Maybe the return of Perot was always planned as "an October surprise." Maybe the millions he spent and the ads he canned were savvy preparations for a daring last-minute raid on the election.

But if true, these are not the actions of the democrat who spoke of town halls, direct access, and a "bottom-up" campaign. They are the actions of a secretive autocrat. They don't describe a man who serves the people but a man who manipulates people.

My father used to say that if a man fools you once, he's a jerk. If he fools you twice, you're a jerk. Only he didn't use the word "jerk."

In the case of Perot, the saddest thing is not his capacity to fool himself or others. It's that this outsider promised to bring new people and new hope to the system. Instead he has brought something very, very old: another large dose of cynicism.

OCTOBER 6, 1992

The California Twins

||||||||||||||||||||||||||||||||||||||||||||||||||||||||||||||||||||||||||||||||||||||||||||||||||||||

San Francisco — From a distance, Barbara Boxer and Dianne Feinstein are linked together like a matched pair of Senate candidates. They share top billing as co-stars of the Year of the Woman Pageant.

And if indeed both these front-runners do win in November, California will get the first prize. It will be the first state in the Union ever represented by two women in the Senate.

This is a probability that surprises even the state's certified political junkies. As Mervin Field, the head of the respected California Field Poll here, says, "If you were in a room last October with a reasonable number of people—stalwart Democrats, stalwart Republicans, and observers—they would have agreed that there's no way in the world California would elect two Bay Area, liberal, Democratic, Jewish women to the Senate."

These women are not, however, as Boxer's campaign manager readily notes, "the Bobbsey twins." They are as different in style as they are in height, and they are succeeding for reasons as varied as their opponents.

Feinstein, measured and moderate, is running against Senator John Seymour, an incumbent so gray that his name is still unknown to nearly half the voters. Boxer, an energetic and genuine L-word candidate, is running against Bruce Herschensohn, a former talk-show host so far to the right of the mainstream that he can't even see the shoreline.

Feinstein and Boxer have, however, benefited jointly from the great California anti-tide: anti-incumbent, anti-Bush, anti-status quo. They share a lot of domestic concerns. As women they share something else. They are running for office in a state which, Field says, "became coed politically before anyplace else."

That's one thing to remember about this election. If women are at the top of the ticket in California, it's not because they are the sudden, overnight sensation of infatuated voters. It's not because of some passing fad for female candidates. It's not a one-election stand.

Feinstein, a former San Francisco mayor and candidate for governor, and Boxer, a member of Congress, are part of a longer, slower, much more important and less splashy trend. Not a Year of the Woman, but an entire generation of women.

Today California not only has two women running for the Senate but 19 women running for 17 of the 52 congressional seats. Most of these women have not come out of the blue or out of the kitchen.

They have come up from the huge number of local offices that govern this state of 31 million people.

"The local offices are our farm teams," says Kate Karpilov of the California Elected Women's Association. With due apologies for the sports metaphor, she reels off the statistics of change.

Twenty years ago only 3 percent of the county supervisors were female. Now it's 28 percent. Fifteen years ago only 10 percent of the city council seats were held by women. Now it's 27 percent. Today about 41 percent of the school board positions in the state are held by women.

When the political planets converged—the recession, the end of the Cold War, redistricting—to make this a time when California voters demanded change, there were large numbers of women ready and eager to make their moves. As Field says, "All the energy and talent that was bottled up has been unleashed. The typical woman candidate in California is just outenergizing the typical male candidate."

The notion, however, that 1992 will be the year of the great leap deserves a cautionary note. Karpilov, for example, prefers to think of it as the year women make, not a baby step, but "a toddler step."

If we triple the number of women in the United States Senate, that would bring the women up to a grand total of 6 percent. If women double their numbers in Congress that would be 13 percent. Even in the California delegation, Karpilov says, the gains "will be only minor blips on the radar screen of parity."

The risk is that 1992 could look like an anomalous, one-time-only special. If so, Karpilov worries about a backlash in the future. "I'm concerned that the public will say, 'You had your year.' "

But even with the California "twins," what we are seeing is not an explosion of female candidates. It's a trickle-up effect. That is the real—if decidedly less glitzy—story of this year and these women.

OCTOBER 16, 1992

Real   People
||||||||||||||||||||||||||||||||||||||||||||||||||||||||||||||||||||||||||||||||||||||||||||||||||||||||||||||

When this is all over, I'm going to miss Marisa Hall. What the heck, I'm going to miss Denton Walthall and Martha Mac-Cormack and Don Jackson and John Donovan.

I'm going to miss the entire cast of voters who did their political jury duty during the debate marathon. The folks who asked the candidates those questions in Virginia. The folks who were enlisted on focus groups for PBS and CNN. The ones who were drafted as token undecideds for ABC or NBC.

As each one spoke into the microphones of assorted broadcasters, it occurred to me that they had become part and parcel of the first Real People campaign. They were added to the burgeoning list of publicly certified Real People.

Real people? Sometime in the last few elections, we stopped talking *average* voters. It seems that nobody wants to be a mathematical mean in this Lake Wobegon of a country where all the children are expected to be above average. Nowadays, hardly anyone running for office refers to his or her constituents as *ordinary* people. The word "ordinary" has become a synonym for "dull."

Nor does anyone wax lyrical today about the *little people* of America. The venerable notion of the *common people* has become both uncommon and unpopular. Even talking about Joe Six-pack is seen as talking down to Joe Six-pack. Not to mention his wife.

At the same time, we became so subdivided and targeted by class, race, gender, region, and zip code that it was hard to find a single word that applied to every person or even every registered voter. So we have opted for "real people."

The candidates know it. At every opportunity during this long campaign, Clinton has talked about his program as "rooted in the real lives of real people." In his convention speech, George Bush said, "We are the party of the real people." At each TV teach-in, Ross Perot insisted that he got in the race because people—real people—put him in it.

For the most part, we seem to be using "real people" to separate the political outsiders from political insiders. Real People are the outsiders in this campaign.

Real People do not belong to the closed circle of politicians, pollsters, political scientists, and media analysts who circumscribe the common wisdom. Real People do not say, "That will drive his negatives up." Real People do not turn off the television debates and tell each other, "Ross Perot launched a torpedo at George Bush, who failed to hit one out of the ballpark but did show he'd go the fifteen rounds."

The fact that we look to Real People, that we prefer the questions they ask and the answers they give, that we find them trustworthy, is surely connected to our growing suspicion about experts. We have turned away from a passion for expertise to a search for authenticity. A desire to find the real thing.

This search started long before this campaign or even the Coke commercials. It began when people grew cynical about actors selling products and the advertisers moved on to such characters as Frank Perdue, Lee Iacocca, and Victor Kiam. Today, advertisers in pursuit of the patina of authenticity shoot commercials as if they were documentaries or home videos.

The political ads too have changed from Ronald Reagan's morning in America to George Bush's *cinéma vérité*. The year's most effective Bush ad employs a purposely jerky camera filming Real People as they question Clinton's trustworthiness.

At their worst these ads' imitation of authenticity can breed a new level of cynicism. Some of it reminds me of the salesman's answer when he was asked for the secret of his success. "Sincerity," he answered. "If you can fake that, you can fake anything."

As a trend, the shelf life of Real People may be fairly short. The spotlight can turn the fresh face into the famous and therefore the dubious. Turn a camera on and any certified political outsider can become an insider.

But so far, the un-star-studded cast of Real People at debates and on television has become our hit parade. Something refreshing has happened. Mark it down in your datebook. In the campaign of 1992, real people were the real thing.

OCTOBER 23, 1992

Baby Boomers Take Charge

|||||||||||||||||||||||||||||||||||||||||||||||||||||||||||||||||||||||||||||||||||||||||||||||||||||||||

It was past midnight by the time Bill Clinton and Al Gore arrived, like elated and tardy rock stars, at the final concert of a grueling national tour.

They were puffy around the eyes and raspy around the vocal cords. But if, as Paul Simon once wrote, every generation throws a hero on the pop charts, this was their moment. The baby boomers' bus tour was, finally, headed for Pennsylvania Avenue.

In the din of the victory celebration in front of the Old State House in Little Rock, the music played the subliminal message of this campaign, "Don't Stop Thinking about Tomorrow." The two men in their dark suits and white shirts, requisite Presidential attire, reached down into the crowd against the final refrain: "Yesterday's gone, yesterday's gone."

At that hour and in that place, it was possible to see and hear one era ending and another beginning.

At the end of this exhausting election, George Bush, a sixty-eight-year-old World War II veteran, the last Cold War President, has been replaced by Bill Clinton, a forty-six-year-old baby boomer and veteran of the war over the war in Vietnam. When all is said and counted, we have witnessed the most striking generational change since the seventy-year-old Dwight David Eisenhower was replaced by the forty-three-year-old John Fitzgerald Kennedy.

But what a different change it is this time. At JFK's inaugural, the bareheaded President issued the eloquent and strident declaration of his generation's ascendancy. "Let the word go forth from this time and place," he said, "to friend and foe alike, that the torch has been passed to a new generation of Americans. . . ."

In that same sentence, JFK offered up the clear, unified description of the men who had just taken power. They were, he said, "born in this century, tempered by war, disciplined by a hard and bitter peace, proud of our ancient heritage."

Where could Bill Clinton find such a clear description for the transition of his generation? These are the baby boomers who have gone through the population like the proverbial pig through the python. Until now, demography is all they've had in common.

Everything that united the World War II generation divided the baby-boom generation. George Bush's war was "the good war." Their generation knew what was expected of men and women. They shared a single attitude toward authority—respectful. They even agree on their drugs—cocktails and cigarettes.

But their children disagreed, and often bitterly, with each other. They disagreed about war, about the roles of men and women, about sex, drugs, rock 'n' roll. They disagreed about taking authority or questioning it.

As the years went by and the predictions of boomer victories went sour, it seemed that the baby-boom generation had trouble coming into power because they couldn't resolve their own deep divisions. In a tough and grueling way, this campaign did some of the work of resolution. In many ways this campaign was *about* generational change.

Bill Clinton's life showed all the fault lines of the baby-boom years. Indeed, he often had a foot on each side of this great divide. He opposed the war in Vietnam, though he didn't head for Canada. He admitted trouble in his marriage, though he didn't get divorced. And he tried marijuana, but he didn't inhale.

His wife too worked this fault line. She kept her name and then took his. She earned four times his salary and delivered his message. She wrote briefs and baked cookies.

The Last Warrior of the Cold War generation bet the bank that he could divide and conquer the baby-boom generation one more time. The Bush campaign inflamed hard feelings about the Vietnam War, pit traditional against nontraditional families, working against nonworking mothers.

Some of it backfired. Much of it just didn't work. It sounded like ancient history. The stuff of the Cold War.

It may be that this generation has been through enough, seen enough, to make peace with itself. To put aside the conflicts of its wonder years for its middle years.

It may be Bill Clinton's place in the intragenerational wars that fuels his real passion to mediate conflicts, to find a center that holds. As he said again to the crowd, "We need a new spirit of community, a sense that we're all in this together."

One thing we do know. The bumper crop of postwar children were YOUNG in capital letters. They were often less eager to take power than to challenge it. They didn't trust anybody over thirty. As a whole, they deferred adulthood, put off marriage, postponed parenthood. And delayed believing they could run the country.

Now, guess what. There's a baby boomer going to the White House. Turn the music up. It's time.

NOVEMBER 6, 1992

ABORTION
WARS

||||||||||||||||||||||||||||||||||||||||||||||||||||||||||||||||||||||||||||||||||||||||||||||||||||

|||||| *Abortion is an argument painted*
in black and white when most people
see shades of gray.

The Alarm Sounds: What If We Lose the Right to Decide?

||||||||||||||||||||||||||||||||||||||||||||||||||||||||||||||||||||||||||||||||||||||||||||||

There were no windows in the chambers of the Supreme Court. The Justices hearing the Missouri *Webster* case were buffered from the sights and sounds of the street, where rights were being defended with such inelegant phrases as "Two, Four, Six, Eight, You Can't Make Us Procreate."

Inside, the argument last Wednesday was cast with far more restraint, far more dignity. But there was drama when Charles Fried took the floor saying, "Today the United States asks this Court to reconsider and overrule its decision in *Roe* v. *Wade.*"

As the spectators tried to read the lips and minds of the Justices there followed a seminal exchange between Fried and Sandra Day O'Connor, the Justice who may be pivotal to this case. "Do you say there is no fundamental right to decide whether to have a child or not?" O'Connor asked Fried.

He answered hesitantly and she pursued. What if, she said, in a future century, we had a serious overpopulation problem. Does the state have a right to require abortions?

This was not some trick hypothetical question that professors use to trip up first-year students. It went to the heart of the matter. The government wants the Court to "reconsider" who has the right to decide the question of abortion: the woman or the state. If it's the state, she asked, couldn't a legislature that disallowed abortion today force it tomorrow?

Fried's response was as quick as it was obtuse. There is a difference, he insisted, between preventing an operation and forcing one. A forced abortion would mean "violently . . . laying hands on a woman and submitting her to an operation. . . ." A forced pregnancy, however, was what? Nonviolent? Benign?

Such distinctions would seem obscure to a woman pregnant against her will for nine months. They would seem specious to the doctor calculating the medical risks of her condition. But George Bush's lawyer saw nothing intrusive in such a pregnancy.

It was O'Connor alone who raised the issue of coercion. Like others who have reservations about *Roe* and about abortion itself, she had concerns as well about individual liberty. If, as she once wrote, abortion was on a collision course with medical technology, then "pro-life" is on a collision course with liberty.

Indeed, the scenario that she described is not as farfetched as it sounds. We do not have to look to the future or to China to see state attempts to control reproduction. We've made our own.

Earlier in this century, there were numerous forced sterilizations in the United States. It was 1974 before the courts ruled that the poor or mentally incompetent couldn't be coerced into such procedures.

Six years ago, in Massachusetts, a court ruled in favor of a husband who wanted to force his wife into a cervical operation so she wouldn't miscarry. She was only protected from this "violently . . . laying hands on" by the *Roe* reasoning of a higher court.

During the 1980s, we have seen as many as eleven cesarean sections ordered by courts. We have had at least one pregnant woman accused of fetal neglect and had others put in protective custody—protective of the fetus.

Even now there is serious debate about whether a pregnant woman could be forced into testing and treatment for her fetus. There are suggestions among those who talk of fetal rights that the government could constrain a pregnant woman's diet and physical activities, stomp out her cigarettes, empty her wineglass . . . or else.

If that is true today, what if the protection of *Roe* were shattered and a woman's rights transferred piecemeal to the government? How freely would the state intervene?

The specter of forced pregnancy is serious enough. There is no real need to tap into Justice O'Connor's fantasy of forced abortion to see the dangers of gutting *Roe*. But pendulums swing. How hard is it to imagine the first financially strapped state practicing coercive family planning? How hard to imagine another group of eugenicists in a statehouse insisting that the brain-damaged fetus of a welfare mother be aborted?

As Harvard Law School's Larry Tribe says, "There's no principled way to say that the government can use women's bodies against their will to nurture the unborn without accepting the other serious and totalitarian implications about privacy." While the Court deliberates the Missouri case, it is worth remembering that if you take away the right of individuals to make decisions about their lives, you cede it to the state. And that is just the beginning.

MAY 2, 1989

The *Webster* Case: How Bad Is It?

Moments after they had begun handing out the stack of opinions to the unruly reporters in the Supreme Court pressroom, hours before the lawyers had finished dissecting 86 pages of opinion and dissent, the phones began to ring at pro-choice offices across the country. They carried one anxious question: How bad is it?

Television reporters had led their stand-ups on the baking marble steps with the news that *Roe* had not been overturned. The right to abortion had survived the first assault of a newly constituted and conservative Court. But just barely.

Access to abortion—the real-life, everyday pathways for the exercise of that right—had been narrowed, threatened, transformed into a maze. Gradually only those women with the proper maps or money might have the right to their rights.

A shifting plurality of Justices ruled in the long-awaited, long-dreaded case called *Webster* that the state of Missouri could ban its health workers, its doctors and nurses and social workers, from taking part in abortions. The state could ban abortion from public hospitals. It could force its doctors to do tests to determine, when possible, whether a twenty-week-old fetus was capable of survival outside the womb.

How bad? In *Roe*, the Court had said that the right to decide the matter of abortion belonged by and large to the woman. In *Webster*, they ruled that the right to decide belongs increasingly to the politicians.

In *Roe*, the Court struck down state limitations on abortion. In *Webster*, the Court invited state limitations.

"Thus," as Justice Blackmun opened his searing dissent, " 'not with a bang but a whimper,' the plurality discards a landmark case of the last generation and casts into darkness the hopes and visions of every woman in this country who had come to believe that the Constitution guaranteed her the right to exercise some control over her unique ability to bear children."

On the steps of the Court, Faye Wattleton, the head of Planned Parenthood, asked rhetorically about these constitutional guarantees: "When did it become a political matter whether Americans have privacy? When did it become a political question whether women had reproductive rights? When did it become a political question whether poor people have the same access to their constitutional rights as the rest?"

The answer to the question "when" was easy: On July 3, 1989, they all became political questions.

During the years when the courts defended abortion, a pro-life strategy flooded the state legislatures with laws that were intended to percolate up through the legal system until the composition of the Supreme Court changed. States passed laws that would have required a husband's consent. They passed laws that would have required that women's names be reported. Again and again, they tried to regulate facilities out of existence.

On Monday, after ruling on one of those cases, the Supreme Court said that next term they would hear three more. Two state laws would put a rising number of obstacles before minors. One would ban abortions not done in the "functional equivalent of hospitals," making costs prohibitive. Slowly, in the post-*Webster* world, law by law, without ever "overturning *Roe*," abortion could remain legal and become impossible.

Justice Scalia, in announcing his own desire to turn the whole matter of abortion back to the legislatures, expressed his distaste for the way that the Court had been "the object of the sort of organized pressure that political institutions in a democracy ought to receive." And if nothing else, on Monday the Court made sure that every political institution in the land will feel that pressure.

For the past sixteen years, the pro-choice people have counted on the courts as their defense, while the pro-lifers have used the legislatures for the offense. If votes were taken today, only nine states would maintain the right to legal abortion. The legislatures that have passed pro-life bills knowing they would be overturned in court have paid no price. Those days are over.

Now every gubernatorial race, every statehouse seat, will become a referendum on sexual politics. The legislatures themselves may suffer from gridlock as abortion bills are rushed into committee in the next weeks and months.

In practical terms, the *Webster* case affects only Missouri. But the national message is clear. Don't count on the Constitution to protect rights. Count votes.

JULY 7, 1989

Sandra Day O'Connor:
One Woman's (Quiet) Voice
||||||||||||||||||||||||||||||||||||||||||||||||||||||||||||||||||||||||||||||||||||||||

In the aftermath of the abortion decision, when the Supreme Court opinions had deteriorated into talk-show shouting matches, I began to have a strange feeling that I had missed something. Or someone. Where was Sandra Day O'Connor in all this?

For months, it was widely assumed that the lone female justice on the bench would be pivotal in the *Webster* case. More than one brief was written directly to her ambivalence. More than one argument was pitched on her wavelength.

In the final count, she was indeed a formidable fifth. She went with one majority in favor of restrictive regulations against abortion. She went with another majority that refrained from overturning *Roe* v. *Wade*. But if her vote was powerful, her voice could barely be heard.

Harry Blackmun wrote a stunning, emotional opinion that he read from the bench. Silent Sandra wrote a dry, highly specific, unmemorable, unquotable opinion, and then skipped court the day the case was handed down.

What happened to the one soprano in the chorus of eight baritones? The only Justice who had ever actually been pregnant? It is entirely possible that O'Connor went low-key on the abortion decision precisely because she is the only woman. Any "only woman" knows what it's like to be in the room when a "woman's issue" comes up and every man turns to her. If she took a step back, if she deliberately chose to opt out of this high-decibel exchange, there is a lot of precedent for that.

But when I went back to search for the shade of O'Connor, and reread the opinion, I found another odd and perhaps highly female cast to it. O'Connor comes across in this opinion as the Court's mediating figure, in search of the middle. She is the Justice of the Peace, trying to reduce conflict between her colleagues and perhaps the opposing forces in the country. Even when it means denying conflict.

Does this remind you of anyone you know? Mom, perhaps?

The *Webster* case came at the end of a remarkably contentious session. If the Justices are ever to have a cup of coffee together, they may need a mediator. Justice O'Connor begins as if she is talking directly to her warring colleagues. Says Harvard Law School's Martha Minow, "She uses every possible gesture to say, 'Hey, you guys don't really disagree,' and 'Hey, there really isn't a problem here.' "

Nonproblem One. The preamble to the Missouri law states that life begins at conception. But O'Connor agreed to uphold this piece of the law because, she said, it's "too hypothetical" to have any real-life effect. No conflict, no problem.

Nonproblem Two. The state of Missouri requires doctors to perform tests on twenty-week-old fetuses to prove their viability. But O'Connor said the state didn't really mean that doctors should do such tests if they were unnecessary. No conflict. No problem.

Nonproblem Three. What about using this case to overturn *Roe*? O'Connor said that the *Webster* decision didn't actually, really, truly, absolutely challenge *Roe*. No conflict and no problem.

Justice Scalia, no slouch in the confrontation department, countered with two full pages calling O'Connor a hypocrite. He said that her efforts to write away conflict between the Court rulings of 1973 and those of 1989 "cannot be taken seriously." (Dear Antonin, there must be another way to put that. Can't a woman ever be taken seriously, even on the Supreme Court?)

I would hate for O'Connor to drop her conciliatory role and join the anti-abortion quartet. But the tone that infuses this and other O'Connor decisions raises some interesting questions about women and judgments—in and out of the Court.

Many who talk about the need for a "female" perspective in law or government or business value women as peacemakers, mediators, compromisers. It is women who frequently translate their children—uh, colleagues—to each other.

But there can be a downside to this value. It's the other model of Mom standing over the fighting kids, insisting, "I don't care who's right, I just want peace and quiet." Professor Minow describes this downside as "a reluctance to face up to conflicts that are there, to use a strategy of avoidance. And it's a failure to state in clear and certain terms the large governing principles for the future."

In a series of decisions, Justice O'Connor has tried to stake out common ground, a valuable piece of turf in this society. But you can't always find it. And you can't always create it.

On the statues that grace our courtrooms, the image of Justice is a woman. But not necessarily a mom.

JULY 11, 1989

Parents, Daughters, and
Consent
||||||||||||||||||||||||||||||||||||||||||||||||||||||||||||||||||||||||||||||||||||||||||||||||||||||

I do not know how long it's been since Father knew best and
Mother knew everything going on in the lives of her children.
Maybe that was never more than an image we carried around in
our heads about our own parents' self-confidence as adults, as heads
of households, as moms and dads.

But if anything has changed in the last generation it is the
erosion of this confidence. As parents today, we are openly uncertain
about how we are doing. How would we rank on a national pass/
fail system? How often, for that matter, are we marked absent?

Our anxiety peaks as our kids enter their teens, the corridor to
adulthood that's often marked by their closed doors. Suddenly the
most sophisticated find ourselves uttering old clichés: It's 4 p.m.
or 1 a.m.; do you know where the children are and what they are
doing?

The worry that kids are out of control, at least out of our control,
runs deep. And parents are increasingly attracted to anything that
holds out the promise that it can strengthen our authority and the
bonds between us and our teenagers.

Today, one of these promises comes wrapped in the spate of
"parental-consent laws." Such laws offer us a shred of knowledge
and control over our daughters' lives. They seem to promise that
at least these girls, whether thirteen or seventeen, won't go through
an unwanted pregnancy and abortion without us.

This is why parental-consent laws have become popular in recent
years. Nearly three-quarters of adults support them, pro-choice as
well as pro-life Americans. They have listened to the supporters of
those laws argue that no minor can have her ears pierced without

parental consent. Why, then, can she have an abortion without permission?

Politicians, in turn, who read the polls and seek some elusive "compromise" on the hot issue of abortion, often pick this one restriction on minors to prove they are "pro-family." Even the Bush administration, shying away from anti-abortion activism, will enter a Supreme Court brief this term on the Minnesota law requiring parental notification. It is considered a politically safe move.

But the issue isn't as simple as it first appears or appeals to us. In real life, minors do not need permission slips to have sex. Once pregnant, fifteen-year-olds do not need to notify their parents in order to deliver the baby. Indeed, once a teenager becomes a mother, she is legally an adult. We don't retain control over child and grandchild.

Most parents who are attracted to consent laws like to assume that every family is like theirs. They assume that girls are exaggerating when they say, "My parents would kill me." They assume the best.

For the most part, girls do tell parents. But not all of them can. As Harrison Hickman, who does polling for pro-choice groups, says, "When people hear the phrase 'parental consent,' they need to think, not about loving families sitting around making decisions. They need to think about young women abandoned and abused." To give an abusive parent more power over a child is more punitive than caring.

So the question behind the political and psychological support for parental consent has been whether we can provide support to "good" families without punishing the daughters of "bad" families.

There may, just may, be a compromise in the offing.

On September 30, a new law went into effect in Maine. It is labeled parental consent. But it might more accurately be called an adult-involvement law.

The state has cut a wider legislative pathway that may ensure adult presence in the lives of pregnant teenage girls, but without putting up barriers to force them into motherhood. A girl in Maine can get permission for an abortion from any family member of her choice—parent, sister, aunt, grandparent. As a second resort she can choose another adult—a minister, counselor, nurse, judge, physician—to accompany her through a counseling and informed-consent procedure.

In the politics of abortion, such a bill is certainly a compromise. It's a pro-choice, pro-family bill, supportive of "good" families without being punitive to pregnant girls. It is one way to separate out the anti-abortion crowd from the majority who worry about girls going through a crisis alone.

For families it is also a compromise. A compromise with reality. Adolescence is indeed a corridor. During this time, our children are neither full-grown adults to be treated as independent individuals nor dependents with no say over their own lives. Gradually the law may be scratching out a middle ground that reflects the truth about adolescence.

OCTOBER 3, 1989

The Gag: Who Decides Who Speaks?

||||||||||||||||||||||||||||||||||||||||||||||||||||||||||||||||||||||||||||||||||||||||||||||||||||||||

If there is any doubt about how abortion has reshuffled the political deck, consider this. On Thursday, a conservative majority on the Supreme Court delivered up a conservative's nightmare. They declared that anyone who takes money from the government must give something back: the party line.

To put it succinctly, the government that pays your rent can buy your speech. Anyone who works in one of the 4,000 federally funded clinics that provide family planning to four million poor American women is now forbidden from using the A-word.

Today if a patient asks about abortion, her doctor is legally required to act like a good government puppet. He or she must pull out the federal script and read: "The project does not consider abortion an appropriate method of family planning."

If the patient persists and asks for a referral, there are more scripts. Her doctor or provider has to refer her for prenatal care to those who "do not perform abortions."

This is the real-life effect of the Supreme Court ruling in a case that came to court bearing the name of Dr. Irving Rust, the medical director of a Planned Parenthood family-planning clinic in the South Bronx. A soft-spoken, Harlem-raised physician, Dr. Rust had worked since 1981 with the guidelines that forbid use of federal funds to perform abortions. But in 1988, when the Reagan administration wrote a set of regulations for Title X that banned even talking about abortion, he balked.

As Dr. Rust said last fall, what was at stake was the relationship between a doctor and a patient, the ability to talk freely and honestly. "If a woman came in with cancer of the ovary and there were three methods of treatment," he explained as an analogy, "could I tell her the government says that chemotherapy is *the* treatment, no matter what I think?"

This was the argument that seemed to worry the newest Justice, David Souter, when the case was heard in court. "You are telling us the physician cannot perform his usual professional responsibility," said Souter. "You are telling us [the government] in effect may preclude professional speech."

But in the end, Souter cast the tie-breaking vote to form a 5–4 majority. In the first, chilling indication of how he votes on the subject of abortion, Souter went with Justice Rehnquist. And Justice Rehnquist went with the government.

These rules, wrote the Chief Justice, weren't meant to inhibit the doctor's point of view but to promote the government's "value judgment favoring childbirth over abortion." The regulations weren't made to "gag" health-care providers but to "simply ensure that appropriate funds are not used for activities, including speech, that are outside the federal program's scope."

In one searing if subconscious comparison, Rehnquist showed just how political the Court's own judgments have become. Funding speech about family planning but not abortion was, he wrote, like funding a center for promoting democracy. The government doesn't also have to promote "competing lines of political philosophy such as Communism and Fascism."

All this smacks more than vaguely of arguments over funding for the arts. Does the government only fund along political lines? If you're on the payroll, do you still have the right to say what you believe or know?

What is a question of medical treatment for Dr. Rust and his patients is a matter of political philosophy for Justice Rehnquist and his majority. What is a concrete crisis in the lives of poor women becomes a wonderful abstraction in the words of the Justices.

Abortion-rights supporters, who are learning the hard way not to depend on the Court, will press Congress to change the regulations. There is a bill wending its way through the Senate that would reverse the guidelines and allow doctors to once again tell a poor woman all her legal options.

But as it stands today, clinics can either take the hush money or cut their services. Doctors can choose between government-prescribed service to poor patients or leaving the clinics. And poor patients will face another hurdle in a double-standard health-care system.

Wasn't it the conservatives who always told us to worry about the long arm of the government? If it's uncomfortable in the examining room at the clinic these days, that's because the government has moved in and put a firm hand over the doctor's mouth.

MAY 28, 1991

Nibbling Away
at a Woman's Right
||||||||||||||||||||||||||||||||||||||||||||||||||||||||||||||||||||||||||||||||||||||||||||||||||||

Kathryn Kolbert likes to say that politics and law are a lot like *Sesame Street*: "You have to learn how to count."

She didn't get this tip directly from Bert and Ernie but from her experience as an attorney defending abortion rights. There are certain numbers that seem especially unlucky for any pro-choice calculator this year. Take the number 12. Last week the House came up 12 votes short of being able to override George Bush's veto and protect the right of a doctor to talk freely to a poor client considering an abortion.

Take the number 600. That's about how many new restrictive laws state legislatures have passed since the *Webster* decision allowed them greater leeway.

Take the number 4 (please). That's the margin in the Senate that confirmed Clarence Thomas to a deciding seat on the Supreme Court.

Now Kolbert's counting has turned to a countdown. The ACLU lawyer is the lead attorney on a case heading down the fast track to the Supreme Court. It comes with a petition that asks the Justices to say once and for all: Has the Supreme Court overturned *Roe* v. *Wade*? Is abortion still a fundamental constitutional right in the United States?

This question has been simmering since Reagan and Bush began appointing new members to the highest bench. The new Court hasn't killed the right established by *Roe* v. *Wade*, but it's nibbling it to death. Indeed, in 1989 the *Webster* decision virtually invited the states to start chomping.

Now abortion-rights groups have said: Enough. In Kolbert's words, "It is time to force the Court to say whether or not *Roe* remains the law."

The case that raises that issue is *Planned Parenthood* v. *Casey*. This case began in the Pennsylvania legislature. In 1989, the legislators voted in favor of a law that restricted abortion by, among other things, requiring a mandatory waiting period, state-written counseling, parental consent, and husband notification.

On October 21, the 3rd Circuit Court of Appeals upheld every restriction except the one forcing women to tell their husbands. More importantly, the court based its ruling on the belief that *Roe* v. *Wade* had already been gutted. Abortion, they said, was no longer a fundamental constitutional right, but rather a "limited fundamental right." This "right," in other words, could be limited by any law a legislature passed and a court thought was "reasonable."

Until now, abortion-rights advocates—carefully counting the numbers on the Supreme Court—have tried to avoid a showdown over *Roe*. It was always the anti-abortion forces that asked for a review of the seminal case. Pro-choice advocates figured women were better off clinging to whatever they could grasp while the cliff eroded under them.

Now, Kolbert's clients, the clinics and doctors who provide abortions in Pennsylvania, have said, "We're tired of dying gracefully. It's time for the Court to decide."

By petitioning the Court for a review, they are risking an earlier and full reversal of *Roe*. But as Kolbert says, any woman within the jurisdiction of the 3rd Circuit Appeals Court—Pennsylvania, Delaware, and New Jersey—has already lost a fundamental right.

The reality is that pro-choice supporters can't, uh, count on the Court. The abortion issue has gradually but inexorably moved out of the legal system and into politics. So now the most important number on the minds of the groups pushing for a definitive answer from the Supreme Court is 1992.

This case is the only one challenging *Roe* that could get to or through the Supreme Court this election year. If the state of Pennsylvania decides next week to join the issue and keep to a speedy timetable, the issue of abortion is going to be front and center in every race.

"I think most people have a hard time believing that the Supreme Court could take away a constitutional right," says Kolbert. "When I say to young women, 'Do you believe that the Court could take away the right to birth control and abortion?' there's a disbelief that permeates their world."

If the Justices, after all, overturn *Roe*—the bedrock of privacy decisions—the right of a woman to decide is going to land squarely in the laps of legislators. And 1992 could be the year when many politicians discover their number is up.

NOVEMBER 29, 1991

The   Abortion   Stalemate

||||||||||||||||||||||||||||||||||||||||||||||||||||||||||||||||||||||||||||||||||||||||||||||||||||||

The anniversary went as expected. After nineteen years of protests and counterprotests that mark the Supreme Court's abortion
decision, everyone knows the drill. Placards of fetuses over here,
posters of coat hangers over there. Sound bites all around.

Of course, the energy level seemed higher this year, and the
sense of urgency heightened. That too was to be expected. After
all, the Supreme Court has decided to hear the Pennsylvania case
this spring. If the Justices overturn *Roe*, or empty it of any last sips
of meaning, the date of the protests may change, but the argument
will go on.

Anyone who doubts that should check the age of the protesters.
They are getting younger, not older.

What a fix we are in. Pro-life and pro-choice forces are more
than polarized; they are mutually demonized. Most Americans feel
deeply ambivalent about abortion—with views that are complicated
and highly personal. But the issue is as public and oversimplified
as a vote. Ambivalence is only heard as two separate voices, arguing
in absolutist terms.

As a country, we would like the issue to go away, but instead
it's shifting into a higher focus. As a people, we rank it low on the
list of national priorities, but it's gaining importance in politics.
It will rage on, in the Presidential campaign, in Congress, where
the Freedom of Choice Act will gain ground, in state legislatures,
in the push to import the abortion pill.

Even Kate Michelman, the head of the National Abortion Rights
Action League, stopped in the middle of the anniversary rituals to
acknowledge, "Most Americans are hungry for some kind of solution

for the controversy. People are tired of battling out the issue in the public domain. They will do battle. But they want to move on and resolve this."

Abortion, she said wearily, "is not a happy event in the lives of women. We don't run around saying this is an experience you need to have a fulfilling life. I work on this issue, but I would like to see nothing more than a country that respects the right and works to reduce the need."

That wish may signal a new direction. During all the years of deadlock, those for and against a woman's right to decide have focused far more energy on abortion than on reducing the number of unintended pregnancies. Indeed, as someone who views the loss of abortion rights with alarm and more than that, a sense of betrayal, I share the current sense of crisis. But this is the time to broaden our perspective—not to dilute the energy, but to enlarge the argument and the audience.

Americans don't want to talk about rights without also talking about responsibility. We can't talk about how to end pregnancy without also talking about how it begins.

As Francis Kissling, the head of Catholics for a Free Choice, says, "We who are feminists talk about women's right to control our bodies. For the right-to-lifers, that right ends at pregnancy. But for the pro-choicers, it often sounds as if the right *begins* at pregnancy."

The tough reality is that in half of all the abortions performed, neither the women nor their partners had used birth control. Just to raise this issue leaves pro-choice advocates open to charges of "guilt-tripping." We know, after all, about birth-control flaws and failures. We know about human frailty as well. We don't subscribe to forced motherhood as a punishment.

But it is also true that those of us who defend the right to choose do not comfortably endorse abortion as a first choice. Those who believe that women are more than wombs do not regard the fetus as mere protoplasm.

Indeed, the same women and men who believe in women's rights support access to abortion as just one part of a much wider vision. That vision is of women who are raised to be strong, self-confident, and responsible. We have to be willing to say in public what we would say to our daughters. And to our sons.

It's hard to broaden the debate during a crisis; far easier to raise the same old banners. But maybe we can only lower the decibels of this debate by staking out this common ground.

People of strong moral sensibilities disagree violently about abortion. That is not going to change. But as Francis Kissling says, "We're going to have to live together in this country." Sometime, before the twentieth anniversary of *Roe*, or the twenty-fifth, or the fiftieth, we have to begin learning how.

JANUARY 28, 1992

A Search for Common Ground

||||||||||||||||||||||||||||||||||||||||||||||||||||||||||||||||||||||||||||||||||||||||||||||||||

Watertown, Mass. — The reports from the front lines of the abortion wars are as dispiriting as ever. Hostilities have only escalated and opponents have now become enemies.

In Utah, two armies fought over the Republican Party platform, using high-decibel ammunition. In Washington, groups for and against abortion rights are waiting in separate trenches for the Supreme Court decision in the Pennsylvania case.

In Massachusetts, Operation Rescue is planning its next clinic assault and the National Organization for Women is training its guards. And in dozens of political races, candidates are recruiting fresh new divisions under the opposing banners of "choice" and "life."

But in a vine-covered building behind a wooden fence in suburban Boston, a small group of family therapists is trying to establish a demilitarized zone. The Public Conversations Project they have created is on a leading edge of the nascent movement struggling to defuse the civil wars.

Their project grew out of a question that director Laura Chasin asked herself and her colleagues in 1990: "Do we as family therapists have skills that can be helpfully applied 'out there'?"

The public arguments in American political life resembled the "stuck conversations" of troubled families. Each member was locked into a hostile, fixed position. But of all these arguments, the one about abortion seemed the most tragically frozen.

"We talked about the unintended consequences of this struggle," says Chasin. "It takes many of the most compassionate and principled people—many of them women—and induces them to take their energy, passion, talent, money, and direct it against each other."

As therapists they had long been in the "pattern-busting, stuckness-busting business." But they wondered, could they do it in the real world?

Over the past year and a half, they invited groups of people to join a different sort of conversation. Some of their names were provided by Planned Parenthood and Massachusetts Citizens for Life; all identified themselves as pro-choice or pro-life.

Under the ground rules, people were not allowed to try to persuade each other. Instead, over three hours and under the guidance of a project member, they talked and listened. They explored stereotypes of each other, acknowledged ambivalence, and watched what emerged from this process.

Some questions indeed led down hopeless dead ends. When does life begin? Is the fetus a person? Who should decide? But of the fifty people who went through the process, only two were totally unable to find new ways of talking.

"The main thing that happened was the way these people perceived each other," says Chasin. "They came in thinking, Oh my God, I'm going to be meeting with *them*. They went out thinking, These people are compassionate, principled, and share concerns that I have."

Indeed, at moments in the videotaped conversations, it is impossible to know the opponents without a label. Which side said, for example, "How do we get people who are in the business of making laws to start thinking about a world in which there would be no need for abortion?"

"These people were in such pitched battles," said another project member, "they didn't have a clue what they had in common." But gradually they uncovered a shared concern about the well-being of children and mothers. Both sides agreed that using abortion as a form of birth control was wrong. They agreed as well about the importance of preventing unintended pregnancy and about the need for sex education.

Chasin and her colleagues harbor no grand illusions that this process will forge a Great Compromise on abortion—take your placards and go home. The project itself is dedicated to dialogue, not policy making.

But once a pattern has been "busted," once people are no longer defined as demons, they hope that the public, like the family, may be able to come up with some solutions. Indeed, there are hints of this success in other parts of this movement.

In Missouri, Wisconsin, Texas, and California, pro-life and pro-choice people are meeting and talking—carefully. Some have jointly endorsed legislation for sex education or funding for poor families.

There is at least one computer network linking thirty pro-life and pro-choice thinkers. And recently, the Public Conversations Project took their model to a church group and a women's group in Mississippi.

Such signs look small against the backdrop of the trench warfare. But they are real testimony to the longing to figure a way out of this endless, polarizing civil strife.

Abortion is an argument painted mostly in black and white when most people see shades of gray. But here, the Public Conversations Project is trying to release fresh ways of thinking, to stake out new ground. The color scheme they have chosen is, in Chasin's word, "green." A much more peaceful hue.

J U N E 2 , 1 9 9 2

A   R i g h t   L e f t   S t a n d i n g   b u t   C r i p p l e d

||||||||||||||||||||||||||||||||||||||||||||||||||||||||||||||||||||||||||||||||||||||||||||||

At long last the Supreme Court managed to stake out some of that elusive common ground in the ongoing abortion wars. On Monday, they issued a ruling that both sides could attack.

Randall Terry, chief guru of pro-life's Operation Rescue, hated this decision. And so did Kathryn Kolbert, lawyer domo for the pro-choice forces.

Standing on the Supreme Court steps, a sputtering Terry said that the three Justices writing for the majority "have stabbed the pro-life movement in the back and reaffirmed the bloodshed." Nearby, a somber Kolbert said, "The Court has taken away the fundamental rights women have had up to today."

The ruling itself made the Supreme Court reporters wish they'd taken that Evelyn Wood speed-reading class after all. It contained five separate opinions spread out over 100 pages. Enough to keep the analysts busy and the spin doctors making house calls for weeks.

What the Supreme Court delivered was a bad-news, good-news, half-empty, half-full cup of decisions. On the one hand, the 5–4 majority opinion written jointly by Justices O'Connor, Souter, and Kennedy reaffirmed a woman's right to abortion. On the other hand, they defended the state's right to expand the barriers between a woman and her ability to exercise that right.

This trio of Reagan-Bush appointees described abortion—better than the Court ever has—as part of the women's rights movement. "The ability of women to participate equally in the economic and social life of the nation," they wrote, "has been facilitated by their ability to control their reproductive lives."

They admitted too that there was no justification for reversing _Roe_ v. _Wade_, except for the personal "disposition" of a new group of Justices. To overturn laws every time you change judges would "seriously weaken the Court's capacity to exercise the judicial power and to function as the Supreme Court of a nation dedicated to the rule of law." The Supreme Court of law would be seen as the Supreme Pawns of politics.

But this majority also threw out the "trimester system" established in the *Roe* decision. Instead, they said states could "regulate" abortion even in the first trimester as long as they didn't place an "undue burden" on the woman.

In the majority view, most of the Pennsylvania restrictions in this case—a waiting period, a state-written medical lecture, and parental consent for minors—were acceptable. Only the mandate that a woman tell her husband was struck down.

It is no wonder that the pro-choice advocates agreed for once with their nemesis, Chief Justice Rehnquist, when he said, "The joint opinion . . . retains the outer shell of *Roe* v. *Wade* but beats a wholesale retreat from the substance of that case." Nor is it any wonder that the pro-life advocates agreed with their new villains, O'Connor and Souter and Kennedy, when the trio said this ruling protects *Roe*.

The decision muddles old allegiances. It muddies the political waters as well.

The Court didn't hand the pro-life forces the victory they expected after twelve years of loyal Republican voting. Clarence Thomas came as advertised, in favor of overturning *Roe*. But Kennedy and Souter and O'Connor took a stand against a ban.

Nor did it hand pro-choice forces a decision with the political punch they were looking for. This decision doesn't make abortion illegal. It "merely" makes it more and more difficult, expensive, or even impossible for poor women, young women, and rural women. That's harder to see, harder to feel, and may be harder to mobilize against.

Abortion rights activists are ready to press the Freedom of Choice Act through Congress and onto the President's desk. An expected veto would put Bush in the spotlight as the person single-handedly denying women the right to choose. Now the Court's decision may mute the power of abortion as an overriding campaign issue.

In this climate and this time, it's reasonable to feel relief at the ruling. The Court has at least put a floor under the deteriorating right to choose. The Justices said states could not ban abortion, but they said so by one vote, by one Justice. Laws like those in Louisiana and Utah and Guam are unlikely to be upheld when they come to the Court.

Justice Blackmun, the author of the 1973 *Roe* decision, put it bluntly: "I am eighty-three years old. I cannot remain on the Court forever, and when I do step down, the confirmation process for my successor well may focus on the issue before us today."

For the moment, we have reaffirmed a tattered right. Or maybe we've just won a short reprieve.

JULY 3, 1992

Corinne Quayle's "Baby"

Spare me the Quayle jokes. This story is not small potatoes. The Vice President spoke from his heart and had his head handed to him.

Last week, Dan Quayle was asked what he would do if his daughter came to him as a pregnant adult. He said, "I would counsel her and talk to her and support her on whatever decision she made." For once he sounded like a father instead of a candidate with a politically correct right-to-life tape on automatic replay.

But he also sounded like a counselor at a Planned Parenthood clinic, a notion that had the whole country smirking. Was he a closet advocate of a woman's right to decide? A lot of folks yelled, "Gotcha!"

Next came Marilyn to say that if this same daughter gets pregnant now at thirteen, "she'll take the child to term." Would she make that decision for her daughter? "We will make it with her."

Poor Corinne Quayle's teenage reproductive system became a subject of intrafamily discussion and public debate. But the dispute between Dan and Marilyn was blown out of proportion.

The apparent disagreement wasn't about Corinne's behavior but about her age. When Corinne's eighteen, she can have an abortion with Dad's support. While she's thirteen, she'll have a baby by Mom's order.

Before you say that this is more Danfoolery, let me remind you that this is how upside down, inside out the abortion issue has become. On the one hand, most Americans agree that a twenty-year-old is more equipped for motherhood than a thirteen-year-old. On the other hand, we are making it harder for thirteen-year-olds to get abortions than their elders.

Before Quayle's now-famous quote about supporting an adult daughter's choice, he rattled off the standard argument in favor of laws restricting a young daughter's right to abortion without parental consent. "My daughter," he said, invoking Corinne again, "if she wants to take an aspirin at school, she has to call and get permission. And if she wants to have an abortion, she doesn't."

His argument about parents and daughters resonates widely in our country and not just among Quayle supporters. The idea that our thirteen- or sixteen-year-old daughters would face a crisis alone, have an abortion without our knowledge, surrounded and counseled by strangers, strikes at the heart of what it means to be a parent. Which is to be involved in our children's lives, their troubles as well as triumphs.

This feeling runs so deep that some thirty-six states now have parental notification or consent laws on the books. Even the Freedom of Choice Act, which would make *Roe* the law of the land no matter what happens in the Supreme Court, leaves this too-hot-to-touch issue of parents and daughters to the states.

Most parents support those laws though we know, deep down, you cannot legislate communication. There is no law that can make teenagers notify their parents before they have sex. They don't need a permission slip to become pregnant. Maybe our daughters can't get an aspirin without our consent, but they can go through pregnancy and childbirth.

Indeed, in practical terms, many of these laws have a very different consequence than we may desire. The most stringent ones requiring parental consent throw up the highest barriers in front of the most vulnerable and youngest girls.

The vast majority of teenagers do come to a parent for help. These girls can get abortions. But only the most sophisticated of estranged teenagers can find their way through the system. Only the savviest can find the money, travel to the clinic, or stand up before a judge, and therefore make their own decisions.

The ones who are not savvy or sophisticated get to be the mothers. At which point, in most states, they are suddenly and ironically "emancipated" into legal adulthood.

It isn't just the parental-involvement laws that affect the young most. Every restriction that makes it more difficult for an adult woman to get an abortion makes it most difficult for a teenager.

As for Corinne Quayle, the unwitting and undoubtedly mortified "daughter" in her parents' public scenario? Together, the Second Couple have reminded us of the double standard of abortion. In the Quayle world an eighteen-year-old gets to be supported whatever her decision. A thirteen-year-old gets to have a baby.

This is no joke. It's the foolishness that passes now for public policy.

JULY 31, 1992

Making Abortion
a Private Matter—at Last

||||||||||||||||||||||||||||||||||||||||||||||||||||||||||||||||||||||||||||||||||||||||||||||

The company always blamed it on the weather. The European manufacturers of the abortion pill were simply, repeatedly, and openly terrified by the American climate.

When anyone asked the heads of Roussel-Uclaf and its parent

company, Hoechst, why they refused to make RU486 available to American women, they would just point to the political atmosphere. In the intemperate, unpredictable American environment, they said, the pill would produce a storm of controversy. They worried that the company would be devastated by a right-to-life boycott.

But my, how quickly the prevailing winds have changed.

There's a pro-choice President in the White House. A frustrated group of Americans has begun negotiating for a Chinese version of the pill. And suddenly, the same company finds our climate rather hospitable. In a shift that would make a weatherman dizzy, Roussel-Uclaf has told the Food and Drug Administration that the abortion pill should be made available here.

It may only be a matter of time before American women have access to the early, nonsurgical abortion that's already been used by 120,000 French women. Indeed, if the early RU486 research is right, Americans may have an effective morning-after pill. And abortion may finally become what it was always supposed to be: a private matter.

These days the most public threat to abortion rights isn't coming from the courts or from the legislatures. The front lines now are the clinics, the parking lots around them, and the sidewalks in front of them.

There's an irony in this turn of events. Early in the movement, such clinics were conceived as low-key, low-cost, neighborhood places where women could comfortably come for all their reproductive health care, including abortion. "If the anti-choice people had designed them, they couldn't have done a better job than we did," says a rueful Barbara Radford, the head of the National Abortion Federation.

Clinics have become the isolated ghettos of abortion providers and the easy targets for pro-life activists. Abortion itself is segregated from the medical world and medical practice.

Over 90 percent of abortions are performed in specialized clinics. Doctors assume they can refer patients to clinics and are less often trained to perform abortions themselves. Only a quarter of gynecological residents are routinely taught the procedure.

Instead of having a clinic in every neighborhood, we have entire states, like the Dakotas, with only one clinic apiece. State restrictions are often written with clinics in mind and there are no abortion providers in 85 percent of the counties nationwide.

The buildings themselves are not user-friendly. They have become easy marks for arsonists and bomb throwers and those—this is the latest—who inject putrid chemicals through the walls. Just to get in, a woman may have to run a gantlet of pickets and self-appointed "rescuers." While someone in the parking lot writes down the number of her license plate so she can be harassed at home.

RU486 could irrevocably change this, for one simple reason: You don't need a clinic to swallow a pill.

Women who must now take long bus rides to distant cities, where they are required by some state laws to wait forty-eight hours, would only have to visit their gynecologist or family physician. Women who must now be escorted along hostile sidewalks to a strange front door could sit in the waiting room back home with patients getting Pap smears and flu shots. Instead of one clinic in a town or state to terrorize, there would be thousands of doctors' offices, HMOs, and college clinics to identify.

The pill does not make surgical abortions obsolete. It is used only in the first nine weeks of pregnancy. Four percent of the French women who took RU486 still needed a surgical procedure. In France, the drug is still restricted to clinics, where most of the country's health care is provided.

But here, RU486, as a morning-after pill, and an abortion pill, could become part of our decentralized medical system. As Radford puts it, "If individual physicians start providing this pill on a regular basis, the anti-abortion people will have to go home."

Finally, after all these years, most abortions could truly become a matter between the pregnant woman and her doctor. What a change in the weather that would be.

FEBRUARY 28, 1993

THE GENERATIONS

||||||||||||||||||||||||||||||||||||||||||||||||||||||||||||||||||||||||||||||||||||||||||||||||||||||||||||

|||||| *The final moment of assuming adulthood may be when we inherit the legacy, become the keeper of traditions, the curator of our family's past and future memories. When the holidays are at our houses.*

Turning the Generations Upside Down

||||||||||||||||||||||||||||||||||||||||||||||||||||||||||||||||||||||||||||||||||||||||||||||||||||||

It is evening when my mother, whose life is booby-trapped by technology, calls. She is having an electronic breakdown. The television set, which once merely and manually went on and off, now requires a series of instructions before it will obey.

There are numbers to be entered on two remote controls that are not remotely within her control at this moment. Something has gone awry.

To avoid an emergency house call, I talk her through the system step by step. The scene is not unlike the old war movie in which a ship-to-shore appendectomy is performed by telephone. Eventually, the patient is saved.

I hang up the phone flush with my own prowess, more than a bit intolerant of my elder's difficulty coping with the television. The word I use is "phobic." The feeling I have is superior.

But my smugness doesn't last long. Within days I am confronted by my own younger generation. They cannot understand why I am not up to speed—their speed—on the equipment we share. Why do I hesitate to program the VCR? Why have we never logged on the new computer program? It's really, we are told, fun. The feeling that I have is of incompetence.

What I am describing is nothing unique to my family. There is a three-generational model of technological life in America. Seventysomething meets fortysomething meets twentysomething.

The model has become the central sitcom of modern times. All across America, ten-year-olds are called from their bedrooms to work the video camera; twelve-year-olds are wrenched from their homework to program the VCR; fourteen-year-olds come home from dates to fix the glitch in the computer.

We find it amusing, take it for granted, and rarely think about the vast revolution that has turned the generations upside down. Technological change has done something our ancestors would have never believed: made experts of the young.

In part, this is the story of America itself. When immigrants came to this country, they left behind not only the language but the cultural knowledge that made them surefooted guides through the old, traditional world. In America, their children became interpreters of new words and ways.

Now each generation emigrates to a new technological country. Elders learn this technology as a second language, haltingly, imperfectly. Children grow up bilingual.

The pace of change seems to make experience obsolete. It's one of the things about being a parent now. Fewer of us have a skill to teach our children. Fewer children apprentice themselves to us as adults. There are times when we lose confidence that what we have to teach has any meaning.

A man becomes a printer and his grandchildren lay out newspaper pages on computers. A woman learns the intricacies of preserving food and her children buy a refrigerator.

One generation has a storehouse of home remedies and the next generation takes penicillin. For every man who teaches his child to fish there is another who tries to learn Nintendo from that same child.

The things that elders still show the young—how to hit a ball, plant a tree, tell a story—have become peripheral to their daily economic survival. They are the stuff of avocation rather than vocation. Indeed, parents and children spend their time together before, after, around work. We have become each other's extracurricular activity.

In all of this, the one subject that the elders are entrusted with as if it had some permanence is "family life." We are told to teach our children "values." But we all forget that values were once learned while watching, while working, beside the older generation.

Values came in the conversation over a shoe last or the hem of a skirt. Respect came from the knowledge of the older generation and the acknowledgment of the young.

The wonder is that technology hasn't severed the cord between generations, but just frayed it. The wonder is that the older generation still is expert in a subject that never becomes obsolete: life.

Skill comes quickly, but wisdom comes, if at all, slowly. Technology favors the young, but the soft information about our human kind, our own behavior, needs aging. In the end, it's not a bad exchange for a little problem with the VCR.

MARCH 29, 1991

Children on Their Own

||||||||||||||||||||||||||||||||||||||||||||||||||||||||||||||||||||||||||||||||||||||||||||||||||||||||||

There is a scene in *Home Alone* when Kevin McCallister stands before the mirror in his parents' bathroom, slaps some after-shave lotion on his tender eight-year-old skin, and lets out a howl. It comes just in time. One bracing shock of reality to remind us that Kevin is not quite yet the man of the house.

For the rest of this delicious movie, the son of the suburbs, the youngest child accidentally left behind in his family's frantic vacation exit, is nothing if not self-sufficient. He protects himself. He protects his home. And in the process, it seemed to this contented viewer that Kevin McCallister protects parents from the worst of their anxieties.

Home Alone is the surprise hit of this season. The smart money in Hollywood never figured it would reach the top. They didn't count on the longing for a family movie in which the hero is a delight, the criminals are comic, and you don't have to put your hands over the kids' eyes.

But it's also a hit because *Home Alone* taps the most primal plot: the fears that kids have about being abandoned and the fantasies they have of being on their own.

Kevin is the latest in a long line of deserted children. Before the McCallisters took off for Paris without their youngest son, an entire anthology of children had learned to survive without parents: The lost boys of *Peter Pan* who had fallen from their prams never to be found again. The children of Disney, Dumbo and Bambi, left motherless in the world.

For a generation, Pippi Longstocking personified a child's fantasy of independence. Even Dorothy, mysteriously orphaned into her Aunt Em's home and then wrenched away by another natural disaster, fended for herself in Oz.

There was never any need for a psychiatrist to analyze this theme. At some point, children become aware of their dependency on adults who aren't always reliable. Parents can be anything from absentminded to abusive, from benignly neglectful to untrustworthy. Even the best of us can be busy or distracted. Even the most secure childhood can be shattered by death or divorce. This recognition stirs a child's longing to be strong.

The theme has taken a harder twist lately as we fear that family life is coming loose at the seams. Steven Spielberg's fractured families had parents too distracted to see even an E.T. in their midst. In *Honey, I Shrunk the Kids*, a harried father absentmindedly put his children in lethal danger in their own back yard. There was obvious symbolism in the dialogue of the quarter-inch children lost in the suburban grass: "We're too small. He can't hear us."

But *Home Alone* does more than appeal to the child's need to believe in his survival. Nowadays parents need to believe it as well. And that's what has changed.

At the risk of turning comedy into sociology, Kevin is a poster child for worries about "self-care," that euphemism for no care. Well over two million kids between five and thirteen are "home alone" every weekday afternoon.

Kevin's parents left on vacation, but most have gone off to work. Kevin's neighborhood was emptied for Christmas, but usually it's empty by 9 a.m. Today's working parents, anxious in their absenteeism, set up hot lines and rules . . . over the phone. We talk about childhood "resilience" and the value of their "independence"—and keep our fingers crossed.

The movie's upper-class family setting, a houseful of expensive electronic gadgets, stands in as a visual accusation often launched against working families: that we are neglecting children for luxuries. Kevin's mother is not the only one who asks herself in crisis, "What kind of a mother am I?"

Onto this sociological backdrop steps an eight-year-old boy saying, "Hey, I'm not afraid anymore." Kevin on the big screen conquering his fear of the furnace. Kevin taking care of himself. Kevin protecting himself, his home and hearth from criminals who are less threatening than comic.

If *Home Alone* is every child's fantasy, it is also every parent's fantasy. It's all there: the universal and anxious wish that, in this uncertain time, the kids will be all right. And the hope for a happy ending.

DECEMBER 18, 1990

Chelsea Chooses School, or Putting Your Kids Where Your Mouth Is

||||||||||||||||||||||||||||||||||||||||||||||||||||||||||||||||||||||||||||||||||||||||||||||||

Washington — Until now there had been no designated Chelsea Clinton beat. Just a smattering of occasional items on the life and times of the First Child-elect.

This was due to an unusual conspiracy of decency on the part of the media, and some atavistic memories of what it was like to be twelve years old. If there is anybody out there who looks back on his or her eighth-grade photo with fondness, please raise your hand. You may leave the room.

So last week, when Chelsea landed on page one of virtually every newspaper in the country, it was a warning shot across the brow of the President's child. Dear Chelsea: From now on, you aren't a kid, you are a symbol. Every move you make, every breath you take, we'll be watching you. Everything you do will reflect on your parents. Welcome to Washington and have a swell adolescence.

The issue was Chelsea's school, Sidwell Friends. The politician who presented himself as a strong supporter of public schools was a father sending his own daughter to private school. Hypocrisy alert? Waffling alarm?

The Clintons said simply, "As parents, we believe this decision is best for our daughter at this time in her life, based on our changing circumstances." *The Washington Post* was understanding. *The New York Times* was disapproving. And *USA Today* asked their readers to chime in by letter, toll-free telephone, or fax machine.

The disappointment of the public school parents, teachers, and principals was palpable. In this city, the schools have been suffering from a sinking sensation. They have been labeled unstable and mismanaged. The test scores are way below the national norm and the dropout rate way above.

There were many who wanted the Clintons' daughter enrolled as a vote of confidence, a pledge to the future, or a magnet to attract middle-class parents in flight. In short, a symbol. What we got instead was one of those uncomfortable ethics seminars that rage among middle- and upper-middle-class parents, especially liberals. Do you put your kids where your mouth is?

I have been in the room any number of times when decisions were made between someone's political beliefs and their parental —what?—responsibilities, instincts, protectiveness?

I've been there when a colleague deeply committed to the inner city and also to his ten-year-old decided that two muggings were enough. He took the kid and ran to the suburbs.

I've been there when a strong advocate of child-care centers finally, abashedly hired a nanny for her own baby. The turnover was too great, the attention too scattered.

I have heard parents who are morally committed to a standard of fairness and equity admit they bought their way out of community problems. A crying child came smack up against a principle.

At other times and in other homes, I have watched parents put their children on the line for what they believe in. But they weren't always sure that was right either.

Push comes to shove at school age. Presidents and other parents want to make the public schools in their city places they want to send their kids. But how to balance what's best for the long run with one childhood's short run?

The guru of children's issues, Marian Wright Edelman, picked private school for her kids. So did Jesse Jackson. Tens of thousands in the capital and other cities moved to suburbs "for the schools." Others pay for parochial schools and not always for the prayers. NIMBY—Not in My Back Yard—becomes Not My Kids.

People may not talk publicly about their unease for the same reason that Bill Clinton—who overexplains everything—didn't explain the reason for picking Sidwell Friends. The ethical conflicts of people with options are a limousine luxury compared to the problems of people without the same options. This disparity is at the heart of the debate about school-choice proposals.

I don't regard Chelsea Clinton's school as Bill Clinton's hypocrisy. She is not a publicly owned child even if she lives in subsidized housing. Her job is not to set educational policy. It's to get educated.

But her father came up against the personal conflict that only happens in a country with a public school system torn by what Jonathan Kozol calls "savage inequalities." This is one parent who can't drop out of the public argument when he opts out of the public school.

There's more at stake than symbolism.

JANUARY 12, 1993

Family Rush Hour
|||||||||||||||||||||||||||||||||||||||||||||||||||||||||||||||||||||||||||||||||||||||||||||||||||||||||||||||||

The geese are overhead, flying south in V formations as crisp as a sharpened pencil. We watched them from the porch in a Maine light transformed by September clarity. Now we follow their lead, proceeding on our own annual migration.

The path we take also heads south, along parallel highway lines. We pass the exit to Kennebunkport, where George Bush has spent his vacation in the Presidential triathlon: fishing at ten, tennis at eleven, horseshoes at noon. Within an hour of home, the roads become clogged with our own species: back-to-school, back-to-work creatures.

With jars of wild blackberry jam wrapped carefully in T-shirts and towels, we are returning to the real world, although why we call it "real" I cannot tell you. Is reality hard-edged and harried while fantasy is soft and leisurely? Is the real world one of obligations and the fantasy world one of pleasures?

Our migration takes only a few hours, but as we reach the city a familiar feeling comes out of its August hibernation. The rush that comes from being rushed. A lick of anxiety accompanies us through the traffic to the airport, where, in some adult variation of the old car pool, I leave my once-child on her way back to college.

And as I watch her, books, bags, guitar, and all, the familiar watchword of the real world comes back into my mind: hurry. The new year has begun. Hurry.

This is what I associate with September as much as clean notebooks and new shoes. We learn all over again to trade our own rhythms for those of school and work and, in turn, we teach that to our children.

In millions of homes there is the same sudden nagging jump-start to the year. It is the sound of our own voices commanding ourselves and our kids: Stop dawdling.

On the streets today, there are kids with straight parts in their hair and lunch in their Batman boxes. Behind these kids there is a private tutor, at least one parent whose alarm bell precedes the school bell, whose workday begins with the urgent morning job of getting everyone out of the house. Someone who wages a small battle against the sleepy summer tug of leisure, or its evil twin, sloth.

This is what morning is like in America. Not the image of ripe Reaganesque fields and flags, but of pressed parents who may regret the sound of their own impatience sprinkling the breakfast cereal. It is the image of kids collected in buses and cars, delivered to buildings, and redistributed to teachers and classrooms. Americans on schedule, on line, productive.

There is no mystery to why we trade our inner pace for a workaday lockstep. There is no living to be made on the sand. Nor is there any mystery to why we become our children's trainers in this pattern. We are driven for the most part by what Barbara Ehrenreich calls succinctly in her new book title *Fear of Falling*.

Even the middle class in America, or especially the middle class in America, is insecure about its economic future and its children's future. That's more true now in an era when the middle is shrinking and many are slipping down or scrambling up. The fear of falling attaches itself to another anxiety—"a fear of inner weakness," as Ehrenreich observes, "of growing soft, of failing to strive, of losing discipline and will."

We fight these anxieties in ourselves by making a virtue out of necessity: hard work. We fight it in our children by driving out daydreams with discipline. Our own days speed up and we teach, even compel, our children to keep up.

If we are very lucky, we find work we like and schools where our children are happy. But it's only when we step aside for a time, a week or a summer, that the pace becomes daunting, unnatural.

Pretty soon, I know, long before we have emptied the last jar of blackberry jam, it will seem routine again. To the children on my street, the school year that crackles with a fresh start will grow as worn and familiar as a chalkboard eraser. Workaday life will seem as normal as wearing a necktie instead of a T-shirt, heels instead of sneakers.

But today, having just left the ocean for the city, I am most aware of the deliberate, even dutiful way we prepare our children to lead the exact life that we find so rushed. The pressure is on. Hurry, kids.

SEPTEMBER 8, 1989

The Passing of the
Good Provider
||||||||||||||||||||||||||||||||||||||||||||||||||||||||||||||||||||||||||||||||||||||||||||||||||||||||||

One blazing hot afternoon, I was the sole captive audience for a Washington cabdriver as he extolled the vices of his city and the virtues of his second wife. "One thing about my wife," he intoned, "she's a good provider."

This was said with such matter-of-fact appreciation that I couldn't help smiling. I had never heard such a traditionally male expression applied to a female without at least a nod, a wink, a hint of some "Mr. Mom" role reversal about it.

But the more I ran that sentence around in my mind, and the more I repeated the driver's line, the more it occurred to me that I rarely hear that kind of kudos applied to men anymore. "He's a good provider"? Even the sound of such a phrase would be vaguely suspect today, as if there were some understood flaw for which this "providing" compensated. At least . . . he's a good provider. Whatever else . . . he's a good provider.

Today among the ads and cards that carry the images of Father's Day, there is no tie, no tool, no electronic toy that carries praise for the Provider into the public arena. What was once the essence of fatherhood, the moral virtue for which a man was rewarded with the title of head of household, seems somehow out of place in our more egalitarian world.

Father's Day—a salute to the solid souls who brought home the bacon, put food on the table, a roof over your head—now carries a different message. The socially approved images of fatherhood are emotional, not financial. They are about love, not money.

Calvin Klein's model father hugging his young son for "Eternity." Another man Ivory Soaping his baby. Hollywood heroes confessing to Enquiring minds that their newest romance is their offspring. Child-raising books that speak pointedly to men.

The definition of a bad father may be the same as it's been: a man who abandons his children. But the definition of a good father is more layered. It's not that the demands of providing have truly lessened their hold, but they have gone underground. And a new structure has been added.

Ask James Levine, the director of the Fatherhood Project, what fathers want and he will report back from the research front: "First and foremost, they still want to be the provider, the economic and physical protector of their families. That's how men feel at a gut level and it's what women expect. We all buy into it.

"Second of all, they want a different relationship with their children than they had with their own father. Part of being a good father is being different from their own father."

What we've done is up the ante on fathers the way we have upped it on mothers. Added one role on top of the other, a new expectation on top of the old.

Even in the two-paycheck family, caretaking is a given for mothers. The headlines are heaped on fathers who change diapers. Even in the changing American family, earning is a given for fathers. The headlines go to the mothers who debate their "choices."

Our grandparents counted themselves successful if they kept their children clean, housed, fed—provided for. But today parents are less likely to judge themselves by what they do for their children—cooking their dinner, buying their clothes. We count our success as parents by what we do *with* our children. So fathering is less about a role and more about a relationship.

Did our ancestors expect intimacy with their children as they grew up? I don't think so. But we do. Indeed, almost every measurement we openly apply to family life is about feelings.

We judge ourselves today largely by our children's psychological well-being—a much trickier calculation. We grade our families by the closeness of the ties formed and sustained. It's a high-maintenance job that can only be accomplished at home.

So working fathers—no longer a redundant phrase—have learned about conflict. They have learned about the conflict between

being a provider and being a parent. The conflict between supporting a home and being in it.

And except for the neckties, Father's Day is getting to look a
lot like Mother's Day.

JUNE 14, 1991

The Biological Clock

|||||||||||||||||||||||||||||||||||||||||||||||||||||||||||||||||||||||||||||||||||||||||||||||||||||||||||||||

My friend has been home, visiting. She has held informal
reunions with college friends, high school friends, all fortysomething and holding. Holding up, that is.

She spreads out the photos before me. What does the old crowd
look like to someone who's never met them. Do some look older?
Others younger? Could you guess his age? Hers?

What strikes me is not my friend's middle-aging peers, not the
range of grays and the width of waistlines, the various shapes that
people in their forties take. It is the ages of the children that lace
these snapshots of back-yard barbecues and beaches.

The eldest of this pack's offspring is twenty-one, she tells me;
the youngest two months. One friend was dropped off by a daughter
who needed the car, another came with a baby in a backpack. Two
couples at the Kodacolor gathering talked wryly about the costs of
college tuition; two others about the price of child care.

I list my own friends' statistics. Children that range from thirty
to three months. Biorhythms that range from hot flashes to morning
sickness. Has our generation produced, or perhaps re-produced, its
own gap?

Those of us who have arrived at mid-life did not follow neat
patterns. We didn't act like what the demographers call a cohort
group. Indeed, if there is something that typifies this generation

of individualists, it is the instinct to rewrite the rules. And the expectation to be young for longer, if not forever.

While my friend was on vacation, the Census Bureau confirmed what we observe: the trend toward later parenting. Four times as many first-time mothers are over thirty now than were in 1970.

Those who have their first children at thirty-two or thirty-five may have their second at thirty-eight or forty. A gallery of women in the current *New York* magazine fit the category of "Mommie Oldest." In their mid- and late forties they beat the biological clock.

There is no parallel feature on "Daddie Oldest" because it is less of a biological feat. But older dads are far more common.

Bent over the snapshots, my friend and I look for hidden clues to the meaning of this trend. What do we make of the parents and children spread across what used to be three generations?

We know from experience that it was often harder for couples who started children, marriages, and careers in one decade. They and their children had to grow up together. Only now do they look relaxed.

We know that the much-planned, long-desired babies of older parents are often valued as a delicious prize for issues that have been resolved, lives that have matured. Their parents have grown into patience and even wisdom. But we don't know how it will be for these babies later.

For a long time, we have been advocates for later parenting. But now with our own nearly grown children and aging parents we dust off our appreciation for the life cycle.

Families aren't just parents and babies, after all, but relationships extended over time. What will happen to this mini-generation of older parents when they face retirement and college tuitions at the same time? Will the financial crunch facing young families find a new reflection in the older model?

What about the dynamics of a sixty-year-old father and an adolescent son? Will rebellion be muted by greater understanding? Or repressed by fear of a parent's age?

The forty-five-year-old parent is hardly a social problem on the scale of, say, the thirty-year-old grandmother. But there is an odd mirror here too. Will the children of older parents have to grow up faster, mature faster to care for parents earlier?

I know how much mid-life Americans pride themselves on staying younger. We run and diet and monitor ourselves into health. We expect to be physically fit. The postponing generation has done everything later and surely, in fairness, should live healthier and longer. But it doesn't always work that way.

Any way you do the numbers, having children later means having fewer years together. And it means fewer children who have grandparents in their lives.

Surely, there is no perfect moment to have children. Every child is subject to and a product of the parents' fate. For the most part, people have children late because that is finally the "right" time in their lives.

But perhaps we increasingly define the right time not just for ourselves but for our jobs or finances or mortgages. We keep one eye on the big sweeping hand of the biological clock that dictates how long we can have babies. But it may limit our view of our life as parents and children together over time.

Looking at these snapshots, my friend and I know pretty much the essential story of young families, their strengths and weaknesses. Now, as more of us come to mid-life reunions with babies in our backpacks, we wonder what the pictures will look like through the next and longer lens.

JULY 21, 1989

Cosby in Charge

||||||||||||||||||||||||||||||||||||||||||||||||||||||||||||||||||||||||||||||||||||||||||||||||||||||||||||||||

At the very end, Cliff and Clair Huxtable waltzed out of their living room, off the set, past the studio audience, and on to that place where all good shows go when they die. The Afterlife of Television Reruns.

The grand finale, the much-ballyhooed last episode of *The Cosby Show*, was bathed in the warm waters of premature nostalgia. It was soft around the edges, comfortable as an old sweater, just what the doctor—Dr. Huxtable—ordered for his loyal audience.

One rite of passage was tied to another. Theo Huxtable was graduating from college. Cliff Huxtable, graying and predictable as middle-aged spread, had seen another child over the thorny divide of adolescence and fully launched.

Mission accomplished. Parental mission accomplished. And, of course, by implication, television mission accomplished.

In some ways, there was always a parallel in the two worlds that Bill Cosby created. Patriarch of the Huxtable household, he was also progenitor of the television enterprise. As both actor and producer, Cosby held to his own standards and ideas.

So this week, those who pay attention to media history may talk about how Bill Cosby saved the sitcom. Those who write about social history may critique the show's role as well in the evolution of racial images.

For many years, the one family that seemed to represent Every-family was also black. The father who became the idealized Every-father was also African-American.

He is praised by many for breaking through a clutter of negative black stereotypes. He's condemned by others for producing a falsely positive picture of rich, professional black Americans. He's lauded for presenting blacks "just like whites." And criticized for the same thing.

But those of us who are neither critics nor historians but mothers and fathers of the *Cosby* era remain most conscious of the other stereotype shattered by this show. Bill Cosby deliberately staged a counterculture revolution against the clueless parent, the feckless father, the out-of-it adult and the in-charge, knowing, smart-if-not-smartass child.

Cosby arrived in 1984, just as the two-working-parent family became the norm. He set up shop just as the baby-boom generation was raising its boomlet. Parents were no longer the Establishment. They were us. And a querulous "us" at that.

As Jay Rosen of New York University put it, "Cosby didn't conform to the absent father image or to the pleading, negotiating, New Age father. In the earlier shows, adults were shown confounded by the child culture. But Cosby knew enough to get the better of the child."

On this show, as Bill Cosby put it himself, "the adults won." They got the better of the children, but for the good of the children.

The messages that spoke to a new generation of parents and children watching this show together were clear. Parents could wield authority without being authoritarian. They could pass on values without laying on trips. They could raise kids without losing their sense of humor or self-confidence.

In the afterlife of reruns, some future audience may imagine that the Huxtables were a typical American family. That's no more true for our time than the Father who Knew Best was for the 1950s.

The Huxtables were a television two-career couple—a doctor and a lawyer—who always seemed to have enough time for their children. Work formed a backdrop for their lives and their bank accounts, but it rarely interfered with their family life. Most of us squeeze family time more tightly than a twenty-two-minute sitcom in a twenty-four-hour day.

Today, at the end of eight years with the Huxtables, it is confidence that seems the most reassuring and strong Cosby trait. It's a confidence that often feels elusive to parents who raise children with more stress and less certainty in real life than on television. But it was comforting nonetheless.

Cosby put an image on the home screen of the families we miss, the parents we admire, and the home life to which we still aspire. It isn't just a coincidence that as the Huxtables go dancing off the family set, a lot of other parents are trying to learn their steps.

MAY 1, 1992

Oh, the Questions
Kids Ask

||||||||||||||||||||||||||||||||||||||||||||||||||||||||||||||||||||||||||||||||||||||||||||||||

San Francisco — At last some good news about the environment. North of here, deep in redwood country, one small woodsy creature has just been saved from the brink of extinction.

The endangered species in question is the Lorax, a stumpy, mustachioed, and furry fellow who sprang from the imagination of Dr. Seuss. For eighteen years, this critter has offered a conservation message to the same children who devour green eggs and ham.

As the central character of an environmental morality tale, the Lorax's role was to speak for the Truffula trees because "the trees have no tongues." Over and over again the Lorax has waged a losing battle against the Once-ler family, who turn every last Truffula tree into sweaterlike Thneeds and flatten the environment into a wasteland.

But this fall *The Lorax* itself, with its zany rhymes and conservation message, felt the sharp edge of the axe. In Laytonville, a small lumbering community, the second-graders who read this tale in class came home bearing questions.

One, an eight-year-old son of a wealthy family that sells logging equipment, said to his mother, "Papa doesn't love trees anymore, does he?" And with that his parents and others tried to evict *The Lorax* from the required reading list.

After a contentious few weeks during which everyone in the district came to know about Truffula tufts and Super-Axe-Hackers, the local school board voted to table the fate of *The Lorax*. They will "review" the entire school reading list.

So for the moment *The Lorax* has survived. But other familiar issues were raised. How much easier it is to take a moral stand in somebody else's back yard with somebody else's paycheck. How hard it is to be morally challenged by your own children.

The loggers of Laytonville are hardly the first to experience this challenge to values and behavior. At one time or another, most of our children come home from school with questions and return from the wider world with a sharp eye for contradictions.

The children fresh from the just-say-no class ask about our martinis and pills. The children who read the labels on the cigarettes ask why we smoke. In one town, those who learn what nuclear weapons do ask why their parents build them. In another place, those who learn about injustice ask why their parents tolerate it.

When these questions are first heard from kids who once thought we knew all, the immediate impulse is to say what the Once-ler said to the Lorax: Shut up. It's an urge to cut off the source of criticism, rather than to answer the endless and uneasy questions: Why don't we take the homeless into our houses? Why are some poor and others rich?

Adults are not used to moral confrontation in their daily lives. The rich and powerful may even be exempt from such challenges. Except by their children.

As Dr. Robert Coles, who has spent a lifetime learning about the moral life of children, observes, "Moral discussion is usually kept abstract to protect us. It's only when it gets concrete, when it starts hitting close to home and close to the pocketbook, that it pricks us."

It's easier to talk about the rain forest in Brazil than the pollution coming out of the plant we work in or the pesticides we spray on our crops. But children remind us of the holes in our rationalizations. They often remind us of the uneasy compromises we have made to work and live with ease.

In their own fresh encounters with right and wrong, they prod us into feeling that we should do something . . . about smoking or injustice or the environment. Their questions force us to explain and expose our own, often muddy reasoning.

The irony in the Laytonville controversy was that *The Lorax* did not say lumbering was itself immoral. Indeed, the author in his real life as Theodor Geisel lives in a wooden house and writes books made of paper. His treatise was about greed and waste. The response was a raised axe.

But when parents react to a child's prodding with alarm, it isn't just because the questions are troublesome. It's because we cannot form an answer that rings right in our own ears.

OCTOBER 17, 1989

The Family Legacy

||||||||||||||||||||||||||||||||||||||||||||||||||||||||||||||||||||||||||||||||||||||||||||||||||||||||

It is my turn now: My aunt, the keeper of Thanksgiving, has passed the baton, or should I say the drumstick? She has declared this a permanent legacy.

Soon, according to plan, my grandmother's dishes will be de-livered by cousin-courier to my dining room. So will the extra chairs and the communal chafing dishes. The tradition will also be transplanted.

But this morning, she has come over to personally deliver a piece of this inheritance. She is making stuffing with me.

In one hand, she carries the family Thanksgiving "bible," a small blue book that bears witness to the recipes and shopping lists and seating plans of decades past. In the other hand, she carries three loaves of bread, a bag of onions, and the appropriate spices.

It must be said that my aunt does not quite trust me to do this stuffing the right way, which is, of course, her way, and her mother's way. She doesn't quite trust my spices or my Cuisinart or my tendency to cut corners. So, like a tribal elder, she has come to instruct me, hands on, to oversee my Pilgrim's progress every step of the way.

Together we peel the onions and chop them. Not quite fine enough for her. I chop some more. Together we pull the bread apart and soak it and squeeze it. Not quite dry enough for her. I squeeze again.

Gradually I, the middle-aged mother of an adult child standing in the kitchen of the home I make mortgage payments on, feel myself again a child. Only this time I find amusement in taking such exacting instructions from my elder. More than amusement. I find comfort in still being somebody's young.

But sautéing the onions until they are perfectly brown (my aunt doesn't like white onions in the stuffing), I start divining a subtext to this recipe sharing. It says: Time is passing. Generations pass. One day I will be the elder.

"I don't think I like this whole thing," I say aloud, sounding like the child I am now. My aunt, who is about to be threescore years and ten, stops stirring the pan for a moment and looks at me. She understands. And for a while it isn't just the fumes of onions that come into our eyes.

The moment passes; I go back to mixing, and my aunt goes back to her favorite activity: bustling. But I no longer feel quite so much the child.

Adulthood arrives in these small sudden exchanges more than in well-heralded major crises. And the final moment of assuming adulthood may be when we inherit the legacy, become the keeper of traditions, the curator of our family's past and future memories. When the holidays are at our houses. The reunions at our instigation. When the traditions are carried on, or cast aside, because of choices that we make.

When we were small, my sister and I used to giggle at assorted holiday tables ruled over by our elders. We would at times squirm under the rule of imposed traditions and best behaviors. A certain prayer, an unfamiliar dish, an eccentric relative could send us to the bathroom laughing.

In time, when we were teenagers and then young parents, we were occasionally rebellious conformists, critical participants at family celebrations. We maintained a slight distance of humorous affection for the habits that the older generation carried on.

We were the ones who would point out that no one really liked mincemeat, that the string beans were hopelessly mushy, the onion-ring topping simply passé, that there was altogether too much chicken fat in the stuffing. It was easy to rebel against the things we could count on others maintaining.

Now I see this from another vantage point, that of almost-elder. I see that tradition is not just handed down but taken up. It's a conscious decision, a legacy that can be accepted or refused. Only once it's refused, it disappears.

How fragile is this sinew of generations. How tenuous the ceremonial ties that hold families together over time and generations, while they change as imperceptibly and inevitably as cells change in a single human body.

So it is my turn to accept the bequest, the dishes, the bridge chairs, the recipe book. This year there will be no string beans. Nor will there be ginger snaps in the gravy, forgive me. But the turkey will come with my grandmother's stuffing, my aunt's blessing, and my own novice's promise.

NOVEMBER 23, 1989

LIVING AND DYING
IN THE HIGH-TECH AGE

||||||||||||||||||||||||||||||||||||||||||||||||||||||||||||||||||||||||||||||||||||||||||||||||||||||||||

|||||| *One infertility counselor who
heard about this "breakthrough"
asked out loud, "When do you say,
enough is enough?" The female body
once said it for us. Now women, like
men, will have to use less predictable
organs: the heart and the brain.*

The Woman and the Womb Mate

||||||||||||||||||||||||||||||||||||||||||||||||||||||||||||||||||||||||||||||||||||||||||||||||||||||||||||||||||||||||||||

The court has declared that she is not his mother, though he grew in her womb, though he came into the world down her birth canal, though her breasts filled with milk for him. Anna Johnson is now officially, legally, unrelated to the boy she bore.

A judge in California has ruled that Anna was just a prenatal "foster parent" to Mark and Crispina Calvert's fetus. She nurtured it, fed it, housed it—but it always belonged to them. The womb was merely rented: When her work was done, the boy-product belonged to his genetic owners.

This is what it has come to, our technological "advances" in reproduction. Dictionaries and precedents and nature are turned upside down. Giving birth to a child is no longer proof that you are its mother.

In baby steps, from Baby Louise to Baby M, from test-tube conceptions to surrogate mothers, we have arrived now at Baby Christoper Michael Calvert—created in a petri dish, implanted in a "surrogate," and awarded to the people who contributed their DNA and RNA.

I have followed this story ever since a pregnant Anna Johnson first claimed her womb mate as her own. I have watched as the court tried to answer the question: Whose child is this?

By and large, I side with the Calverts. They willed the existence of this baby. They conceived it. They chose Anna Johnson to be their surrogate. The single mother of a three-year-old had made this deal.

Johnson's sense of abandonment by the Calverts and her growing attachment to the fetus and then the boy were tragic proof that human nature is more complex than a contract. But to have given her custody of the boy would have been akin to allowing zygote-napping, a theft of the Calverts' genes.

As for the effects of shared custody on the child, I also agree with the judge. As he said, "I think a three-parent, two-natural-mom claim in a situation is ripe for crazy-making."

But the questions that arise out of the business of surrogacy are themselves ripe for crazy-making. The case of the Calverts' "miracle baby" has, if anything, strengthened the entire case against payment-for-pregnancy.

This was not, after all, only a tale about the importance we place on genes. It was a tale about the importance of commerce.

Surrogacy for strangers is a business. However much is said about altruism, well-to-do women are rarely moved to sell their bodies.

The Calverts were not wealthy when Crispina met Anna as hospital workers. But they had $10,000 to offer and Johnson had what they wanted: a womb. With the exchange of money, the Calverts became the employer, Johnson became their worker, and baby production their enterprise.

But society can ask whether such a private agreement should be allowed. We can ask whether pregnancy is just another service industry. Is the uterus a spare room available to any boarder for a price? Is the child another product we can buy?

In two or three more baby steps of change, I can imagine what some ethicists fear: a breeder class of women for couples who can't bear their own. Here at last is a job you can do in your spare time at home with little training.

It is fair to ask about the moral limits of commerce. If we let a woman rent her uterus, then perhaps she can lease any subsidiary rights that might adversely affect that fetus. The right to eat what she wants, go where she wants, even to choose her own medical care.

The judge said that Anna Johnson made a "substantial contri-bution" to the existence of Christopher Michael. Anyone who has been pregnant could list that "contribution" in varicose veins, sleep-less nights, the great lumbering takeover of one body by another. In the labor that is indeed labor.

Those who say that women are free and intelligent enough to decide for themselves if they want to "sell" this "contribution" have little understanding of the economic constraints on freedom. This is why we impose limits on our medical commerce. We cannot sell a kidney. We should not be able to sell a pregnancy.

There is no way to stop a genuinely altruistic act of surrogate motherhood. But there is a way to end pregnancy as a commercial activity. Make payment illegal. Make the contracts illegal. Take surrogacy off the sale rack.

Until we do that, we are guided by the laws of the marketplace. Let the buyer and the seller beware.

OCTOBER 26, 1990

Discovering Designer Genes

So another pair of genes has been discovered in our biological closet. It happens regularly these days. A group of scientists go mucking about in the private corner of our DNA and come out with something new.

This time, Boston researchers have uncovered a mutant gene. The mutant P53 can produce cancers that "run in families" like a train crashing over the generational track.

In one of the eighty families they studied with the rare Li-Fraumani syndrome, seven of thirteen members had cancer at a young age. Many relatives had experienced so much of the disease that it was considered a family curse. Indeed, people in families who carry this defect have a 50 percent chance of cancer by age thirty—and now they can know the odds at birth.

The study reported in *Science* magazine may be the first such documented genetic cancer link, but it's not the last. Nor is this cancer link the most devastating of the genetic discoveries.

We already know the genes for Huntington's chorea and sickle-cell anemia, for cystic fibrosis and muscular dystrophy. We are learning what makes some susceptible to aneurysms and may learn what makes others prone to alcoholism.

The Human Genome Project, set up to map chromosomes over an internal human space as vast as any universe, will seek out some 100,000 genes stretched out over the DNA. But there will be a "lag" between the knowledge and the cures. We are discovering diseases faster than we can fix them.

What will happen as scientists learn what "runs in families"? Those families will have to decide what they want to know, and what they want others to know. As we learn about genetic susceptibilities, we will all have to think about the nature of risk. And as we delve into DNA, we will have to reconcile the idea of equality with the facts of biological inequality.

Genetics is going to change the nature of our health-conscious society. Today, after all, we prefer to pin illness on human behavior. We talk of risk *behaviors* and risk *factors*. It's comforting to look for the smoker in the heart-attack victim, to search for the fat in the diet of the deceased.

Our second most popular culprit for illness is the environment. We are obsessed with risks that range from asbestos to Alar, from dioxin to Equal.

But these risks are the ones we share. We are all presumably in danger from the environment; we're all able to alter our behavior. If you are what you eat, after all, you can change your diet.

What happens as we discover that some of us are more susceptible from birth than others? Some at greater risk, biologically, to certain diseases and certain environments, even work environments? What happens when we add genetic risk to the list?

When doctors take a family history, that history isn't always assumed to be destiny. But when family membership itself becomes a factor, will this create another social division?

Today, it often seems that race, religion, ethnicity, and gender compete with the ideology of the melting pot. In many ways, talk of diversity is challenging the traditional language of equality.

Could biology exaggerate this? Could it create another class—

a biological underclass, uninsurable, unemployable. The Joneses have a mutant P53. Nice people, but you wouldn't want your daughter to marry one.

If this sounds like a dark outpouring of science anxiety, let me lighten it. The genie and the gene are out of the bottle. The possibilities of the research are stunning. Moreover, this time scientists are studying ethics along with genetics. For once, they aren't leaving social concerns to a mop-up crew.

But as Eric Juengst, a director-philosopher with the Human Genome Project, recognizes, "The challenge is how to protect our commitment to social and moral equality in face of the fact that we are biologically diverse and, against some parameters, unequal."

Americans have long wrestled with differences and democracy. On the one hand, people have uneven abilities; on the other hand, we are all equals.

Now we are facing a biological variation on that theme. In a country based on the notion that all people are created equal, scientists are uncovering our designer genes. They are not always a comfortable fit.

DECEMBER 11, 1990

The Father of
Them All

||||||||||||||||||||||||||||||||||||||||||||||||||||||||||||||||||||||||||||||||||||||||||||||||||||||

About a dozen years ago, a California entrepreneur went into the business of producing or, rather, reproducing whiz kids. He opened a sperm bank for Nobel Prize winners in the hope of propagating a generation of geniuses.

He called it the Repository for Germinal Choice and I called it a phallic symbol . . . without the symbolism. The only thing higher than the IQs of the donors was their EQs, ego quotients. They went right off the chart.

In retrospect, however, they were modest men. Now we have the more bizarre story of Dr. Cecil Jacobson, an infertility specialist in Alexandria, Virginia. He operated a "sperm bank" that favored one donor: Dr. Jacobson.

The doctor was accused of two sorts of fraud. Misleading a number of women into believing that they were pregnant when they weren't and that their bodies mysteriously and sometimes repeatedly "reabsorbed" the dead fetus. Misleading patients who were promised an anonymous semen donor.

The first set of charges draw a portrait of extraordinary cruelty, a doctor who added a vicious cycle of hope and grief to the emotional roller coaster of infertility. The second set of charges surrounding his "success stories" is even stranger.

When Dr. Jacobson allegedly told one patient, "God doesn't give you babies—I do," he wasn't bragging about his medical skills. Nor was he being paternalistic. He was being paternal, literally. Genetic testing introduced at the trial proved that at least fifteen of the babies conceived under his care bear his genetic imprint. There may be sixty others who could also call Cecil "Dad."

The story of Papa Doc is riveting not only because Jacobson had a distinguished reputation. Not only because he violated assumptions of trust when he turned a doctor-patient relationship into that of sperm donor and recipient, or father and mother. The case raises uneasy and rarely asked questions about donor insemination itself—the oldest, most widespread, and least debated of the "treatments" for infertility.

During the trial, Dr. Jacobson admitted to the use of his own sperm in "isolated circumstances." He tried to explain away this surreal behavior as sound medical practice. His sperm was fresh, healthy, and disease-free. He turned his own seed into nothing more than a good clinical specimen. Give that science a cigar. His testimony separated sperm from sex or fatherhood, distancing genes from relationships.

Had his patients known what was happening between the time the doctor left the examining room and his return with a vial of sperm, I suspect they would have leapt off the table. At least one woman who testified in court was unnerved at how much her newborn daughter "looks just like him."

But what the women and their husbands also wanted was an anonymous infusion of genes. They too wanted the sperm without the man, the donor without the father. Which goes to the essence of donor insemination.

In the last dozen years there have been great ethical debates about dividing motherhood into the sum of its parts. Egg donor, gestational mother, surrogate mother, birth mother, adoptive mother. We've had heated debates about whether women should donate their eggs or rent their wombs. We've read articles by birth mothers and by the children who have sought them out.

But very little has been said about the scientific parsing of fatherhood, about the far larger population of sperm donors, or the 138 sperm banks, or the 30,000 babies conceived by donor insemination every year. The majority of families don't tell the children about this heritage. The country hasn't debated the ethics of paying for sperm. The donors don't join support groups for birth fathers. It is rare indeed that donors check on the family of their prospective child. We treat sperm donors like blood donors.

Papa Doc was, to put it mildly, a special case. It's hard to know what was in the mind of a medical "baby maker," a father of seven children in his marriage, when proffered another brood. But the clamor over this case comes in part from a change in attitudes toward fathers. We are, finally, uneasy about any disconnection between men, sperm, and fatherhood. We are trying to strengthen the lines between male sexuality and responsibility, fathers and children.

Dr. Jacobson gave his infertility business the, uh, personal touch. Now the rest of us are in for a round of second thoughts on sperm donation. It fits the times. After all, today fatherhood is something you do, not something you donate.

MARCH 3, 1992

Baby Girl Genes

|||||||||||||||||||||||||||||||||||||||||||||||||||||||||||||||||||||||||||||||||||||||||||||||||||||||||||||||

The woman beside me pats her rounded stomach and rolls her eyes to the ceiling, exclaiming, "Is she ever active today!" The "she" in this action won't be born until March. But my pregnant companion already knows the gender of this gestation.

I have grown accustomed to the attachment of a pronoun to a fetus by now. Most of the women I know of her age and anxiety level have had "the test" and gotten the results.

Over the past two decades, through amniocentesis and then CVS and sonograms, a generation of parents has received a prenatal exam, a genetic checkup on their offspring. They have all been given new information and sometimes new, unhappy choices.

But the "she" playing soccer in the neighboring uterus is a healthy baby. And the woman is more than pleased with both of those pieces of knowledge.

What if she were not? What if she and her husband had regarded the sex of this child as a devastating disappointment?

I wonder about this because, in the news, doctors report success on the road to developing a simple blood test on pregnant women to determine the sex of the fetus. The geneticists are excited because such a test could allow safer, widespread testing. It could help those worried about gender-linked inherited diseases.

But this test may increase the possibility of abortion for sex selection by those who regard gender itself—the wrong gender—as a genetic flaw.

The repugnance to abortion-by-gender runs deep in our culture. Both pro-choice supporters who believe that abortion is a serious decision and pro-life supporters who believe it is an immoral decision unite in opposing sex selection as the most frivolous or sexist of motives.

It is the rare person who defends it on the grounds of population control or pure parental choice. It is a rarer American who chooses it. Indeed, the only countries in which sex selection occurs in discernible numbers have been those such as India or Korea where daughters have long been unwanted. It is almost always female fetuses that are aborted.

But gender testing and the capacity for gender choosing—before and after conception—is an ethical issue in this country too. This is the first but hardly the last time that the new technology will be available to produce designer babies.

Today, genetic testing is valued in America because it leads to the diagnosis of diseases that cause pain and death and disability. Eventually it may lead to their cure. But in the future, we also are likely to have access to much more information about genes than we need medically. We may be able to identify the gene for height, hair color, eye color, perhaps even athletic ability or intelligence.

There will always be parents who, out of ego, or some perverse view of children as a perfect product, want to pick and choose genes according to a master plan. Should society encourage or allow that? Must doctors perform tests and turn over information to patients to do with as they will?

John Fletcher, an ethicist at the University of Virginia, suggests a line to be drawn around our right to know. "Any kind of genetic knowledge that isn't related to a genuine disease," he says, "is on the other side of the line."

Since gender, like hair color, is not a disease, he believes that the medical profession can refuse testing and disclosing for two reasons. To prevent abortion-by-gender and, in a wider moral context, to keep genetic research on the right track.

Americans haven't yet learned how to say "no" to knowledge. Doctors may feel uncomfortable, even paternalistic, withholding information from people about their own bodies, genes, fetuses. The state of Pennsylvania has banned abortion for sex selection in the bill that goes into effect this month. Such a ban is not only impossible to enforce, but says nothing about the future dilemmas of reproductive knowledge.

At the moment the moral consensus against sex selection is holding. The medical profession should at least state, in public and in unity, a strong position against gender selection and a moral prohibition against genetic eugenics.

But in the longer run, the rest of us may be called upon to ask whether our curiosity about gender is worth the risk that others will misuse that information. It may be wiser to learn if it's a "he" or a "she" the old-fashioned way.

JANUARY 5, 1990

Beating the
Biological Clock

||||||||||||||||||||||||||||||||||||||||||||||||||||||||||||||||||||||||||||||||||||||||||||||

Not long ago, after a midnight session with a male friend who was considering fatherhood at fifty, I decided that middle-aged men suffer from a distinct biological disadvantage. They don't go through menopause.

This was a fairly quirky, contrary point of view. My friend did not long for the growth experience of hot flashes. It is more often women who resent the biological clock ticking loudly over their leisurely plans.

If anything, the female fertility deadline seems positively un-American, unfair. We are, after all, citizens of a country that believes in endless choices and unlimited options. Moreover, this biological destiny seems like a remnant of inequality: If men can have babies in their seventies, why not women?

Still, it seemed to me that the biological clock was a useful warning system about the life cycle. It was a way of saying that life changes and time runs out.

The female advantage was a built-in reminder that options have to be exercised and choices have to be made. And if women focus more on the press of time and are less surprised by aging, maybe it's because of the ticking sound in their ears.

Now it appears that the biological alarm has been turned down. We are reading headlines that would have confounded our grandmothers: "Menopause Found No Barrier to Pregnancy." Doctors have discovered a way to beat the clock. Post-menopausal women can become pregnant.

If this were just another entry in reproduction technologies, it would be unsettling enough. In the same month, we heard from California of a surrogate hired to carry the genetic offspring of another couple.

Now we learn that women can become, in essence, surrogate mothers for the children they want to raise. Seven women in or past menopause became pregnant with eggs donated by younger women and fertilized with their husband's sperm. More are on the way.

The emotional offshoot of this technology is complicated enough. Essentially, a pregnant woman can now carry a child conceived by her husband and another woman. How would that feel over time? How much pressure will an infertile woman feel to produce her husband's child instead of adopting? And in case of divorce, would the genetic parent have first psychological and legal claim?

Such queasy ethical questions trail behind each man-made variation on nature's theme. But this time the news is on the breaking of the age barrier.

I don't think pregnancy will become a popular retirement activity. I don't think it will be something for women to do in their sunset years when, at last, they have time.

Those most affected by this new option will be infertile couples, those who came to marriage late or menopause early, or have exhausted other biological possibilities. For these people, each new "miracle baby" produces another crop of questions: How far can they stretch their will and their wallet? How much of life should be focused on reproducing life?

The promise is that women can keep their biological door open, at least with the help of a stranger. The problem is that it also prevents closure. It changes the way we think about life.

Among the seven who got pregnant was a woman who had undergone a range of fertility treatments for an entire decade. Moreover, when this pregnancy ended in tragedy—a stillbirth—she decided to try again.

When you remove nature from the equation, there is a whole new set of calculations to be made. They bear, not surprisingly, a strong resemblance to the ones that men have faced.

A forty-five-year-old woman has, on the one hand, a thirty-five-year life expectancy, more than a younger mother had a hundred years ago. A new mother at fifty may be healthier than her predecessor a generation ago.

But a menopausal mother becomes a senior citizen with teenagers and a Social Security recipient paying college tuition. She may become dependent on her children just as they become independent. The issues become energy, and age gaps, and the real midnight on the biological clock: mortality.

One infertility counselor who heard about this "breakthrough" asked out loud, "When do you say, enough is enough?" The female body once said it for us. Now women, like men, will have to use much less predictable organs: the heart and the brain.

NOVEMBER 6, 1990

Nancy Cruzan's Right to Die I

||||||||||||||||||||||||||||||||||||||||||||||||||||||||||||||||||||||||||||||||||||||||||||||||||||||||||||||

On the morning Joyce and Joe Cruzan came to the Supreme Court to ask permission to bury their daughter, the obituary page in my newspaper suddenly took on a very different dimension.

Most of the people in those columns had died of "causes"—heart disease, cancer, pneumonia. More than a few died of a "long disease" or a "brief illness." But it occurred to me that morning that nobody had listed that other common cause of death: a human decision.

The obit page gave no hint of the dramatic choices made by their families. There was no sense of the urgency, the pain, and the uncertainty involved in the choices to prolong living or prolong dying. It was as if these people had died quietly in their own beds surrounded by their own people.

That is, of course, not what happens. Every year, two million Americans die, 85 percent of them in an institution. Of those deaths, 80 percent involve a decision by someone to do or not to do something.

The "something" may not be as dramatic as turning off a respirator or taking out a feeding tube. It may be the decision not to resuscitate a parent with Alzheimer's. It may be the decision to say no to another operation or medication when that cancer will soon be listed as the cause of death. But it is nevertheless a human decision.

The Cruzans went to court just to get the right to make this decision. They had to sue for the grimmest of victories, a merciful end to their daughter's imprisonment in a permanently unconscious state of life. But their unhappy journey through the legal system has sent a message to the rest of us.

This case came to the Supreme Court because Nancy Cruzan had never documented her own wishes. Nancy's father believes deeply that if his daughter woke up for just one moment, she would be appalled at her fate. But Nancy was twenty-five and had only left a comment to a friend that she wouldn't want to be a "vegetable."

The reason the fate of her bloated body, permanently fixed in a fetal position, arrived at the doorstep of the Supreme Court is that the state court didn't accept the evidence of her intent. They maintain that the question was unresolved: How would she want to live? And, therefore, who would decide?

An irony in this case is that the two opposing sides have one thing in common. Both Joe Cruzan, the father, and William Webster, the ambitious pro-life attorney general of Missouri who is fighting Cruzan, have living wills. They will each get to decide.

As for the rest of us? Somewhere between 10 and 15 percent of Americans have signed a living will, a declaration about their own wishes. In its most generic form, the living will available through the Society for the Right to Die states simply this:

"If I should be in an incurable or irreversible mental or physical condition with no reasonable expectation of recovery, I direct my attending physician to withhold or withdraw treatment that merely prolongs my dying. I further direct that treatment be limited to measures to keep me comfortable and to relieve pain." Anyone can write such a statement, sign it, and have it witnessed.

There are forty state statutes governing living wills. Such a document doesn't, indeed can't, cover all the questions of medical treatment that arise in a crisis. A more comprehensive will was published last June in the AMA's *Journal*. Most forms suggest that we also designate someone to act in our behalf and that we be as specific as possible about our attitudes and desires.

Despite limits, a living will can help prevent the living death that we have seen in the bedside horror stories of Karen Ann Quinlan and Nancy Cruzan. And it can help families.

Days before the Cruzans came to court, I took part in a class discussion on this issue. There I was struck by the fact that half of the students, though only in their twenties, already had some first-hand experience. They could replay, in great detail, the moral struggles of their families to do the right thing, to do what a parent, grandparent, aunt, or uncle would have wanted.

It left me wondering how many of the survivors carried a measure of uncertainty and guilt. It left me believing that they deserved guidelines along with the responsibilities for another's life and death.

By spring, the Supreme Court will have determined the fate of Nancy Cruzan. But for the rest of us, the American way of death-by-decision now demands decisions by the living.

DECEMBER 12, 1989

Nancy   Cruzan's   Right
to   Die   II
|||||||||||||||||||||||||||||||||||||||||||||||||||||||||||||||||||||||||||||||||||||||||||||||||||||||||||||||||||||||||||||

Death did not come gently to Nancy Cruzan.

It took almost eight years from the car accident that left her unconscious to the death certificate. It took almost three years from the time her parents asked to end treatment to the time a Missouri court agreed. It took twelve days from the moment the feeding tube was removed to the moment she stopped breathing.

The last week in the life of the young woman whose body was locked in a fetal position and whose mind was permanently obliterated was not easy either. Pickets appeared on the hospital lawn. Protesters forced their way onto her floor. Reporters stood death watch, sending out updates on the deteriorating condition.

Joe and Joyce Cruzan, for their part, spent days in their daughter's room and nights in the mobile home set up on the hospital lawn. But in the end they wrested from the state and from modern medicine the terrible right to bury their child.

Her death did not come gently to any of the Cruzans.

I will spare the family any message about the larger good in their loss. They have been through enough. I can only imagine how this ordeal prolonged and distorted their mourning. There is no upbeat, sunny side for the family.

But for those of us who knew not Nancy Cruzan but the inanimate Cruzan case, there is an extraordinary legacy. The Cruzan case, like that of Karen Ann Quinlan, became a story that made America talk publicly and at length about death in the technological age.

In the press, the case was often cast as the right to die versus the right to life. In the courtroom, especially the Supreme Court, it was about the right of families versus the right of the state.

But in the everyday language of Americans talking to each other, Nancy Cruzan's terrible fate made spouses as well as lawyers, friends as well as legislators, talk about the quality of life and the quality of mercy. We were forced to confront the paradox that the same technology that can save us can also doom us to what Nancy's own doctor called "a living hell."

As Daniel Callahan, the director of the Hastings Center, said in a sort of eulogy, "There is the balance of Greek tragedy here. We want the very advances that have given us this problem."

For much of human history, the medicine man or woman was also the caretaker. Medical mercy meant helping people, and helping people often meant helping them to die peacefully.

But in our lifetime, medicine improved in its ability to save life and doctors redefined kindness as a cure. Death became a technological failure. As Callahan says, "The National Heart and Lung Institute is not set up to allow us to die more peaceably from heart disease but to cure it."

Our gratitude to science, our own passionate pursuit of medical salvation, now comes with increasing unease about this same technology. We fear that there may be too much of a good thing. That we can't stop it.

This is what Nancy Cruzan came to represent as she lay twisted, bloated, unconscious, in her hospital bed. As people came to feed her what the hospital ludicrously called "supper." As the doctors described her condition as a "persistent vegetative state." As others argued—is this better?—that they had seen tears in her eyes.

She came to represent the unintended consequences of technology, the side effects of our best intentions, the cruelty of our modern medical mercy. She came to represent something worse than death.

In time, people may wonder why Americans spent so much time arguing about sustaining one unconscious woman while so many others in our society died for lack of medical care. They may wonder how, on the brink of deliberate killing of thousands—in war—we paid so much attention to the quality of one life.

But every family that has been prompted to talk aloud about life and death, every hospital that has been forced to think about aggressive treatment, every medical school that has been prodded to teach young doctors about dying, has a piece of Nancy Cruzan's legacy.

May she, at long last, rest in peace.

JANUARY 1, 1991

Dr. Death's Suicide Machine

||||||||||||||||||||||||||||||||||||||||||||||||||||||||||||||||||||||||||||||||||||||||||||||||||||||||||

On June 4, Janet Adkins, a woman in fear of losing her mind to Alzheimer's disease, traveled to Michigan for a back-alley suicide. The doctor that she found to expedite her wish was Jack Kevorkian, an M.D. and a maverick, that word we use to describe both crusaders and loose cannons.

Dr. Kevorkian drove his vehicle, his suicide-mobile, his welcome-to-death wagon, to a park in Oakland County, north of Detroit. There, in the back of a van, the doctor hooked up his patient to a machine. After saying thank you, we are told, Janet Adkins, fifty-four, lover of music and mountain climbing, pushed a button that released a lethal drug into her body.

In the days since that fateful, fatal encounter, Mrs. Adkins has been eulogized by her minister as "a pioneer in the battle for death with dignity." Dr. Kevorkian has been both lionized and vilified as he makes his way through the headlines and the talk shows, daring the authorities to turn the maverick into a martyr: "If it's legal, let me do it. If it's illegal, stop me."

And in these same days, questions of life and death—what kind of life? what kind of death?—have been raised in the public consciousness with a new scenario attached to them.

In some ways, Dr. Kevorkian is too easy a target for this discussion. With a ghoulish passion, the retired pathologist and self-described "obitiatrist," or death doctor, has advocated everything from experimentation on death-row inmates to a chain of nonprofit suicide clinics. "My motto is," he says, "a rational policy of planned death."

From all accounts, Dr. Kevorkian was in no position to judge Mrs. Adkins's illness, the extent of her depression, to offer counseling or alternatives. It is impossible to justify the role played by a stranger/physician—one eager for a test case—in providing the weapon for suicide. But in some ways, the attention to Dr. Kevorkian's personality begs the central questions about life and death and medicine.

I believe that there is such a thing as rational suicide. If a person is old enough or ill enough. The hard part is defining "enough." When Dr. Bruno Bettelheim ended his life some weeks ago, it seemed to me that he deserved moral permission for his act. The stories about Janet Adkins are less clear.

Alzheimer's, diagnosed a year ago, had robbed her of her music and pockets of her memory. By some standards she wasn't far gone enough to give up on life. But it's fair to suggest that it wasn't just her sense of loss but her bleak vision of the future that caused this preemptive strike against the debilitating disease.

Dr. Kevorkian says that Mrs. Adkins had asked her doctor what he would recommend for her when she was finally in a vegetative state. The doctor, according to Kevorkian, said "he would tell her husband to shoot her." If that is true, he offered nothing. She could exercise her will now or lose it.

The future Janet Adkins faced is one that other elderly and ill recognize. Most of us have the desire to live as long as our minds are working. But at precisely the moment we might choose to die, we may have lost the capacity to make that choice. How many suicide pacts and acts are based on that fear?

The desire to control death may be a modern conceit, a kind of hubris against nature. But it is one based on modern technology. The terrifying specter of our age is a body attached interminably to a machine. The terrifying specter is a doctor who won't let us die, won't let us decide.

Janet Adkins's death landed in the news just as ethicists and doctors await the Supreme Court decision about Nancy Cruzan, the thirty-two-year-old who has been in a permanent vegetative state for over seven years. They are waiting to hear if the Court will allow a family to remove a feeding tube.

There are some who believe that the slippery slope leads directly from Nancy Cruzan's hospital bed to Dr. Kevorkian's death-on-wheels. If we remove a feeding tube, soon we will have the chain of suicide clinics.

But I suspect that just the opposite is true. It is the fear of ending up "a vegetable" that drives many to extremes. It's the terror of the life-support machine that makes the suicide machine an attractive alternative.

There may always be rational suicides, always be cases in which a doctor's moral obligation to ease pain and suffering supersedes the demand to prolong life. But if we can be confident of humane treatment, if we can retain a measure of control over our lives even at their end, there will be few suicide seekers in the back alleys of medicine. And Jack Kevorkian will be remembered as a maverick without a cause.

JUNE 15, 1990

Medical Overkill

||||||||||||||||||||||||||||||||||||||||||||||||||||||||||||||||||||||||||||||||||||||||||||||||||||||||

Washington — It is late at night, and we are talking about health care the way Americans do, in personal stories that begin with words like "my mother" or "my friend" or "I." This time we are talking about the end of life. How it often ends. How we would choose it to end.

In the last months we have borne witness to two deaths, two technological grand finales to good humane lives. Two men we know went out of life in full medical regalia—tubes and respirators galore—like some horrifying fireworks display of What Medicine Can Do, Circa 1993.

One of our friends has, in her hands, a hospital bill some seventy pages long and 200,000 insurance dollars deep for her brother's last month of what barely qualified as life. Another colleague is trying to tally up, just for the macabre curiosity, what Medicare paid for her husband's last days: the cost of coma.

Their mourning and our evening is made uneasy by the feeling that maybe too much had been done to these men in the guise of doing everything for them. There was a point, somewhere in the dying process, when medicine took over, when one decision led to another inexorably.

We share other such stories of times when all thought-out plans, all the family discussions, had simply been finessed, short-circuited by the hospital imperative to do one thing and then another. The medical people had gone step by step down the road to the respirators.

Our conversation this night is not just personal, though. It's colored, I am sure, by the recognition that a new man has moved into the White House not far from where we sit. He has promised a new health-care policy as part of his hundred-day hit parade.

Two sets of words come together, one after the other, as if they were inseparable: health care and hard choices. But the truth is that we haven't even been able to make the easy choices yet.

One thing we know is that the costs of health care went up some 14 percent last year. We know that over a third of all Medicare expenses go to the treatment of people in the last months of their life. Whether they want it or not.

There are studies that echo our personal conversations. They show that Americans worry that at the end of life they will receive too much medical treatment and too little pain relief. Now there is, as well, a survey that says doctors and nurses who treat dying patients worry that they *give* too much treatment and too little pain relief.

Health-care providers who answered the survey by the Education Development Corporation were four times as likely to be concerned about overtreatment as about undertreatment. Half of them said they had acted against their conscience in providing health care: They had offered treatment that was "overly burdensome" to patients. Two out of three believed that patients didn't get enough help or information to make decisions.

So we have some rare agreement among patients, families, doctors, nurses, even ethicists that the terminally ill should be treated with fewer tubes and more tenderness than is often the case. But still the stories accumulate. And so do the costs.

To mention money is to be immediately suspect. As Susan Wolf, an ethicist who helped with the survey, says, "The cost-containment argument makes people suspicious that there's a hidden motive behind stopping life-sustaining treatment. That it's not just about effecting the patient's wishes." It raises the specter of an accountant behind the physician deciding who lives and who dies.

Nevertheless, when we talk of health care and hard choices in the same breath, we mean medicine and money. We mean the allocation of dollars to transplants and prenatal care, to the elderly and the young, breast cancer and AIDS. We envision groups competing with each other for attention and dollars.

The stories of medical overkill of the dying are about times when the ethical and financial bottom lines might converge. They represent moments when doing what is humane also saves money.

If we cannot stop treatment for those who don't want it, if we can't respect the wishes of the dying and their families, if we can't make the easy choices, what hope do we have to make the rest? These are decisions that will take place not just in one white house but in a hundred hospital rooms a day.

People are forever asking, Where do we start the debate about health care? One place to begin is at the end.

FEBRUARY 2, 1993

CLOSE TO HOME

‖‖

‖‖‖‖‖ *Can Max, who straightens the fringe on his rug, find ultimate happiness with Nora, who has a half-eaten sandwich under the sofa? Can a woman who stores her dirty dishes in the sink find contentment with a man who gives her a Dustbuster as a present?*

Picking Rites

||||||||||||||||||||||||||||||||||||||||||||||||||||||||||||||||||||||||||||||||||||||||||||||||||||||||||||||

Casco Bay, Maine — It is early morning, but the clock that this woman watches so dutifully all year is unimportant here. The tide is what matters. And mussel beds do not stay open twenty-four hours a day.

So she is up and dressed for success in this venture. On her feet, a pair of blue-and-gray reef walkers. Above them, faded green cotton pants rolled up to the knee and bearing berry stains from seasons past. Above that a red T-shirt and a blue baseball cap advertising the local market.

In the city where she lives most of the year, this fashion style could be faithfully described as dork, full dork, or, in the language of fashion, dorque. To complete the overall look, she is carrying a vintage mesh potato sack for her hunting and gathering.

Thus attired, the woman heads down the dirt road to the ocean. She passes by the blackberries, their prickly branches heavy with breakfast fruit. She barely stops to inspect the raspberries that have acquired the fine mold that signals the end of their season. She will come back to them later.

At the water's edge, she makes her way over the rocks whose vast crop of mussels are only temporarily exposed to the air. Carefully, she clambers over this space, lifting great clumps of seaweed, as small crabs scamper away. She carefully chooses her spots, places where the biggest blue-black mussels have the fewest barnacles.

She is shopping, fussy as any buyer for a trendy urban kitchen, picking the finest foods available at the market. But what a different sort of marketplace this is. As she loosens the beards that connect these mussels to the rocks, she finds herself overwhelmed by the natural bounty of this season and this place. By the ease of putting food on her island table.

Mussels, raspberries, blackberries, mackerel. These are the free meals that she gathers from this island. What, she muses ironically, would it take to get such delicacies in the city? How many extra steps have been put between us and dinner in the urban obstacle course? An education to get a job to get a paycheck to get a car to drive on roads that are paved to get us to the store from one direction and the food from another. That is just the beginning.

What does it take to bring home the bacon or berries in the city? Another random list forms in her head: an alarm clock, a lipstick, pantyhose, gasoline, a bank card . . . money moving around the elaborate circuit we call the economy. What does it take here? Two hands.

For most of the year, the woman on the mussel flats "makes a living." She produces sentences in a building constructed for people who make and sell sentences in return for paychecks deposited and withdrawn in banks created for their convenience and their debt. The reward for people who "make a living" is, if they are lucky, a few weeks in a place where it seems possible to simply live. And to live simply.

If the woman sounds romantic about the country, she is not really. She has no desire to live off the land in February. She has watched her neighbors here do the hard work of bringing in that other island crop, lobster. Water doesn't wholly insulate this place from the world.

She knows that people want more than fish and berries. They want heat in the winter, beds in their homes, college for their kids. They want candy bars and VCRs.

But she also knows that as these wants expand like a mail-order catalogue, something else is added to the American wish list. The longing for time.

Ask families what they want and the same answer comes out: time. Some tell the pollsters that they would exchange money for time, literally buy it if they could. Others express it in a desire to shortcut the complicated and unnatural cycle that takes them around the days like a stock car in an interminable race.

So on a summer day, up to her ankles in the rising tide, she is grateful for what is here for the picking, mussels and peace of mind. Walking back this country road with tonight's dinner, she is saving time, aware as only a city dweller can be, of the luxury in living hand to mouth. How simple life is when you can want what is at hand.

AUGUST 20, 1991

Groundhog Day

Somewhere in the middle of *Groundhog Day*, Bill Murray turns to the man sitting beside him at a bar and says in a voice of utter despair, "What would you do if you were stuck in one place and every day was the same and nothing mattered?"

This is the philosophy of life that the rather obnoxious and egocentric weatherman has brought to this delicious time-warp fantasy. Murray has gotten stuck, truly stuck in Punxsutawney, Pennsylvania, where he went to cover the February 2 festivities.

For the weatherman, there is literally no tomorrow. Or, to be more precise, tomorrow is another today. He wakes up the next morning to the same morning, and he's the only one who knows it. Moreover, he is doomed to relive the day until he gets it right.

To the jaded moviegoer, *Groundhog Day* may well be to February 2 what *It's a Wonderful Life* is to December 25. It presents the possibility of human renewal—only this time with a sense of humor.

To the jaded female, it also presents the possibility that even a self-centered cad can eventually get it. Given time enough, Andie MacDowell, and a dozen slaps across the face, any man is educable. After endless reruns of the skirmish of the sexes, this one becomes, uh, sensitive.

But sitting in my popcorn perch, I'm willing to bet that the appeal of this hit movie comes less from the fantasy it evokes than from its echoes of real life. Especially real life at mid-life.

What would you do if you woke up in the same place and every day was the same?

For most people, middle age is a little bit like that. It's long past the time of life when most of us were building our careers, beginning our families, and nesting. It's the maintenance stage when an extraordinary amount of energy is going to upkeep—keeping up the commitments you have. One morning inevitably looks a lot like the one before it.

Of course, the time-warp stories that make it to the silver screen are usually about some young person yearning to get back to the future. Or about mad scientists trying to jump into an entirely different dimension.

The daydreams of youth that Hollywood usually respects are about breaking away. The daydreams of middle age that get screen plays are most often centered on starting over.

Books also tend to divide the adult life cycle into dramatic passages. We are regaled with theories that show us facing a dead end, following an exit sign out of the old rut and choosing a new beginning. The words mid-life and crisis are joined at the (expanding) hip.

But in real life, those of us who do not want to start over in the middle face a very different test of renewal. Daily renewal. Getting up in the same place, doing the same things—only making it matter.

Most of us don't want to throw everything over and go to live in Tahiti with the tennis pro. We don't want to have a post-menopausal baby or a second career in brain surgery. So we have to figure out how to make the best of what we have.

Making the best of what we have, I might add, is not second best. It's not the siren call of a mid-life depression inviting us to settle. It is, rather, a demand for active engagement in caring for what and whom we value.

That is what's touching about *Groundhog Day*. Our trapped weatherman has to learn this the hard way. His life is reduced to one inescapable day. It's the entire deck he's been dealt, the allotment of flowers he can arrange, the whole cast of characters in his life.

He goes through stages of feeling trapped, depressed, and living as if there's no tomorrow. He finally comes to the not-so-profound-but-still-pretty-rare realization that he can change his world by changing himself. That there's a lot of learning that goes into perfecting one day.

If this movie were a Zen lesson, it would be about living in the now. If this were a twelve-step program, the moral would be: One day at a time. If it were an environmental poster, it would read: Think global, act local.

But as a prescription for mid-life when the outlines of our lives are pretty clear, it's about making the best of what you have . . . over and over. Making small repairs and improvements so that the commitments of mid-life—the work you do and people you love —don't become a trap. They become and remain the town in which you choose to live even when you have options.

If that sounds hopelessly sappy, well, blame it on the movies. But after watching Murray, I will never tell you to have a nice day. How about making a few, nicer days.

MARCH 12, 1993

The Neatness Gap
||||||||||||||||||||||||||||||||||||||||||||||||||||||||||||||||||||||||||||||||||||||||||||||||||||||||||||||||||||||||||||

Call it an occupational hazard, but like most journalists, I have a tendency to destroy every nice romantic fantasy with some flat-footed realism. No matter how I may suspend judgment in the darkened movie theater, by the time I reach the parking lot I am writing a postscript to the happy endings.

So I left *White Palace* as Susan Sarandon and James Spader were beginning their happily-ever-after. And as I was beginning my what-happens-next.

It wasn't the age gap between these two that stuck in my deconstructionist imagination, although much ado has been made of the steamy love affair between a forty-three-year-old woman and a twenty-seven-year-old man. When we were younger, the older woman was cast as a predatory Mrs. Robinson. Now baby boomers are Mrs. Robinson's age, and suddenly she's wise and sexy. Makes sense to me.

Nor was it the class difference between the hash slinger and the yuppie that led me to worry about the trouble ahead. Hollywood is forever telling us that class is no barrier to true love as long as you are earthy, good, sexy, and very, very thin.

But what struck this postscript writer's mind was the ultimate difference that has left so many more lovers in the lurch. The neatness gap.

Can Max, who straightens the fringe on his rug, find ultimate happiness with Nora, who has a half-eaten sandwich under the sofa? Can a woman who stores her dirty dishes in the sink find contentment with a man who gives her a Dustbuster as a present?

Opposites may attract when you are talking about class and age. But housekeeping? If this were a prenuptial quiz, the question would be: Which makes marriage happier: (a) the simultaneous orgasm or (b) the single standard of cleanliness. The answer, of course, is (b). But it's much harder to achieve.

How do I know this? Needless to say, I have never left a half-eaten sandwich under the sofa. I finish the sandwich. (I leave the wrapper.)

But I belong to that group of females who are very quiet when other women complain that their husbands leave socks on the floor. Let me put it this way: My husband believes, as a matter of deep moral conviction, that clothes should be turned right side out *before* they go into the washing machine.

In the days before our two families blended their laundry, he lived in an apartment that could be described (by me) as Spartan-

Japanese. I lived in a home that could be described (by him) as Early Childhood Chaos. With dog.

His kitchen had surfaces. Mine had them too, of course, although they hadn't made an appearance for some time. He regarded the dishwasher as something to be run. I thought of it as a convenient storage space. He liked the refrigerator clean (without anything to eat). I liked it full (of mold).

When these opposites attracted more than dust, I got weekly cleaning help. He cleaned up for the cleaning help.

We have made compromises, of course. If, for example, I leave the table during breakfast without posting a guard at my half-empty coffee cup, he accepts this as an invitation to clear the cup. If I catch him with my half-full coffee cup, I accept this as an invitation to stab him with my fork. It all works out.

We still have separate cars. You could eat off the floor of his car. You could read off the floor of mine. My husband still longs to achieve the pristine quality of nature. I still believe that nature abhors a vacuum and a vacuum cleaner.

He cannot understand how any human being—let alone one he loves—can walk up the stairs without picking up the shoes on the landing. I cannot believe that anyone—let alone someone I love—cares whether a pair of shoes is on a landing or in a closet.

Deep in the hearts of couples like us who share space but not standards, each sees this difference as a character flaw. One person's free spirit is the other's dirty slob. One person's orderliness is the other's anal-compulsive obsessiveness.

In *White Palace*, love conquers all this. We are led to believe that Max is loosening up when he drinks Perrier out of a bottle. We are supposed to assume that Nora is straightening up when she sets the table and brushes her hair.

Hollywood is grand for fantasy, but they have come up against something harder to resolve than age, sex, race, class, or creed. In six months it won't be the wrinkles around her eyes Max finally notices. It will be the ring around the tub.

Older woman, younger man? Working-class, rich? When all is said and done, neatness counts. So too does messiness.

NOVEMBER 9, 1990

Tribal Wedding

||||||||||||||||||||||||||||||||||||||||||||||||||||||||||||||||||||||||||||||||||||||||||||||||||||

The usher greets the woman at the door to the church and inquires politely, "Are you with the bride's families or the groom's families?" It is the plural that stops this guest for a moment at the threshold. The bride's families? The groom's families?

The usher is, of course, accurate in his pin-striped propriety. If the church architecture were as up-to-date as his etiquette, there would be more than two aisles. The pews would be divided into four equal parts.

The young man and woman who are about to be wed were raised in kinship patterns familiar to anthropologists who study our culture of divorce. They each have parents and stepparents, four sets of family friends, a quartet of households and people who care about them. They are loaded down with extras.

Their ceremony this morning doesn't join two families. It takes place at a four-way intersection. This is a scene of earlier accidents. So the woman answers the usher carefully. She is with the bride's mother. He seats her accordingly.

As the music begins, this friend of the bride's mother is conscious not only of the costumes but of the choreography. The ceremony is as detailed, as elaborate, as any religious rite of passage. But the concern here is less for sacred proscriptions than for family. The two had staged their event, carefully avoiding the taboos of hurt feelings.

The bride walked down the aisle by herself because, she said publicly, a modern woman doesn't have to be "given away." Privately, she had worried about choosing between the father who gave her life and the stepfather who raised her.

The groom invited both pairs of parents to stand up for him, couple by couple. He insisted publicly that it was only fair since they had shared custody of his childhood. Privately, he admitted it would be awkward to see Mom and Dad reunited at his own altar.

Even the peripatetic photographer had gone along, carrying a lineage chart in her equipment bag beside lenses and film. She could be seen keeping track of the family quadrants as well as the f-stops and the guests as well as ASA ratings. There would be, of course, four separate albums.

By the time the ceremony was over, the cake was cut, the dances were danced, the guest found herself on a corner of the lawn, talking briefly with the bride. Scanning the assembly, the young woman said to her mother's friend with palpable relief, "It went well, didn't it?" "Without a hitch," said the guest, and the two smiled at each other familiarly.

It occurred to the guest then that the confident and kind woman she had known since childhood had felt like the manager of this event more than the bride. It occurred to her that in other tribes the elders staged ceremonies for their children. But in the culture of divorce, the children were often the ones who held the responsibility.

If she went back through the snapshots of this bride's life, the guest could remember a girl who managed things almost from the moment of her parents' divorce. A six-year-old who packed her own bag for visiting. A twelve-year-old who bought a dress for her father's wedding all by herself.

Moreover, every event that brought her parents together had been shadowed with an unavoidable tension. It didn't matter that their divorce was what we call "civilized." Birthdays, graduations, each big day that brought the tribe together had been something to get through. Without a hitch.

A product of this culture, the bride was now a skilled negotiator: competent, independent. Raised in a background so similar they might have come from the same "old country," her husband had become an accomplished manager, a fine-tuned listener and mediator. They were the success stories, a credit to their own kind.

And yet, like their own kind, they had lost the parental umbrella at an early age. Christenings and grandchildren would go on in the pattern of shared custody, now multiplied by two. Holidays were likely to remain productions, more than celebrations, with rotating families. They would be the ones who kept track of turns, of trees, of turkeys. Yet they felt a loss of family that came with this surplus of families.

The guest counted their blessings. The bride had "handled" divorce well. The groom had muted the open hostilities between his parents long ago. But the new couple didn't want their own children to go through these same rites of passage. This is one thing about the adult children of divorce, the guest noted: They rarely want to pass on the totems and taboos of their own traditions.

So today, a friend of the bride's mother, watching this marriage of two of a kind, silently sends her best wishes. To these people of good and strong will, good luck from the tribe.

JULY 24, 1990

The Truth about Squirrels

As a child of the 1950s, I was taught to think of the squirrel as a lovable, furry role model of the American work ethic. The creature who frequented my schoolbooks worked his tail off all fall collecting the acorns of assorted oak trees. When winter came around, he survived by just nipping over to little tree grocery store for his three square nuts a day.

I should have known better, I am sure. The only tree in our apartment courtyard was an ailanthus, not an oak. The squirrels in our neighborhood seemed to spend most of their time perfecting their electric tightwire act.

But these were the Cold War years, when all good little animals

were expected to do their part for the great anthropomorphic prop-
aganda machine. Remember the three little piggies? The boring,
brick-house piggy was the one who survived the big bad wolf. You
get the idea.

Since then I have learned the truth about urban squirrels, and
of course about the economy. Squirrels may indeed put away their
acorns for a snowy day. But they don't have a clue where they put
them.

Their survival—indeed, their complete takeover of the city—
has nothing to do with the virtues of the good old 1950s: industry,
husbandry, loyalty. They thrive on the economic tools of the 1990s:
ingenuity, adaptability, flat-out nerve. And, of course, sunflower
seeds.

Which brings us to the subject at hand. The case of the Wallenda
at my window. Named after the humanoids, the Flying Wallendas.

For the better part of three years, I have been happily feeding an
assortment of basic winter-hardy New England birds out of a modest
plastic bird feeder at my second-story window. My Audubon kitchen
life-list includes the squabbling finch family, several pairs of titmice,
some overbearing blue jays, subdued junkos, sparrows, and an occasional downy woodpecker, or, in this case, downy plasticpecker.

The first hint that a somewhat heavier visitor had taken up a
post at the window was the discovery that the seed cups were being
knocked to the ground. The second hint was Wally himself performing a flying leap from fence to electric wire to tree branch to
window feeder. Degree of difficulty, 7; execution, 5.7.

This feat was matched by an extremely large mammal, female
and human, lunging at the window, knocking in anger, and yelling
at a squirrel not remotely my own size. Degree of difficulty, 1.
Execution, 3.5. Factor of absurdity, 9.8.

For several weeks, Wally and I performed our duet. He worked
on his acrobatics with the passion of an apprentice in a circus training
program. I worked on my bird-feeder defense hysterics. The difference, however, was that he improved his act.

Sometime during February he learned to execute a soft landing
in the feeder with one graceful motion. It would have taken him
less time to learn, I am sure, except of course that feeder was squirrel-
proof. Did I mention that?

Never mind the 1950s squirrel, that dutiful hunter-gatherer. By my observation there is nothing as impressive and determined as a nineties squirrel conquering the latest technology. After one month, he could not only get at the seeds, he could balance directly on top of the food under a small—equally squirrel-proof—overhang, thereby gaining food and shelter simultaneously. Degree of difficulty, 9; execution, 9.3.

A nineties kind of squirrel, he didn't just work hard, he worked smart. Indeed, he began exhibiting pride in his accomplishment and boldness at his feat. I, on the other hand, have been reduced to his co-dependent, or his audience. If the feeder is empty, he stares directly through the window at me until I put down my newspaper and get him some more seeds.

Does this mean that I can't defend my own home bird feeder against a measly squirrel? The problem is that I belong to the old economy. I have to go to an office to write the words that get the paycheck that puts bird food in the feeder. I have to squirrel away savings—just like I was taught—while he spends all day learning new skills. He wins.

Let it not be said, however, that I am hopelessly mired in oldthink. I'm a nineties kind of gal. After all, I used to run a bird feeder. Now, after extensive retraining, I can proudly announce that I am operating a squirrel feeder.

MARCH 12, 1993

Nine E-Z Steps to Weight Loss

||||||||||||||||||||||||||||||||||||||||||||||||||||||||||||||||||||||||||||||||||||||||||||||||||||

Once again we have come to that wonderful time of the year when the Xmas Glutton wrestles that gatekeeper of conscience,

Willpower, to the ground and rushes headlong into a corporeal takeover of the human pleasure centers.

Cheerful and, need I say, roly-poly, the spirit of Yule Gruel arrives at a million office parties strewing chocolate truffles over the word processors and sprinkling taco chips over the microchips. He then flows on toward the family dinner table on a river of eggnog, infecting perfectly normal aerobic, waist-watching Americans with feeding frenzy. And leaves in his wake a population that is 75 percent saturated.

Good little boys and girls of any age greet this annual visitation in the same spirit as their forebears. We open our mouths in welcome and do not close them again—except to swallow—until New Year's. At that point, we vainly attempt to return the annual Xmas Glutton gift: five-pound packages of fat, nicely divided and suitable for application on either hip.

And what do we discover? This is a nonreturnable item and we forgot the sales slip.

The Xmas Glutton tradition stems from the days when our Neanderthal ancestors gave each other seasonal gifts of suet. This may explain why they never left their caves until spring: They didn't want to be seen. That, however, was before the mirror had been invented.

But today, when self-hate follows indulgence with alarming speed, a collection of *Homo sapiens* have assembled to help others of their species resist the Xmas Glutton. As a public-service venture, we have put together a list that will help average Americans avoid the holiday body buildup without committing themselves to an institution or getting a ski mask without a mouth hole.

Without further ado, we offer you Nine Ways to Lose Weight During the Holidays.

1. Have a baby. Admittedly, this is not a route open to everyone. It requires a good deal of planning. But it is the only surefire way to drop seven pounds overnight between Christmas and New Year's.

2. Go in for elective root canal. This is a multistage dental procedure that makes eating as attractive as, well, root canal.

Try to schedule the Novocain shot for thirty-five minutes before the office Christmas party and again before the New Year's Eve bash. This gives you at least three hours during which you can't taste anything without dribbling. The advantage of this over having a baby is that it costs less than college tuition.

3. Read the *New England Journal of Medicine* before any holiday celebration. This will convince you that anything you are about to be served is potentially lethal. Hard-core cases should jot down references to cholesterol on their shirt cuffs, to which they can refer when the cheesecake is passed.

4. Join a religious cult that only eats one color food a month. December is blue. Okay, it's green, but hold the avocado.

5. Get a new puppy, unhousebroken, and take him with you everywhere. This has several advantages. The puppy will eat everything before you can. Your hands will be full. You'll both be asked to leave the party. It's also less painful than root canal.

6. Have twins. Double the weight loss.

7. Get divorced. Granted this may seem extreme, but it is a staple of the ever-popular High Anxiety Diet. Half of the people lose weight because they are too anxious to swallow. The other half are anxious to get down to their dating weight. But no matter how much you want to lose, it is best not to combine a divorce with having twins.

8. Hire a food stylist instead of a chef for your parties. A food stylist works for the photographer, not the diner, and glazes turkey with shellac instead of honey. He will produce a feast for your eyes. Let them see cake.

9. Put on a bathing suit and do not take it off until 1990. This will provide a handy and constant reminder about your current shape. It will also rule out any possibility of going out in public, where the Xmas Glutton lurks even now, waiting to dip this entire list right into the chocolate fondue.

DECEMBER 22, 1989

Saying Goodbye to Sam

||||||||||||||||||||||||||||||||||||||||||||||||||||||||||||||||||||||||||||||||||||||||||||||||||||||||

The rug has gone to the cleaners. The bowls have been through the dishwasher. The leash has been put away. The leftover food has gone to a neighbor's dog.

Still the house is full of Samantha's shadows and sounds. I hear her tags jingling from the hall. My husband opens the front door carefully, as if she were still sleeping near it. I catch myself putting a cereal bowl down on the floor. We both instinctively think about letting her out, letting her in.

This, we say to each, is what people must mean when they talk about a phantom limb. It takes time to get used to what isn't there. What isn't here anymore is Sam.

Sam was no wonder dog. She had no tricks to speak of, unless you count her agility at emptying wastebaskets. She was no candidate for David Letterman unless he is fascinated by dogs that eat apple cores. She did what most of her kind do today: She kept a family company while the kids were growing up. It was her job.

If Disney made films about the lives of ordinary canines, I could contribute a few on the Urban Adventures of Sam. The time she jumped out of my sister's second-story window. The time she was mugged by a more aggressive street dog. The time she was hit by a car. The time she gave birth on the staircase. The time she found her way home across three miles of traffic. The time (times) she wound up in the pound.

Now it seems like such a cliché: The kids leave, the dog dies. Puff the Magic Dragon and sixteen years have passed.

Old age came in its time and we saw it in her pace. She simply slowed down. For years Sam would show her impatience with the two-footed species by racing circles around me. Then one year I became impatient at her pace. The next year, she gave up distance running altogether. Then she gave up the stairs.

Gradually there were more days when we caught her falling, or leaning against the wall, when she didn't hear us or see us, when she seemed confused and crippled. There were days when we began to think about what the vet had called so discreetly "other choices." Of which there was only one.

Maybe in the rural societies they take these things more easily. By these things I mean life and death. The power to choose life or death.

Maybe it's the times. Today we confront the questions of mercy killing with a battery of ethicists and double-handed questions. On the one hand this, on the other that. Maybe the same human questions have infiltrated our treatment of animals.

In any case, as Sam noticeably failed, I talked about this with everyone I knew. What are the parameters. How do you know when there is too much misery? Or pain for that matter? Were we selfishly keeping her alive because we couldn't bear to be accomplices in her death? Was it wrong to make a life-and-death decision based on crippling? On incontinence? On confusion? How do you assess your responsibility to a creature in your care?

Many had been through this before, but they offered no certain advice, not even the friend who insisted that I was being excessive in my anxiety. He said to me wryly, "Hey, we're talking about a dog. We're not talking about a parent."

But I know no one who found this an easy exercise of their power, their ownership. There are very few guidelines about love and death.

In the end, Sam saved us from uncertainty. It was her last gift. On Friday afternoon, she fell down and couldn't get up. We wrapped her in a blanket and drove her to the animal hospital, where the vet told us what we knew: She was dying. We came home without her.

For all the talk, all the vain considering of "choices," the moral decisions came upon us suddenly, in crisis. I suppose that is always true. Suddenly we have to choose between life and death: a few more days of life and instant death. Choose now. This decision was at least clear.

The vet, a kind young woman, tried to ease my way as she eased Sam's. But cradling Sam for the seconds it took for the injection, the seconds it took to stop breathing, I felt, literally in my hands, how faint the line is that we draw between life and death.

Now, maybe, when the rug comes back I won't think of it as hers. Time goes by. But today the house still seems to echo with her tinkling name tags.

JUNE 9, 1989

Shopping in the Chromosome Mall

||||||||||||||||||||||||||||||||||||||||||||||||||||||||||||||||||||||||||||||||||||||||||||||||||||

On the seventh day before Christmas, the couple went out together to shop for presents. And came home with a bundle of revelations.

Until then, mind you, the pair appeared to be a very model of compatibility. They shared everything from a passion for calamari to an impatience with Mario Cuomo.

No predetermined sex roles skewed their partnership. Indeed, they were capable of sharing a kitchen, a checkbook, and a tennis court without contemplating spouse-icide. Who would have guessed that a gender gap of massive proportions would come unwrapped over gifts?

This is what happened: They entered the store side by side. He walked directly toward a display case, spotted a pair of earrings for his daughter, checked the price tag, and said—this is a quote— "These are nice. I'll buy them."

The entire elapsed time of this shopping trip? About forty-three seconds.

It is entirely possible to regard this as normal—if you belong to the subset of human beings who also think it's normal for 250-pound men in padded uniforms to make a living crashing into each other to move a ball down a field. She, however, was stunned.

This is how the woman would have done it: She would have (1) checked out every item in the store; (2) agonized over whether this daughter already had a pair of round earrings; (3) held the blue color up against the lavender; (4) checked the round against the square; (5) thought about the implications of one daughter's earrings against another daughter's scarf; (6) worried about blue, asked for cherry red; (7) wondered if there was another pair on sale; (8) picked the black ones.

Minimum elapsed time? Forty-three minutes, including a break for aspirin.

The couple thus discovered after these many years what every Christmas salesperson learns their first season on the job. By and large, women go shopping; buying is just the end result. Men go buying; shopping is the dreaded necessary means.

In any given year, most of the woman's friends approach Christmas shopping as a marathon event of twenty-six days' and twenty-six malls' duration. Most of the man's friends approach it as a three-day dash. They start later, panic harder, and purchase faster.

The woman devised a sexual Santa quiz: One friend at work bragged recently about a one-day blitz, breaking the record for presents per hour. Another friend admitted to collecting goodies all year—just a few more to go. Check the gender on your answer sheet.

The woman wonders if there is any research to explain this sexual gap in consumer style. Is it possible that it's all nature, not nurture? Her foreplay, his focus? Perhaps it's a gift of the Chromosome Magi—XX for shopping, an XY for buying.

What would the sociobiologists have to say? Would they pin it on our ancestors? His anthropological forebears were geared to pursue any mammoth that came into view. Hers went cruising the designer bushes, picking only the ripe berries out of the patch.

The right-brain, left-brain crowd might find the dividing line in the cortex. On the right side, women regard shopping as an art, while on the left, men regard it as an analytical chore. She wants to be creative; he wants to get the job done.

And what spin would modern gender watchers put on the shopping differences? According to the current cultural divide, men are directed toward goals and women toward relationships. He wants to make a decision; she wants to make everyone happy.

Maybe men see a shirt on the counter, while women see a relationship. What does this shirt say about how well I know someone, understand them, can give what they want?

Surely it takes less time to buy a tie than an emotional statement. A forty-three-minute gap if there ever was one.

By the time the couple has returned home, packages in hand, the woman has turned a shopping trip into a sociological tract. But sorting out her bundles and revelations, it now occurs to her that maybe this is just a case for Single-Sex Shopping.

There is, you see, a postscript to their seasonal adventure. In the kitchen, he takes out the results of his speed-shopping and pauses to wrap them with meticulous, time-consuming care. She takes out her carefully chosen presents and sloppily Scotch tapes them into their wrappers with abandon.

So much for small motor coordination and chromosomes. One good thing about gender roles, she thinks. They can almost always be exchanged.

DECEMBER 24, 1991

A Room of Her Own

||||||||||||||||||||||||||||||||||||||||||||||||||||||||||||||||||||||||||||||||||||||||||||||||

The room at the top of the stairs is beginning to look like a museum permanently displaying one exhibit. This one would be labeled: The American Teenager, Circa 1980.

Almost four years ago, the permanent resident vacated this space to become a college student. She is now twenty-one years old. The room and its artifacts are frozen at age fifteen.

The mother who lives here year-round comes in to look over the contents from time to time. There is the bookshelf whose time line extends from Dr. Seuss to *Our Bodies, Ourselves*. There are the stuffed animals and the memorial to James Dean. There are the walls covered with posters and the doors covered with bumper stickers of places visited in 1983, 1984, 1985.

But lately what the woman sees in this memorabilia, this back-to-the-future decor, is the stuff of an emotional time warp. The space feels melancholy, like a waiting room. The walls seem to expect the return of a missing child, when in fact it is a young woman who comes home these days.

So the mother has gotten the urge to peel off the layers of the past, to pack the items of childhood away, and to paint over history and start fresh. She wants to greet the student this summer with a more updated color scheme.

But when she makes her offer of renovation, it is greeted by its absentee owner with something less than enthusiasm. On the other end of the line, the mother hears a small, surprised—childish?—question: "Why?"

The mother talks rationally about the paint peeling over the desk, the stickers that make the room look like a pickup truck. Then, hearing the hesitancy in her daughter's voice, she asks archly, "Come on, do you want this room to remain a shrine to your adolescence forever?" And the student answers, "Yes." Only a long-distance laugh lightens her seriousness.

When the woman hangs up the phone, having lost round one, it occurs to her that something more interior than decorating may be going on in this dialogue. Maybe they weren't just talking about paint chips. Maybe they were talking about growing up and growing apart.

This woman has heard many people on the cusp of adulthood talk about the difficulty of getting parents to accept and grant their independence, their separateness, their difference. It is a running theme of these years.

When they go home, for a week or a summer, they say that it's hard for parents to acknowledge how much they've changed. But these young do not talk about—because they don't always know—the difficulty they have letting parents change, letting home change.

How many people moving onto the shaky turf of independence want the security of knowing that they can go home again? How many want to believe that they can be children again? There is comfort in the idea that parents, like bedrooms, are freeze-framed in their old places: not demanding but available, always there in case of emergency.

For parents as well, there is a conflict in these middle years. The desire to be there if needed comes up against the desire to change and fill their own lives. They want to be welcoming but not to be waiting. They want to be more than custodians of an empty nest.

This woman, surveying her former child's room in its pris-teen beauty, knows how often the home takes on the symbolic weight of this separation. She knows a freshman who felt bereft this year when she moved to college and her parents moved to an apartment. There was no home for the holidays.

She knows a thirty-year-old embarrassingly upset to discover that the space he hadn't used in ten years was now a den. There was no room for him anymore. And she knows a forty-five-year-old unexpectedly stunned when her parents left for Florida. The site of her childhood went up for sale.

The mother was running ahead of herself. She doesn't want to board up this bed, or make a final statement about separation. It had taken more than a little while to accept her child as an adult. Shouldn't a room graduate high school when its owner graduates college?

But the business of renovating family relationships, she knows, is tricky. As families grow up, parents as well as children start to juggle old ways and ties, to balance their sense of independence and their sense of belonging. In the lives of adult families, it turns out that making room for each other is more than a matter of paint.

APRIL 17, 1990

Knocko

||||||||||||||||||||||||||||||||||||||||||||||||||||||||||||||||||||||||||||||||||||||||||||||||||||||||||||||||||||||||||||||||||

Casco Bay, Maine — I am in the bushes, digging out the bittersweet vines wrapped murderously around a tree, when the cardinal comes back into view. The bird, in all his finery, flies across the lawn, undulating in great long crimson loops. And then ends his elegant flight pattern by crashing directly into the barn window.

Mission accomplished, he retreats to a nearby bush. From this launching pad, he commences his afternoon of battering. The bird I have come to call Knocko attacks the glass once, twice, a dozen times, before he takes off to fight another time.

I have been watching this routine for weeks. The first time I saw him perform his Great Window Crash, I felt like the audience at an airshow when the careful choreography of the planes suddenly turns into a midair collision.

Like any guilt-ridden eco-worrier, I assumed that it was my fault. Last year some cardinals had nested inside the barn; this year, we replaced the window. Was the bird trying merely to get home through the pane?

But as Knocko went another and then another round with the window, it occurred to me that he must be fighting. With his own mirror image.

Did this splendid and birdbrained creature see an enemy in the reflection of the windowpane? Did he come out attacking—day three, round twelve—an imagined rival? Himself?

Watching Knocko knock out his brains and aware that I am no naturalist, I call the Audubon Society, where a field ornithologist confirms my own mischievous diagnosis of Knocko's behavior. The cause, in one word, admits Simon Perkins, is testosterone.

At this time of year, Perkins tells me, males often smash themselves against windows, hubcaps, even rearview mirrors. "What they see in their reflection is an intruder in their territory and they attack it. They won't give up as long as their hormone level is up."

Lest he be guilty of stereotypes—politically incorrect for those of us who deal higher up on the food chain—Perkins adds that occasionally a female will do it as well. But by and large, banging your head against a mirrored wall is a male activity. Testosterone, he adds traitorously to his sex, "is a universal hormone that makes all males do very strange things."

This sort of behavior, built into their systems long before there were windows or hubcaps in the world, is now entirely unfit for the rigors and traps of modern civilization. "Even if they don't injure themselves or blow themselves out immediately, they only have a certain amount of energy in their short lives," says Perkins. "It's like a gas tank. What you use now you won't have later."

Knocko and his like harm not only themselves but also their families. "Raising young is an extremely expensive task. To have to expend more energy on an imagined foe is," he says conclusively, "not good."

Simon Perkins is no sociobiologist. Nor am I. Leaping from birds to humans or from cardinals to generals is a risky business. Furthermore, neither of us wants to be accused of male bashing. After all, the cardinal is doing quite enough male bashing for both of us.

But this week at least, even in Knocko's territory, people are asking whether George Bush's decision to fight in the Gulf was the product of thought or a hyperactive thyroid. So we're entitled to worry a bit about nature, nurture, and warfare.

In the aftermath of the Cold War as well, men and women are wondering if Russia was ever the real threat. Which of today's enemies are a figment of our imagination? A mirror image?

And while we are on the subject, it isn't just ornithologists who notice that "raising young is an extremely expensive task." Nor is it just environmentalists calculating how much money has gone to fools' fights instead of children. The task of separating real and false foes is a central one for any life built on instinct but dependent on reason.

Ah, but for Knocko at least, there is good news, a cure. The man from Audubon tells me that my cardinal's hormone level will be down in another week or two. In the meantime I am instructed to cover the window. With one blanket, carefully placed, I can wipe out an enemy and save a small friend.

What is this? Think globally, act locally? Today, with a punch-drunk cardinal at my window, he makes it sound so easy.

MAY 24, 1991

Aging and Airbrushing

||||||||||||||||||||||||||||||||||||||||||||||||||||||||||||||||||||||||||||||||||||||||||||||||||||||||||||||

There is a condom on the coffee table. It's been there for weeks now, in a photograph, displayed genteelly between the manicured fingertips of Elizabeth Taylor, the way her grandmother might have held a teacup.

The image is meant to be startling, I suppose, the cover for a story about Taylor's gutsy work for AIDS. But whenever I glance down at the portrait I think more about the message in Taylor's face than the one in her hand.

This is what has captured my attention: Elizabeth Taylor at sixty, airbrushed within an inch of her life. Elizabeth Taylor at sixty, nipped, tucked, lifted—?—out of her peer group. Elizabeth Taylor at sixty—not exactly *National Velvet* but somewhere between *Cleopatra* and *Virginia Woolf*. Looking thirty-five and holding.

Is this what sixty looks like? At its best? Or at its worst?

In the past decade, we have charted the middle-aging of female models and role models. Women who are fortysomething are being allowed out in public although they almost always wear a label that reads: "still." Still attractive at forty. Still youthful at forty-six.

But gradually it has occurred to me that women are only being given an extension on aging. They are not being given permission to age gracefully. The culture is telling women they can be younger longer. It is not welcoming old women.

So, I wonder, is this progress for women or progress for the beauty business? Must we *still* be still attractive at fifty-five? Will we *still* want to be still youthful at sixty-five?

I belong to the generation that has made menopause a subject for best-seller lists and polite conversation. Sometimes my friends sit at lunch unabashedly gossiping about the choices other women make, women who are older but not necessarily wiser, about how to age.

Did a slimmer, drug-free Liz Taylor buy a new face to go with her new life? Or to go with her new, younger husband? One friend calls it a positive act. Another calls it depressing.

Did Jane Fonda, physically fit beyond most women's dreams, buy new breasts? One defends her right to fight aging. Another cites her sad pursuit of youth as proof of low self-esteem.

When any television broadcaster or actress goes under the plastic surgeon's knife, one will defend it as pragmatic. Another will ruefully describe it as defeatist.

The other night, a friend called to read a line spoken by Carolyn Heilbrun, a scholar and detective story writer. "I used to be thin," Heilbrun told a reporter, "but after fifty-five, I said, 'Oh, the hell with it.' "

My friend laughed with delight and promised to tape this remark to her refrigerator. But I know that her refrigerator holds nothing inside that could contribute to middle-age spread.

This gossiping we do is not idle at all. It's a conversation, full of curiosity and anxiety, about age and power and invisibility. A conversation about the future.

What is it that Germaine Greer wrote in her great, sprawling, infuriating, and illuminating unmade bed of a book, *The Change*? "There is no accepted style for the older woman; no way of saying through dress and demeanor, 'I am my age. Respect it. . . .'

"She has a duty to go on 'being attractive' no matter how fed up she is with the whole business. She is not allowed to say, 'Now I shall let myself go. . . .' Yet if a woman never lets herself go, how will she ever know how far she have might gone?"

How far to go? Any one of us can come up with a handful of appealing images of old ladies from painter Georgia O'Keeffe to Gray Panther Maggie Kuhn to, of course, Katharine Hepburn. All women who went far. But it's hard to chart a path through that second awkward age between middle and old.

In the world we live in, safe sex is more acceptable fare for a magazine cover than a sixty-year-old face. In this world, it takes more confidence, more nerve, more power for a woman of a certain age to look that age than to carry a condom in public.

But today, I will put aside the portrait of the movie star with the lavender eyes and put aside these thoughts as well. A new issue of the magazine has arrived at my door bearing a new image. On the cover is Candice Bergen. She is, of course, *still* beautiful at forty-six.

NOVEMBER 20, 1992